THE DEATH OF
PSYCHOTHERAPY

THE DEATH OF PSYCHOTHERAPY

From Freud to Alien Abductions

DONALD A. EISNER

Foreword by Tana Dineen

Westport, Connecticut
London

Library of Congress Cataloging-in-Publication Data

Eisner, Donald A., 1943–
    The death of psychotherapy : from Freud to alien abductions /
Donald A. Eisner ; foreword by Tana Dineen.
        p.   cm.
    Includes bibliographical references and index.
    ISBN 0–275–96413–2 (alk. paper)
        1. Psychotherapy—Evaluation.   2. Psychotherapy—Philosophy.
    I. Title.
    RC480.5.E365   2000
    616.89'14—dc21   99–22138

British Library Cataloguing in Publication Data is available.

Library of Congress Catalog Card Number: 99–22138
ISBN: 0–275–96413–2

First published in 2000

Praeger Publishers, 88 Post Road West, Westport, CT 06881
An imprint of Greenwood Publishing Group, Inc.
www.praeger.com

Printed in the United States of America

The paper used in this book complies with the
Permanent Paper Standard issued by the National
Information Standards Organization (Z39.48–1984).

10 9 8 7 6 5 4 3 2 1

To Ardyne, Danielle, and Courtney

Contents

Foreword by Tana Dineen   ix

Introduction   xi

1. Science and Fiction in Psychotherapy   1

2. Psychoanalytic Psychotherapy   21

3. Cathartic Therapies: From Primal to *est*   45

4. Recovered Memory Therapy   67

5. Humanistic Psychotherapy   95

6. Behavioral and Cognitive Therapy   117

7. Strategic Family Systems Therapy and Neurolinguistic Programming   143

8. Spiritual Therapy   163

9. From Buddha Psychotherapy to Alien Abductions   185

10. The Death of Psychotherapy: Conclusions   205

Selected Bibliography   227

Index   229

Foreword

A fundamental assumption, which has become almost a cornerstone of American society, is that psychotherapy, however it is packaged and sold, is somehow good for us. Recent statistics indicate that upwards of half of the U.S. population, at some point in their lives, turn for help to a psychotherapist.

As a business enterprise, psychotherapy appears to be thriving. People have come to rely on it in their pursuit of comfort, good feelings, success, and happy outcomes. But is there any proof that these customers are getting what they pay for?

Several years ago, when I was first starting to voice this question out loud, I submitted a proposal to the American Psychological Association, suggesting that a mock trial be held at their annual meeting. The title for the event was to be "Psychology on trial: Can the profession survive and should it?" I had assembled a panel of prominent lawyers, sociologists, and psychologists. Our agenda was clear. We wanted psychotherapy examined and judged in the cold light of scientific evidence. Not surprisingly, the proposal was turned down: the "powers that be" were not willing to bring this issue under public scrutiny.

These same "powers that be" will not take kindly to Don Eisner's book for, in many ways, he has done what we had hoped to do, and he has done it well. Melding his extensive knowledge of psychotherapy, gleaned from his education and experience as a psychologist, with his training and skill as a lawyer, he has put psychotherapy on trial.

In *The Death of Psychotherapy* he has carefully and meticulously presented the evidence. Chapter by chapter, he looks at the popular varieties of psychotherapy and shows that, despite the claims and supportive studies, they all lack the essential proof of effectiveness. He doesn't deny that some, even many, people feel better after talking to a therapist. But he does challenge that this is due to anything special or specific to any of the treatments.

For centuries, placebos or sugar pills have made people with physical problems feel better. Early in this century, Emil Coué gained fame by encouraging people to tell themselves that "every day in every way, I'm feeling better and better." As Don Eisner suggests, without proof of an active ingredient, psychotherapy should be recognized as nothing more than a sugar pill or an expensive Couéism.

He makes a good case for concluding that there is no active ingredient. While I expect that the organizations which promote psychotherapy will make every effort to ignore or dismiss the evidence, people deserve to be given the facts. At the very least, consumers should have the opportunity to weigh the information for themselves.

Consumer protection is a familiar term. Before important shopping trips, we tend to seek out information about how products have been tested and to find out whether or not there is any support for the claims made by advertisers.

Recently one of the most trusted sources of such information, *Consumer Reports*, addressed the topic of psychotherapy. In a survey of thousands of its readers it asked, "does therapy work?" One would have assumed that, given their approach to toasters and cars, they would have examined each type or model, describing their strengths and weaknesses. Not so! They lumped them all together and concluded that therapy helps simply because the people who chose to fill out a questionnaire claimed that they felt better.

The Death of Psychotherapy does what *Consumer Reports* might have done. It looks at the different therapies offered to consumers and tells them what they need to know. Before spending their money on any type of psychotherapy, people would be well advised to examine the evidence offered here.

Tana Dineen
Author of *Manufacturing Victims:
What the Psychology Industry Is Doing to People*

Introduction

I entered the field of psychology in 1970. In the 1980s, I began law school and became a practicing attorney in 1988. This book emerged from the confluence of the two disciplines. My specialization in law was psychotherapy malpractice. What I began to notice as I took the depositions of both the defendants and the plaintiffs' treating therapists was the inexactness of the therapy that was provided. Many therapists testified that their approach was eclectic.

Thus, a major impetus for this book originated with the observation that many therapists did not adhere to a specific type of therapy but seemed to proceed on an ad hoc basis with the justification that adjustments or modifications were made in order to better treat the patient.

A second significant inspiration was Masson's *Against Therapy*. His diatribe against psychotherapy is cited in the text that follows. What I derived from Masson's book was that therapists do not practice what they preach. At that point, I began a preliminary survey to assess whether there were any empirical and well-validated studies that supported the efficacy of psychotherapy. What emerged is an evaluation of many of the popular present-day therapies.

Thanks are due to: a former client, who permitted me to quote a part of her journal; Matt Maibaum, Ph.D., for his comments on an earlier draft of portions of this book; Frederick Crews, Ph.D., who made incisive comments on chapters involving psychoanalysis and recovered memory therapy; Susan Kennedy, for typing and editing the first draft of the manuscript; John Donohue, project editor, and Betty Pessagno, copy editor, who made the book readable; and Nita Romer, acquisitions editor at Greenwood Publishing Group, for her support of the project.

Chapter 1

Science and Fiction in Psychotherapy

Since virtually the beginning of human existence, individuals have been suffering from emotional problems and difficulties with everyday living. It has only been in the last several hundred years or so, however, that formal attempts have been made to deal with emotional problems. A type of treatment that has evolved over the last 100 years is called psychotherapy. Psychotherapy is a technique in which one person (the psychotherapist) generally engages in a verbal interaction with another person (the patient).

Interestingly, psychotherapy cannot be precisely defined. In California, psychotherapy is defined as "the use of psychological methods in a professional relationship to assist a person or persons to acquire greater human effectiveness or to modify feelings, cognitions, attitudes and behavior which are emotionally or socially ineffective or maladjustive."[1] A similar definition relates to the amelioration of distress in cognitive, affective and behavioral functioning.[2]

What exactly are the psychological methods or principles that produce the improvement in human effectiveness? Corsini and Wedding assert that the therapist should have "some theory of personality origins, development, maintenance and change along with some method of treatment logically related to the theory."[3] The California Business and Professions Code (section 2903) states that the procedure producing improvement in cognitive, affective and behavioral functioning "involves understanding, predicting and influencing behavior."

As is obvious, the procedures, techniques or theories as to how psychotherapy is performed are never defined. Not too surprisingly, different therapists may not agree as to what is considered psychotherapy.[4] Apparently, psychotherapy is something psychotherapists do. Corsini and Wedding estimate that as of 1994, there were over 400 different systems of psycho-therapy.[5] There is no line of demarcation or guidepost distinguishing mainstream psychotherapy from "fringe" psychotherapy, let alone outright quackery.

Neither the California Business and Professions Code nor the definition in Corsini and Wedding indicates whether a particular technique needs to be scientifically verified.[6] Thus, there is no requirement that psychotherapy needs to meet any minimal standard of scientific scrutiny or verifiability. If a method or principle is psychological in nature and is performed by a psychotherapist, then the procedure qualifies as psychotherapy. Under this vague and amorphously contoured definition, the following is considered psychotherapy, for example: In psychoanalysis, metaphorical unconscious mental contents are examined. It is theorized that neurotic symptoms may be due to "undischarged emotional tension connected with the repressed memory of a traumatic childhood sexual experience."[7]

Cognitive Behavior Therapy, on the other hand, evaluates how a person thinks and attempts to reduce maladaptive self-views by problem-solving strategies and reality testing.[8] Listed as separate psychotherapeutic techniques are meditation and Yoga. Meditation focuses on training attention in order to bring one's mental processes under greater voluntary control.[9] Yoga refers to an area that includes "ethics, lifestyle, body posture, breath control and intellectual study."[10]

Similarly, informing a client that he or she was abducted by aliens or fomenting this belief as causally related to current mental functioning is within the ambit of psychotherapy. Even astrologically oriented psychotherapy would seem to qualify under this rubric if performed by a psychotherapist. In contrast to exploring unconscious determinants, a psychoastrological analysis uses a fixed point in time to describe and explain human behavior.

In *The Myth of Psychotherapy*, Szasz argues that psychotherapy is not a medical treatment. He reasons that psychotherapy is simply a rhetorical approach wherein one person engages in conversation with a second person. "Virtually anything anyone might do in the company of another person may now be defined as psychotherapeutic."[11] What is needed in order to qualify as psychotherapy are proper credentials and a gullible audience. In a somewhat more therapist-friendly view, Frank states that therapeutic techniques and concepts are "primarily rhetorical devices to persuade or convince the patients of the therapist's healing power"[12] and that the efficacy of "most psychotherapeutic methods depends . . . on how successfully the therapist is able to make the methods fit the patient's expectations."[13]

The question remains: Where is the factual basis for psychotherapy? If there is no scientific basis underlying psychotherapy, then Szasz is essentially correct. Namely, the so-called therapist and the so-called patient are merely indulging in a mutual exchange of myths in which the psychotherapist attempts to impart a particular world view and explanatory concept to the patient. The patient in return reports a perhaps similar world view or notion, and that is when the two individuals embark in a mutual, mythical fantasy excursion into story land—something akin to Alice in Wonderland meets the Wizard of Oz.

PSYCHOTHERAPEUTIC APPROACHES COVERED IN THIS BOOK

Psychoanalysis is covered in Chapter 2. Freud formulated the first major psychotherapeutic technique over 100 years ago. Since then there have been at least 40 modifications of psychoanalysis. However, since the theoretical basis with respect to the psychodynamic and unconscious underpinnings of behavior is very similar, the major focus is on classical psychoanalysis.

By the middle of the twentieth century, Carl Rogers developed a "second force" in psychotherapy (Chapter 5). The humanistic approaches did not dwell on unconscious motivation as a determinant of behavior but rather focused on unconditionally accepting patients as they were and assisting them to reach their potential.

Several forms of therapy can be directly traced to Freud but have made monumental adjustments. A variety of cathartic therapies espouse the notion that uncovering an earlier trauma and ventilating feelings will lead to emotional well-being. Thus, Primal Therapy and Bioenergetic Analysis employ emotional catharsis as the vehicle to dealing with mental disorders (Chapter 3). In addition, various physical and verbal attack therapies include catharsis as a key element in altering a person's emotional state.

In Communication Systems and Strategic Therapy, the focus is on directly attacking the patient's problem from within a family system orientation (Chapter 7). Neurolinguistic Programming (NLP) assesses how people process information in the visual, auditory and kinesthetic modes.

The third major force in psychotherapy is behavioral therapy. Systematic desensitization attempts to gradually reduce a person's fears and anxiety. Implosion Therapy attempts in a paradoxical fashion to initially increase anxiety in order ultimately to reduce anxiety. Many therapists at present employ what is termed the cognitive-behavioral approach. The cognitive aspect focuses on how a person's thoughts affect emotions (Chapter 6).

Psychologists and mental health professionals have asserted that a significant cause of emotional disorder is repression of childhood sexual abuse, and with certain types of therapy, the memories of abuse can be recovered (Chapter 4).

A variety of spiritual approaches rely on the notion of extracorporeal entities as causative agents in psychopathology (Chapter 8). Four different therapies are covered in Chapter 9. The blending of the East and West is found in the form of Buddha Psychotherapy. In Thought Field Therapy and

Palm Therapy, new explanatory concepts and modes of therapy are presented. Lastly, as 100 years of therapy are at hand, some therapists contend that a person's problems can be traced to alien abductions.

THE SCIENTIFIC METHOD

It is not the intent of this book to argue or even suggest that the scientific method is the only way to move forward, in terms of extending a knowledge base, or that human beings may not be helped by means of psychotherapy. Rather, it is simply to emphasize that there is no other way at present to demonstrate that it is psychotherapy in and of itself that may be effectuating improvement in an individual's emotional or mental state.

Freud essentially considered psychoanalysis as a scientifically based methodology. Thus, he claimed that psychoanalysis was a natural science,[14] and therefore he looked for scientifically based causal explanations of psychopathology.[15] Freud's clinical wisdom and acumen were the basis of his scientific approach. For psychoanalysis, the validation of Freud's theory and methods emanated from clinical observations.

Two hallmarks of the scientific method are replication and generalization. In this approach various experimental variables are manipulated in an attempt to analyze relationships between cause and effect. The scientific method generally assumes that time runs forward and that effects occur subsequent to causes. Thus, earlier events that may be traumatic to an individual may be construed as causes of later psychopathology (effects). The task of the psychotherapist, particularly the psychoanalytically oriented psychotherapist, is to archaeologically excavate psychic trauma that may have occurred earlier in a person's lifespan and to use this as an explanatory tool to shed light on the person's subsequent emotional disturbance.

The therapist should base his therapeutic method on validated etiological factors and techniques. The validation of a causal explanation or therapeutic technique comes from a series of experimental and clinical research. To do less means that the psychotherapeutic enterprise is based on intuition and speculation.

GENERALIZATION

If psychotherapy techniques were effective in only a limited population with limited clients, then its utility would be greatly circumscribed. For example, if psychoanalysis had been effective only in the Victorian era, there would be little applicability to present-day populations. Similarly, if there were something unique or idiosyncratic about the person or people rendering the psychotherapy, then there would be extremely limited generalizability to other therapists. It may be that the technique cannot be transferred to other practitioners because there is something different about the psychotherapist who perhaps innovates the approach.

The issue of generalizability of psychotherapeutic effectiveness relates to the personality, age and sex of the therapist as well as to the patients' demographics, including psychodiagnostic categories.

For example, a psychotherapeutic approach might be helpful with persons who are suffering from one particular mental disorder but may have limited or no effect on other mental disorders.

One area of concern is extrapolating data from infants and children to adults. Two major designs for examining age trends are cross-sectional and longitudinal. In the cross-sectional, various ages are compared at the same time: a group of 20-year-olds, 30-year-olds, 40-year-olds, and so on. If reasoning ability is being assessed, the results may very well show that 40-year-olds outperform the other groups. The problem is that age and generation or culture are confounded. Since different people are being compared, it is not always clear what is responsible for the results. In this example, it should be noted that behavior was being directly observed and measured.

In the longitudinal design, the same group or individual is followed over a course of many years. Thus, intellectual capacity can be repeatedly measured over the course of a lifespan to assess the course of cognitive rise and decline.

When psychotherapists extrapolate backward from adulthood to childhood or infancy, they are treading on treacherous scientific grounds. Research conducted on normal children may or may not have any bearing on anxiety or depression in a young adult. Comparison of present clients with research conducted 30 or 40 years ago suffers from the contamination mentioned above.

Thus, the clinician generally relies on the reports of psychologically scarred children in order to generate hypotheses for adult treatment. For example, the well-known study by Spitz (1946) indicated that social deprivation in an institutional setting leads to depression, withdrawal, weight loss and death.[16] The lack of maternal stimulation was seen as a key factor in the severe emotional deficits. Spitz's study concluded that infants are psychologically fused with the mother in the womb and are akin to a conjoined twin. With abrupt separation, as in a foundling home or hospital, the baby does not thrive and loses the capacity for independent functioning.[17]

If the adult patient in the therapist's office was not reared in such extreme circumstances, is it reasonable to generalize backward to find analogous problems with the maternal bond? Do the problems of adult neurotics in any way relate to these unusual circumstances? Without adequate longitudinal studies on a variety of populations, the therapist is confounding age, culture, diagnosis and severity of the environment when attempting to decipher the patient's mental status based on studies of extremely dysfunctional infants. As discussed further in Chapter 2, the speculation reaches a zenith in post-Freudian formulations.

Every year or so, new psychotherapeutic techniques are offered to the public. In drug research, pre-testing is usually done in order to ascertain safety and effectiveness and to determine whether the new medication works in more than just one sample. In the case of psychotherapy research, a whole host of factors need to be considered such as the therapist's personality and the client's psychodiagnosis, age and sex. When examining a number of studies, despite different therapist personalities or demographic characteristics, are the results similar? If, however, the results could not be replicated in different parts of the world, or with different samples of patients, for example, then other explanations for the alleged effectiveness of the therapy need to be entertained.

A rather striking example of the problem associated with generalizing to an appropriate population can be found in the history of Clark Hull's theory. Hull was a well-respected psychologist at Yale University who wrote a text on hypnosis in 1933.[18] Ten years later, he wrote what was to become perhaps the most cited and influential book of that decade: *The Principles of Behavior.*[19]

In a classic text on theories of learning, Hilgard and Bower devote 44 pages to Hull's systematic behavior theory. Freud's chapter on psychodynamics covered 29 pages.[20] It was Hull's view that his theory of motivation would have applicability across the social sciences. It was expected that his theory would provide a comprehensive explanation of human behavior.

Fast-forwarding a decade or two, it might be expected that his theory would form the basis of a behavior therapy or some other psychological theory. In a well-known introductory abnormal psychology text, however, Hull is mentioned only in a fleeting footnote.[21] The virtual disappearance of the theory and its influence can be explained in one word: *extrapolation.* That is, Hull's monumental and careful experiments were conducted primarily on laboratory rats. Unlike Skinner's work for example, Hull's ideas could not readily be extrapolated to humans.[22]

The way to ensure generalizability is to embark on a number of clinical investigations with different relevant populations in different locations, perhaps over different time periods. Thus, in developing a new drug, the scientific community would be looking for what is termed *replication* in assessing the effectiveness of a psychotropic medication in reducing depression. For example, although one study or two studies may show that the administration of a particular antidepressant reduces symptoms of depression, these few studies would not be enough. The results must be repeated so that any possible experimental artifacts or flaws can at least be minimized or randomized out.

DEPENDENT AND INDEPENDENT VARIABLES

In the experimental method, two types of variables are involved. First is the *dependent variable*, which is considered the measurement of change, i.e, improvement in emotional functioning. Usually, the clinician is seeking to assess change in mental status; i.e, is the person showing fewer symptoms of anxiety or depression, for example. The second variable is the *independent variable*. It is what the clinician does in order to effect improvement. It is the variable that may be manipulated, such as a treatment modality. Actually, in psychotherapy research it is not easy to manipulate independent variables because a person may simply call up a psychotherapist and not, strictly speaking, participate in a research project. Thus, there are several alternatives to the experimental approach, as will be described below, including the case method and survey reports, which was the method employed by *Consumer Reports*.

In evaluating the measure of change, the question is asked: To what extent have the patients' lives improved? How are their lives different? How has their mental condition improved, changed or worsened? The next question is: How does one measure change in psychotherapy research? Do we ask patients? Do we ask clinicians or a combination of both? Further questions relate to whether or not psychotherapists are treating the same mental conditions in the first place.

In order to determine if change takes place, many studies evaluate the change in level of depression, for example. In attempting to determine a diagnosis of a patient, the *Diagnostic and Statistical Manual of Mental Disorders* (DSM) has been used traditionally over the last several decades. The current version is the DSM-IV.[23] (One other interim publication, DSM-III-R, was a modification of the DSM-III.) The DSM scheme presents a multitude of problems, not the least of which may be a lack of reliability in setting out the diagnostic criteria. One critic has stated that the diagnostic formulations may be nothing more than a "disguised set of moral, highly culturally bound descriptions about those behaviors that are to be tolerated and those that are to be stigmatized and extinguished."[24] Kovacs (1996) further states that the underlying fraud of the DSM system is revealed by the apparent fact that diagnostic material as to inclusion or exclusion is based on the taking of votes. Thus, the determination and designation of what constitutes psychopathology was based on opinions and not empirical research.

Basing the DSM schema on various theoretical orientations may hamper research not only because it is difficult to make a particular diagnosis, but because different investigators may use slightly different criteria for inclusion in a study. The leading psychoanalytic researchers on Borderline Personality

Disorder state that the criteria in the DSM-III-R are "hardly adequate for research and clinical practice."[25]

There may be an even more significant problem: inter-rater reliability. An individual who is expressing a certain cluster of symptoms may be seen for an initial 50-minute diagnostic interview. Imagine that in a hypothetical study this interview is audio- or videotaped and then is given to ten experienced clinicians who are asked to ascertain what the diagnosis is, say, based on the DSM-IV. How satisfactory is it if only five of the ten psychotherapists agree on the diagnosis? Amazingly, there appears to have been no follow-up research in the last two decades subsequent to the DSM-III as to what the inter-rater reliability is between the diagnostic formulations. It is as if the 1980 version of the DSM-III set the standard, which was not particularly high in various diagnostic categories. Despite the tinkering with some of the diagnostic categories and the addition of some new ones, no follow-up has been made to verify or ascertain whether there is significant agreement among various clinicians.

A fascinating research project would be to present therapists who have different diagnostic orientations (perhaps some who are psychoanalytic, behavioral or family systems–oriented) with psychodiagnostic interviews and ask them to render a diagnosis. If the agreement were to hover around 50, 60 or 70 percent, much would remain to be done in terms of improving the clarity and specificity of a particular diagnosis. Compare this with the diagnosis of dental caries and submit ten x-rays to a variety of dentists. Would there be over 90 percent agreement in terms of rendering a conclusion that these individuals had cavities in their teeth?

In the absence of substantial agreement on underlying emotional problems, it is difficult to conclude that a particular therapeutic technique is effective with a given psychodiagnosis. Therapists who do not even attempt to assess the patient's diagnosis can offer little in the way of explaining how the patient changed, let alone measure whether a change actually occurred. Rather, these therapy approaches may simply rely on a patient's self-report or the clinician's subjective assessment. When a patient is in therapy, she may likely tend to focus on improvements and offer statements evincing positive change in emotional outlook.

The next way of assessing improvement or change might be through psychological testing. This is a gigantic category and can only briefly be touched upon in this book. The usefulness of psychodiagnostic testing may lie in the use of certain so-called objective assessment measures such as the Beck Depression Inventory, which is a self-rated inventory taken by the patient and scored by the clinician.[26] It is obvious to the patient what the test is about. The scoring is rather straightforward in which items are given a number and are added up. The overall score reflects the level of severity of depression. The Beck Depression Inventory allows for some objectivity in terms of measuring symptoms of depression, especially at different points in therapy or in a research project.

Other tests that attempt to establish a diagnosis, such as the Rorschach Ink Blot Test, would seem to have limited utility in rendering an accurate diagnosis.[27] To the extent that any of the research is using unverified or unreliable measures, this will create a major flaw in a particular experimental or case method approach. A possible virtue of this test is that the subject (patient) does not know what it is measuring. Use of the Rorschach Ink Blot Test, however, has been called into serious question by a number of investigators and clinicians in that it appears to have a severe problem in terms of demonstrating anything reliable.[28] Thus, when psychological tests such as the Rorschach, figure drawing or new and experimental tests are used to formulate a psychodiagnosis, questions may be raised as to the underlying accuracy derived. It should be noted, as Dawes further points out, that use of the Rorschach for other purposes such as making decisions about an individual in a legal setting is highly questionable.

ARTIFACTS AND BIAS IN MEASUREMENT

Measurement of change by the experimenter or clinician may be subject to the effect of bias and is a variable in and of itself that may need to be fully examined. A vested interest in a particular technique may lead the therapist or clinician to evaluate the procedure in a more positive light. In addition, a therapist may see change where none exists.

In a study of perceived effectiveness of therapy, a group of behavioral and psychoanalytically oriented therapists were shown extracts from early and late therapy sessions. Unbeknownst to the therapists, the interviews were created so as to be ambiguous and in fact to portray no behavioral or psychological change. The subjects/therapists were asked to indicate if any change had taken place between the sessions. The results indicated that the analytically oriented therapists rated the patients as improving when in fact there was no such improvement.[29]

The problem of expectancy effects may be anticipated in studies where the clinician has a vested interest in the outcome. A major pitfall is evident when the experimenter delivers and supervises all treatment conditions. The investigator may show more enthusiasm for his favored treatment and perhaps unintentionally convey a number of cues to the subjects.[30] Even in a well-controlled study, the effect of allegiance to a particular psychotherapeutic technique is a factor that may need to be considered. Thus, it may not be so surprising that, more often than not, positive results emanate from the proponents of a particular theory and that negative results seem to emerge from researchers who may not necessarily advocate that particular therapeutic approach.

In order to show the generalizability of a particular psychotherapeutic modality, clinical studies are needed from several different settings and locations, especially those that are not under the direct control of the major proponent of the given psychotherapeutic approach.

DEMAND CHARACTERISTICS AND PLACEBO CONTROL

In establishing cause–effect relationships, the experimenter, as well as the clinician, attempts to connect a particular treatment procedure with improvement in the patient's condition. The notion is that the therapist is providing an actual active therapeutic ingredient that is responsible for producing the improvement in the patient's life and mental functioning. The problem is that significant artifacts may be responsible for producing the change in the patient's condition.

Experimental drug research has used a certain methodology in an attempt to control unwanted artifacts. One such attempt is the implementation of placebo controls. What happens here is that a random group of subjects is given the active ingredient such as an antidepressant, whereas another group of randomly selected subjects is given an inert inactive placebo. In the so-called double-blind placebo control study, neither the experimenter nor the subject knows which group receives which particular treatment. The theory then is as follows: If the patients receiving the actual drugs improve, whereas the subjects receiving the inert substance do not improve, then the differences may be attributable to the ingredient in the psychopharmacologically active antidepressant drug.

Without adequate controls, artifact and bias can result from characteristics not only within experimental studies but from the psychotherapeutic environment as well. When observing the environment of experimental or clinical settings, there are certain cues that have been referred to as demand characteristics.[31] The demand characteristics or cues include the sources of information that the subject may receive prior to arriving at the actual experimental scene: There may be rumors about the experiment and certain information provided while they are being recruited. The subject or patient may be responding on the basis of expectation and not necessarily to the "real" experimental or clinical elements.

Orne and Scheibe (1964) conducted a study on sensory deprivation in order to ascertain if unwanted cues or demand characteristics contaminate the variable under examination, i.e, the effects of sensory deprivation on a person's cognitive and perceptual functioning.[32] They attempted to distinguish so-called real effects from placebo effects such as in the above-mentioned psychotropic studies.

In prior research all sensory cues were minimized, which included isolating individuals from visual, auditory, tactile and other stimulation for extended periods of time by totally immersing a person in a tank of water. Following actual extensive sensory deprivation, there has been distorted perception, hallucinations, lack of concentration and increased disorientation.

Orne and Scheibe believed that cues from the experimental situation could contribute to the physical and auditory and visual distortions. Subjects were not deprived of any sensory information and were simply put in a room where they could work on an arithmetic task; they were told, however, that if they wanted to escape, they could do so by pressing a red emergency alarm. They were greeted by an experimenter who wore a white medical coat and took a brief medical history. Most significantly, the subjects were informed that they were to report any unusual visual imagery, fantasy or feelings, as well as any problems with concentration and disorientation. The subjects were informed that such feelings were not unusual when one was placed in the present type of situation.

In the control group, the subjects were met by an experimenter who wore business clothes and did not take a medical history. The subjects were in fact informed that they were part of a control group. Thus, demand characteristics were minimized in this group.

At the end of the experimental period, the experimental group showed more significant cognitive deterioration and sensory alteration as contrasted with the control group. Some examples include the walls of the room starting to waver, objects in the room being animated, seeing colors where none existed, transformation of numbers into inkblots, changes in the size of the room, or forgetting where the room was located.

Orne and Scheibe concluded that, since there was in fact no sensory deprivation, it appeared that the demand characteristics—namely, the experimenter's erroneous but authoritative statements and behavior—appeared to be associated with the changes in cognitive and sensory awareness.

The astounding findings can be applied to psychotherapy in that a number of demand characteristics are involved; namely, psychotherapists strongly believe in their psychotherapeutic approach, which will carry a strong expectation that change will take place. Books and articles are disseminated to the public regarding the expected clinical improvement. With the rapid communication networks and marketing, it takes only a few years for a particular psychotherapy approach to become well known to the mental health community and the public sector. The whole idea of going to a psychotherapist is to try to improve one's emotional condition. Thus, the patient believes that change will occur. If demand characteristics are involved, then it is not the psychotherapeutic technique that may be the active ingredient producing change in a particular individual, but rather the therapist's and patient's expectation of change.

Without adequate experimental controls, these elements are inextricably intertwined. Thus, what one is left with is no more than a general placebo to explain the possible changes in a patient's performance, expectations, feelings and behavior. "Improvement, resulting from any form of therapy cannot be taken as evidence for the efficacy of the particular technique, unless behavior change can be shown to be greater than that due to faith and the efficacy of the therapist and the techniques used."[33] Without some control for therapists' and patients' expectations, which includes demand characteristics and other inherent factors in the psychotherapeutic arena, no conclusion can be reached that the so-called independent variable is in fact directly related to the measurement of change. A person's reaction or response to therapy is contaminated by artifacts, including clinician bias, so that cause/effect relationships are clouded.

THE IDEAL CLINICAL RESEARCH STUDY

A tremendous amount of research over the last 50 years has been concerned with the issue of the clinical effectiveness or efficacy of psychotherapy. The question is whether psychotherapy is more effective than no treatment or whether one form of therapy is superior to another. One of the major aims of the vast amount of research is to find the key active ingredients of psychotherapy. Thus, what is it that determines whether or not psychotherapy works?

Seligman has outlined eight areas that should be included in an ideal study of the efficacy of psychotherapy.[34] If these conditions or factors are met, then there may be some assurance that the therapeutic approach and the etiological explanations regarding psychopathology have some validity.

First, the patients or subjects are randomly assigned to treatment and control groups. For example, if 20 potential patients called for an appointment at a university clinic, one-half of the group would be arbitrarily assigned to a treatment condition and the other half to a control group. The control group could be a no-treatment group, which should be a less effective method of dealing with the emotional problem of the patients.

There should be rigorous controls of the patients in the study, such that there is another group who receives a credible placebo. The intent is to control various influences such as rapport, expectation of gain and sympathetic attention. The rationale is to control for demand characteristics so that it may be possible to differentiate between the alleged active therapeutic agent of change from the patient's expectation or desire to please the therapist.

In order to improve quality control, the treatments should be based on printed or published manuals. The therapists receive training, in part, from detailed narrative descriptions of the treatment protocols. Accuracy of their fidelity to this specific psychotherapeutic approach could be assessed via videotaped sessions with ongoing feedback and supervision. Presumably each therapist would provide the identical treatment. In drug studies, the active biochemical ingredients are always virtually identical. Thus, the independent variable, i.e., type of drug, remains constant, despite who dispenses the medication.

The problem in private practice, however, is that the clinician may not be supervised or adhere to any treatment protocol or therapy manual. Psychotherapists tend to make minor or major therapeutic adjustments and devise various strategies as their careers develop. Therefore, any results obtained in a monitored study cannot necessarily be extrapolated beyond the research study.

The next requirement is that there should be a fixed number of sessions that the patients are seen. In designing a study to contrast several different theoretical approaches, it might be unfair to compare one group receiving 20 sessions of therapy with another group receiving 200 sessions. On the other hand, if it takes several years of psychoanalysis to produce significant changes, it can be argued that short-term psychodynamic therapy should be contrasted with Behavior Therapy, for example.

The measurement of change should be clearly operationalized. Here, reference is being made to the dependent variables. What is being measured should be clearly and concisely defined so that other investigators can determine what is being measured. It would be wasteful for researchers to imagine that they were assessing the same thing only to find out that there are any number of ways to conceptualize or assess the key outcome measures. One problem covered below is the way Carl Rogers defines the necessary and sufficient ingredients needed for psychotherapeutic change (see Chapter 5). Thus, there should be specific discrete definitions of what constitutes clinical improvement. An example of change may be a score on the Beck Depression Inventory, which shows a decrease in depressive symptoms after six months of Cognitive Therapy.

An ideal study would keep the clinicians and raters blind as to who is in the control versus active experimental group. In reality, psychotherapy studies can only be "single" blind in that the clinician, at least, will know whether they are proving the clinically active product or are simply monitoring a group discussion control group.

In order to determine what type of treatment works for a particular type of client, only one DSM-IV diagnosis should be included in the study. If there are loose diagnostic criteria, even including patients with several diagnoses, it will be unclear what type of therapy works for what particular type of mental disorder.

Lastly, it is important to have follow-up assessment for some time after termination of the study. For example, what would it mean if, after three months following the investigation, the improvements in therapy had dissipated?

CASE STUDY AND REPORT

A drastically different approach to illuminating whether psychotherapy is effective is the case study report. There are no experimental manipulations or a control group. Psychoanalysis developed largely as a result of the case study method. A psychoanalytically oriented therapist would write down background material, including important developmental events, along with patient fantasies and dreams and other self-reports. Inferences on an individual's functioning were based on information that is usually considered anecdotal and refers to "impressions, judgments, and inferences of the client or therapist."[35] Moreover, these reports are essentially subjective evaluations and are distinguishable from more objective measures, including standardized questionnaires and direct observations.[36]

In essence, the case study method does not have experimental controls. Of course, it is difficult or impossible to exclude alternative explanations for the behavior under question. A major problem with the case study is that information is not, in many instances, verifiable. Anecdotal reports are filtered through the eyes and brain of the psychotherapist who initially espouses or advocates a particular point of view. Numerous additional explanations may be given for a particular behavior or result. Prior to the advent of tape recorders and camcorders, it was not at all clear that the therapist or clinician had accurately recorded the essence of what had transpired in the course of the clinical case studies.

A second problem is that some of the elements in the client's own history cannot be verified. To give an example, Kazdin summarizes the case history of a patient who entered into psychoanalysis.[37] Although the patient was a vegetarian, apparently this was not a presenting problem.[38] He began avoiding meat at the age of five, at which time he apparently reported having seen a sack of chickens being slaughtered. The onset of the patient's vegetarianism was further elaborated in psychoanalysis and was related to "the patient's idea that eating meat might transfer to the patient's uncontrolled animal impulses, or other acts of animals and incorporation of dead flesh would bring him closer to his own death, that eating meat would have an animal devour him from within, and similar beliefs."[39]

Thus, there is a chain of causal connections made by this psychotherapist who attempts to connect earlier presumed traumatic events to later emotional problems or mental status. The problem is that it is not possible to verify whether the events occurred in the first place or whether they were imputed to the client by the therapist, or developed in the client after he became a vegetarian.[40]

Lastly, there is the problem of clinician bias. Such bias could take many forms, not the least of which is that the writer may make the facts fit the theory under discussion. A series of case reports or anecdotes does not accumulate into an experimental verification of a theory or the etiological underpinnings of psychopathology. Generally, a clinician is not going to report facts or cases that do not support his therapeutic rationale and technique. It appears that virtually any data can be interpreted to fit any theory. Thus, case reports, anecdotes and testimonials do not provide adequate empirical data as to the effectiveness of psychotherapy.

FIELD REPORTS OR SURVEYS

A third method used to ascertain whether therapy is helpful is the field report or *consumer survey*, which may generate further hypotheses as to how to identify the active ingredients in terms of improving a patient's condition. A survey report focuses on getting participants to indicate whether or not psychotherapy was helpful or effective. An efficacy study examines one type of psychotherapy with a comparison group under well-controlled conditions.[41]

Even though some of the experimental and clinical research may support the efficacy of psychotherapy, particularly cognitive behavioral approaches, in treating certain symptomatologies, Seligman states that the efficacy study "is a wrong method for empirically validating psychotherapy as it is actually done because it omits too many crucial elements of what is done in the field."[42]

One way to alleviate these problems of the efficacy study, according to Seligman's view, is to look at a *Consumer Reports* survey that was conducted in the *field*. In 1995, *Consumer Reports*[43] published a supplementary survey regarding psychotherapy and drugs sent to about 180,000 readers. Included in this survey were approximately 100 questions about automobiles as well as mental health. The *Consumer Reports* readers were asked to fill out a section on mental health, "If at any time over the past three years you experienced stress or other emotional problems for which you sought help from any of the following: Friends, relatives, or a member of the clergy; a mental health professional like a psychologist or a psychiatrist; your family doctor or support group." A total of 22,000 readers responded, and approximately 7,000 responded to the mental health questions. Approximately 4,100 went to some combination of mental health professionals, family doctors and support groups. Out of this sample, 2,900 saw mental health professionals.

Questions included what type of therapist they sought out or whether there were any problems such as anxiety, panic, phobia, depression, emotional state at the outset, the emotional state at the time of survey, group versus individual therapy, duration and frequency of receiving therapy, type of therapy including psychodynamic, behavioral, cognitive, and "feminist." Other questions dealt with the outcome—how much therapy helped, as well as satisfaction with therapy.

There was a multi-dimensional measure of therapy effectiveness consisting of:

1. *Specific Improvements.* "How much did the treatment help with the specific problem that led you to therapy?"
2. *Satisfaction.* "Overall, how satisfied were you with the therapist's treatment of your problem?"
3. *Global Improvement.* The responders described their overall emotional state at the time of the survey compared with the start of the treatment. This was based entirely on their self-report.

Seligman states that despite methodological flaws, which will briefly be discussed in a moment, there is empirical validation of the effectiveness of psychotherapy. In asking whether psychotherapy helps, he notes a number of clear-cut results. Specifically, treatment by mental health professionals usually worked. Most of the respondents indicated that they got a lot better. "Out of the 426 people who were feeling very poor when they began therapy, 87 percent were feeling very good, good or at least somewhat better by the time of the survey."[44] Furthermore, long-term therapy produced more improvement than short-term therapy, meaning that the longer the persons stayed in therapy, the more they indicated that they were improved. Interestingly enough, persons in Alcoholics Anonymous did especially well and were reporting improvement scores significantly above scores achieved through treatment by mental health professionals.

Although this was a field approach, Seligman addressed a number of methodological flaws. First, there may be sampling bias in that only persons who are more likely to report improvement in mental health functioning returned the questionnaire. This field report includes individuals who were readers of *Consumer Reports* and who took the time to respond. As noted, there were only 7,000 responses to the questions on mental health issues. Thus, it may be that persons who didn't like their therapy or didn't improve in therapy were less likely to take the time to respond to this survey.[45]

Of course, there were no control groups in the study, and this particular report cannot address whether talking to other sympathetic friends or time alone would have produced just as much improvement as treatment by various mental health professionals. Without a control group, it is difficult, if not impossible, to say whether or not some people improve without treatment; i.e., do some people show spontaneous remission?

One other methodological flaw is that the outcome measures or the dependent measures seem to be somewhat global and lack specificity; i.e., there is not a precise objective assessment method such as the Beck Depression Inventory to assess reported changes in an individual. For example, it appears that the concept of therapeutic improvement was combined with how much the person was satisfied with (or liked) his or her therapist. Despite the large number of methodological weaknesses inherent in this study, it does appear that at least some people are willing to report that their mental or emotional state has improved after seeing a therapist.

The major problem that remains is that there are no data in this type of field study to indicate whether the psychotherapist provides any active ingredient responsible for the apparent improvement in emotional and psychological functioning. What can be stated is that patients who are in therapy, particularly those who remained in therapy for up to at least three years, have a subjective belief that, as a result of seeing a psychotherapist, they feel better.

Any conclusion that a customer satisfaction survey demonstrates that psychotherapy works needs to be taken with a grain of salt.[46] The *Consumer Reports* study does not in any way scientifically confirm or validate that the necessary ingredient to feeling better is showing up at a psychotherapist's office. Nor does it show what it is about going to a psychotherapist's office and receiving treatment that is the central factor in producing change.

CAN PSYCHOTHERAPY SURVIVE?

Many critics have argued that psychotherapy should be abandoned.[47] Some therapists are indeed harming patients, are condescending, and are espousing a particular position and demand that the patient adhere to their view.[48] Sometimes clearly negative outcomes are a result of engaging in psychotherapy.[49] Most psychotherapists, however, are not dangerous, nor do they harm patients. The question addressed in this book is whether clinicians have reliable tools based on sound research. Despite assertions of positive outcomes, the major issue is whether there is any clinical evidence that therapy is effective.

The difficulty psychotherapy faces is that there has been very little scientific research to bolster the claims for its effectiveness. Many therapies have been promulgated without any scientific support whatsoever. The only viable therapy is the technique or method that can be reasonably verified and replicated over several well-designed studies. Case reports, consumer satisfaction surveys, anecdotes and testimonials do not suffice as substantial evidence.

Because human interactions are so complex, it may be suggested that the scientific method is irrelevant. To those who argue that the scientific approach should be ignored, it can be answered that in so doing, one is inviting chaos.[50] There would then be no possibility of demonstrating the scientific validity or viability of the psychotherapeutic method or the underlying theoretical mechanisms. There might only be a haphazard advancement, if at all, with no way to confirm or replicate anyone else's results.

If the scientific method were abandoned, all that would remain would be speculation, conjecture and intuition along with myths. The exchange of rhetoric and myths from patient to therapist and vice versa does not form the basis of a scientific endeavor.

The critical question is whether a factual basis exists for the alleged active ingredients in psychotherapy as well as the purported positive results that are superior to no treatment or just giving advice in a supportive environment. Without adequate clinical investigations, including appropriate experimental controls, one can only speculate about the nature of the verbal interaction between therapist and patient. Without scientific backing, one is left to ponder whether what happens in therapy is based on something specific to the treatment or is mainly the result of a placebo encased in a series of rituals.[51] Without this attempt, the so-called active ingredients responsible for affect change in therapy will remain a mystery.

NOTES

1. California Business and Professions Code, section 2903.

2. Corsini, R. J. & Wedding, D. (Eds.) (1995). *Current psychotherapies* (5th ed.) (p. 1). Itasca, Ill.: Peacock Publishers.

3. Corsini & Wedding, *Current psychotherapies* (p. 1).

4. Corsini & Wedding, *Current psychotherapies* (p. 2).

5. Corsini & Wedding, *Current psychotherapies* (p. 10).

6. Corsini & Wedding, *Current psychotherapies* (p. 1).

7. Arlow, J. A. (1995). Psychoanalysis. In Corsini & Wedding (Eds.), *Current psychotherapies* (pp. 15–50).

8. Beck, A. T. & Weishaar, M. (1995). Cognitive therapy. In Corsini & Wedding (Eds.), *Current psychotherapies* (pp. 229–261).

9. Corsini & Wedding, *Current psychotherapies* (p. 388).

10. Corsini & Wedding, *Current psychotherapies* (p. 388).

11. Szasz, T. (1979). *The myth of psychotherapy: Mental healing as religion, rhetoric and repression* (p. xviii). Garden City, N.Y.: Anchor Press/Doubleday.

12. Frank, J. D. (1995). Psychotherapy as rhetoric: Some implications. *Clinical Psychology: Science and Practice, 2* (pp. 90–93).

13. Frank, Psychotherapy as rhetoric (pp. 90–93).

14. Freud, S. (1959). Some elementary lessons in psycho-analysis. *Collected Papers. S. E.* (J. Strachey, Trans.), Vol. 23 (pp. 281–286). London: Hogarth Press and the Institute of Psycho-Analysis. (Originally published in 1940.)

15. Grünbaum, A. (1993). *Validation in the clinical theory of psychoanalysis: A study in the philosophy of psychoanalysis* (p. 5). Madison, Conn.: International Universities Press.

16. Spitz, R. A. (1946). Anaclitic depression. In *Psychoanalytic study of the child* (2nd ed.) (pp. 313–342). New York: International Universities Press.

17. Mitchell, S. A. & Black, M. J. (1994). *Freud and beyond: A history of modern psychoanalytic thought* (p. 41). New York: Basic Books.

18. Hull, C. L. (1933). *Hypnosis and suggestability: An experimental approach.* New York: Appleton-Century-Crofts.

19. Hull, C. L. (1943). *Principles of behavior*. New York: Appleton-Century-Crofts.

20. Hilgard. E. R. & Bower, G. H. (1966). *Theories of learning* (3rd ed.). New York: Appleton-Century-Crofts.

21. Coleman, J. C., Butcher, J. N. & Carson, R. C. (1980). *Abnormal psychology and modern life* (6th ed.) (p. 60). Glenview, Ill.: Scott, Foresman.

22. Skinner, B. F. (1953). *Science and human behavior*. New York: Macmillan.

23. *Diagnostic and statistical manual of mental disorders* (4th ed.). Washington, D.C.: American Psychiatric Association.

24. Kovacs, A. L. (1996, Winter). We have met the enemy and he is us. *AAP Advance* (p. 19).

25. Kernberg, O. F. & Clarkin, J. F. (1994). Training and the integration of research and clinical practice. In Talley, P. F., Strupp, H. H. & Butler, S. F. (Eds.), *Psychotherapy research & practice: Bridging the gap* (pp. 39–59). New York: Basic Books.

26. Beck, A. T. & Steer, R. A. (1987). *Manual for the revised Beck Depression Inventory*. San Antonio, Tex.: Psychological Corporation.

27. Dawes, R. M. (1994). *House of cards: Psychology and psychotherapy built on myth* (p. 150). New York: Free Press.

28. Dawes, *House of cards* (p. 150).

29. Weiss, S. L. (1972). Perceived effectiveness of psychotherapy: A function of suggestion? *Journal of Consulting and Clinical Psychology, 39* (pp. 156–159).

30. Kazdin, A. E. (1980). *Research design in clinical psychology* (p. 295). New York: Harper & Row.

31. Orne, M. T. & Scheibe, K. E. (1964). The contribution of nondeprivation factors in the production of sensory deprivation effects: The psychology of the "panic button." *Journal of Abnormal and Social Psychology, 68* (pp. 3–12).

32. Orne & Scheibe, Psychology of "panic button" (pp. 3–12).

33. Kazdin, *Research design in clinical psychology* (p. 331).

34. Seligman, M.E.P. (1995). The effectiveness of psychotherapy: The *Consumer Reports* study. *American Psychologist, 50* (pp. 965–975).

35. Kazdin, *Research design in clinical psychology* (p. 12).

36. Kazdin, *Research design in clinical psychology* (p. 12).

37. Kazdin, *Research design in clinical psychology* (p. 26).

38. Friedman, S. (1975). On vegetarianism. *Journal of the American Psychoanalytic Association, 23* (pp. 396–406).

39. Kazdin, *Research design in clinical psychology* (p. 26).

40. Kazdin, *Research design in clinical psychology* (p. 26).

41. Seligman, Effectiveness of psychotherapy.

42. Seligman, Effectiveness of psychotherapy.

43. Mental health: Does therapy help? (1995, November). *Consumer Reports* (pp. 734–739).

44. Seligman, Effectiveness of psychotherapy.

45. Hall, J. A. (1996). Using reader surveys as scientific data. Talk prepared for symposium entitled "The Consumer Reports article on psychotherapy: Does it help?" American Psychological Association Convention, Toronto, Canada, August 11.

46. Dineen, T. (1998). *Manufacturing victims: What the psychology industry is doing to people* (2nd ed.) (p. 179). Montreal: Robert Davies.

47. Masson, J. M. (1994). *Against therapy* (p. 24). Monroe, Maine: Common Courage Press.

48. Campbell, T. W. (1994). *Beware of the talking cure: Psychotherapy may be hazardous to your health* (p. 310). Boca Raton, Fla.: Upton Books.

49. Mohr, David C. (1995). Negative outcomes in psychotherapy: A critical review. *Clinical Psychology: Science and Practice, 2* (pp. 1–27).

50. Schaef, A. W. (1992). *Beyond therapy, beyond science: A new model for healing the whole person.* San Francisco: HarperCollins.

51. Campbell, *Beware of the talking cure* (p. 22).

Chapter 2

Psychoanalytic Psychotherapy

This chapter presents a brief overview of the psychoanalytic method and the attempts to validate psychoanalysis by means of dream interpretation and analysis of the transference relationship. Both case studies and clinical research are critically examined.

Sigmund Freud initially formulated psychoanalysis during the latter part of the nineteenth century. At the heart of psychoanalytic theory is the proposition that the origin of psychopathology is repressed childhood traumatic memories. The retrieval of these memories occurs by lifting the repression, which then produces beneficial results.[1] The essence of psychoanalytic technique is the investigation of repressed trauma by means of dream interpretation, transference and free association.

PSYCHOANALYTIC THEORY

Freud divided the structure of personality into three spheres: the *id*, the *ego* and the *superego*. The id is the original system from which the ego and superego emerge. It is an undifferentiated matrix, which contains everything that is inherited including instincts.[2] The ego is a set of regulatory functions that serves to control id impulses and acts as a reality check. The superego functions as an internalized moral arbiter, which develops in response to parental directives.[3]

Freud postulated a psychosexual theory of development. The *oral phase*, he proposed, extends from birth to eighteen months. The source of gratification centers around feeding and includes the organs related thereto: the mouth, lips and tongue. One contention is that a person whose oral needs have been satisfied tends to be more optimistic.[4] On the other hand, a person who experiences problems during this phase may become gullible in adulthood. Thus, a gullible person is someone who will swallow anything.[5]

The *anal phase* lasts from eighteen months to three years. The main source of pleasure comes from retaining or expelling feces. During this phase significant interest is shown in bodily functions and products. Parental toilet training can help to shape adult personality. Anal characteristics that may emerge in adulthood include being wasteful with money, letting go of feelings through explosiveness and holding on tightly to money, i.e., stinginess.[6]

The *phallic stage* lasts from ages three to six in which gratification centers around the sexual organs. This age sets the stage for the *oedipal* conflict in which boys turn their sexual desires toward the mother. By harboring such desires, however, the child fears his father as a rival. As a result, the boy begins to experience what is termed castration anxiety. In order to resolve the oedipal conflict and avoid castration, the boy renounces his sexual interest in the mother and identifies with the father. Freud labored, perhaps not too successfully, to work out analogous developmental dilemmas for young girls.[7]

After passing through a *latency stage*, a person enters the *genital stage* in which there is a transformation from a "pleasure seeking narcissistic infant into a reality-oriented socialized adult."[8] A successful analysis may be needed, however, in order to reach the fully mature genital character.[9] In Erikson's ego psychology,[10] developmental tasks and conflicts extended into adulthood and into old age.

REVISIONS OF THE THEORY

The twentieth century witnessed innumerable extensions of classic psychoanalysis. There have been at least three major diversions from psychoanalysis, including the defection of the "big two," Adler and Jung, as well as the interpersonal theory of Sullivan.[11] *Freud and Beyond* refers to at least 38 other revisionists.[12] Virtually all of the post-Freudians and alternative analytic therapies can be considered psychodynamic in their shared belief and focus on unconscious motivation.

One of the major revisions is the object relations approach. In general, object relations therapists assess the internal and external world of the patient.[13] The patient has an internal representation (self) of the external objects in the environment. The analyst attempts in the therapeutic setting to elucidate the patient's earlier infant interpersonal relationships with significant others.

There have been significant revisions within the objects relations camp, so that now there are several different and even conflicting theoretical positions.

PSYCHOANALYTIC TECHNIQUE

Analysis of transference was one of the major hallmarks of psychoanalytic technique. In therapy, the analyst remains "neutral" and impersonal, thereby allowing the patient to project perceptual distortions onto this unbiased professional. Freud theorized that, in the transference relations, the patient was "unconsciously re-enacting a latter-day version of forgotten childhood memories and repressed unconscious fantasies."[14] In adult interpersonal relations, unconscious "conflict-laden attitudes" infiltrate from prior childhood interactions with important adults.[15] According to psychoanalytic theory, the patient has no conscious awareness that she is reacting to important present-day figures based on thought patterns and reactions from the distant past.[16] Thus, the early childhood reactions are inappropriately applied to adult situations. This mistaken and unconscious misapplication of feelings toward a stranger, i.e., the therapist, is termed Transference. The patient may view the therapist as a father or lover, thereby transferring feelings from another time and place into the therapeutic arena. The psychoanalyst uses this so-called transference neurosis as fodder for the psychoanalytic session. The origin of a person's psychopathology is recapitulated by means of the transference.

What occurs in early age, though repressed and not known to the patient, flashes before the analyst like a video cassette when the patient shows such significant misinterpretation as to who the therapist is and what they are doing. By viewing this presumed veridical psychological video, the therapist has sufficient data, so that at the proper time they can offer interpretations to the patient. The patient, however, may display *negative transference*; that is, the patient does not accept the interpretations and attempts to impede the therapist's efforts.[17] With persistence, however, the therapist offers insight that is accepted, permitting the patient to overcome her cognitive and affective distortions and hence the neurosis.

Although analyzing transference relationships is one of the most critical aspects of psychoanalysis, it should be noted that various psychoanalytic schools have different positions on how to deal with and interpret transference.

Countertransference refers to perceptual, cognitive and affective distortions that the analyst experiences toward the patient during the course of therapy. Lurking in the analyst's past may be unresolved conflicts that he unconsciously transfers onto the patient in the present-day therapy session. Psychoanalysts, in particular, undergo rigorous training at analytic institutes, for example, to illuminate and eradicate countertransference problems. When countertransference issues emerge in therapy, the analyst either receives peer supervision to work out the problem or terminates the patient. Unchecked countertransference can lead to a therapist acting out another role such as a parent. In such a scenario, which often results in litigation, the therapist may give the patient the keys to his home, or may have the patient move in, and may request that the therapist be referred to as the parent, and so on.

As with transference, there are differing views on how to deal with countertransference. For some psychoanalysts, countertransference is an unavoidable problem that needs to be eliminated. Other analysts find countertransference helpful and in some instances believe that appropriate disclosure of their own feelings is necessary and helpful.[18] Thus, many post-Freudians are more than just a passive mirror or blank slate.

How does a therapist distinguish between negative transference and countertransference? First, a potential psychoanalyst undergoes personal psychotherapy to flush out the blind spots and bias (see below, however). Second, by means of the transference lens, he can see by means of psychic time travel to the patient's historic past and discover what actually happened. So the analyst, by viewing the re-enactment of prior conflicts, has direct knowledge of the patient's early childhood. But what if the "videotape" is faulty? If so, then the analyst has defective tools in separating his own reactions from the patient's. What would be happening is a bouncing back and forth of transference reactions from patient to therapist. Without a psycho-historical time machine, the therapist must rely on clinical judgment about the accuracy and veridicality of events in the patient's early development. In the objects relations form of psychoanalysis, the therapist must display a high degree of clinical acumen in that transference implications are extrapolated from infancy.

Successful psychoanalysis requires that patients' "principal conscious acts, thoughts, and feelings be traced to their *actual* unconscious determinants."[19] Thus, analysis of the transference relationship, for example, presumes that real events are being ferreted out of the unconscious and really happened. Without concurrent validation, such as medical reports or parental observations, it is difficult, if not impossible, to verify the alleged critical events that emerge in analysis.

The veridicality of reported developmental events did not seem to concern Freud or some of his followers.[20]

Whether actual trauma or fantasy is at the root of psychopathology remains debatable in current psychoanalytical circles.[21] Initially, Freud theorized that the cause of adult neuroses could be traced to childhood seduction. His second view presented the notion that the traumatic past might be invented and that the seduction was only imagined.

Thus, clinical judgment as to the truthfulness of the patient's unfolding history is irrelevant. It is enough that the patient verbalize a scenario of trauma, and, under "early" or "late" Freud, the proposition of traumatic causation will be supported.

Narrative truth has been distinguished from literal or historic truth.[22] In

Spence's view, veridical reconstruction of a patient's past history is virtually impossible. Rather, the analyst's therapeutic effectiveness relates to the presumed or mythical narrative that the patient weaves in the therapy session. The stories are not based on archeological excavations into the patient's real past but are verbalizations that may sound creditable to the patient as to what actually transpired.

At first, Freud attempted to plumb the unconscious via hypnosis. Under hypnosis, pathogenic memories emerged, only to be forgotten when the patient arose from the trance.[23] Other patients could not be easily hypnotized.[24] Because of the uneven results, hypnosis was abandoned. Subsequently, Freud introduced the technique of free association. Interestingly, psychoanalytic historians have construed free association as a midpoint between a hypnotic trance and the normal waking state.[25] The patient lies on a couch and does not look at the analyst. The patient is directed to say whatever comes to mind, no matter how nonsensical or unrelated to previous material. The patient is directed not to censor her thoughts. As a result of this technique, the analyst obtains raw data from the patient's unconscious and eventually is able to detect the hitherto repressed desires of the patient. The patient's emotional blocks are circumvented, allowing the therapist to tap into the crucial veins of the unconscious.[26] Thus, free association was deemed as a valid investigative tool that leads to the detection of the actual cause of mental illness.[27]

DREAMS

Freud viewed dreams as the royal road to the unconscious. *The Interpretation of Dreams* (1900) may be his crowning achievement.[28] Dreams, Freud stated, provide clues to hidden thoughts and links to earlier developmental periods. In psychoanalytic theory, dreams are seen as disguised fulfillments of buried conflicted wishes. The motive of a dream is based on a wish that emanates from repressed infantile mentation.

The true or underlying meaning of a dream is called the latent content. What is actually sensorially experienced in a dream is called the manifest content. If a mini-camcorder were placed in the brain to detect dreams, what would be seen if the cassette were observed would be the manifest content. On the other hand, the latent content needs to be interpreted and run through the filter of the analyst. The hidden meaning of the dream is not immediately obvious in part because of distortions (condensation, displacement and symbolism) that conspire to prevent the dreamer from realizing the unacceptable latent dream content.[29] The basis of a neurosis is identical to that of a dream: "A compromise is struck between an unacceptable thought or feeling and the defense against it."[30] The unpleasant material gains access to consciousness only in disguised form.[31]

Mitchell and Black offer a brief example of psychoanalytic dream interpretation: The patient was a woman named Gloria who dreamed she was five years old.[32] In the dream she felt great excitement about her father returning home from work. Upon his return, she noticed something on his shoes that may have been dog feces. She felt threatened by what was brought in. As a result of free associations, the following was seen as relevant to interpreting her dream. At the age of five, a brother was born. She had a vague notion of her father's role in impregnating her mother. She recalled her feelings of jealousy in that her father had given the mother, and not her, the baby. According to Mitchell and Black, the dream may be interpreted as follows: Both as a five-year-old and as an adult, Gloria was attached to her father and his penis. The interest in his penis is displaced in the dream and symbolized by his shoe. Her brother was "a piece of shit . . . and marred her erotic relationship with her father."[33] This manifestly strange dream conceals her hidden childhood wishes, rages and fears. This dream displays her unconscious childhood wishes and the defenses against the wishes, which are blended together in a compromise fashion.

CASE EXAMPLES

Dora

One of the classic cases presented in extensive detail is that of "Dora."[34] A Freudian critic regards this case as one of the greatest in the literature of psychiatry.[35] Spence, writing in the *Journal of the American Psychoanalytic Association*, regards Dora as must reading in almost all institutes.[36] Since treatment lasted no more than three months, the analysis was not complete and hence was considered only a fragment. Nevertheless, Freud made a number of bold and sweeping conclusions that derived from his ongoing formulation of the psychoanalytic method. As Freud notes, he based his publication on his memory. At that time, approximately 1900 or so, there were no recording devices: "the record is not absolutely—phonographically—exact, but it can claim to possess a high degree of trustworthiness."[37]

One of the intriguing aspects of this case is that Dora was not a self-referral; her father referred the patient to Freud. At age 18, Dora presented with a number of organic or somatic symptoms including a cough, tiredness and loss of consciousness. Most significantly, there appeared to be a depressed mood (low spirits—*Verstimmung* in German) along with an implication of suicidality. Dora had written a letter or note that Freud interpreted as a wish possibly to commit suicide.[38] Freud apparently never saw or read the note, but he took the import to reflect a desire to end her life rather than the less innocuous meaning of ending her life circumstances.

What might have made this woman unhappy? It seems her father's friend, Herr K, had made passes at Dora. Her father provided little or no support for Dora, who claims she was revulsed by Herr K's advances. Dora's mother also was of little help. Although Freud never met her, he was able to make the following observation: "I was led to imagine her as an uncultivated woman and above all as a foolish one who concentrated all her interests upon domestic affairs. . . . She presented the picture in fact, of what might be called the 'housewife psychosis.' "[39] Not to leave other women out of the picture, traces of the housewife psychosis are said to be found in normal housewives who obsessionally clean and wash.[40]

Freud further detailed Dora's symptoms: the disgust at Herr K's kiss. Relatedly, when retelling the story, Freud found a sensory hallucination when Dora seemed to actually feel the body pressure of Herr K. In addition, without offering details, Freud deduced that during the kiss, Dora felt not only Herr K's lips but also the "pressure of his erect member."[41] A third related symptom involved the avoidance of men engaged in "affectionate conversation."[42]

Freud explained these symptoms within the context of his developmental theory of personality. He claimed that the disgust Dora experienced was evidence of repression in the erotogenic oral zone. Overindulgence of thumbsucking in infancy seems to be a factor in the aforementioned repression. As Freud notes, her self-gratification via thumbsucking was similarly described by other patients who later became "anaestethic and hysterical."[43] In addition, Freud asserted that the pressure of the hypothesized erect penis "probably led to an analogous change . . . in the clitoris."[44] Due to displacement, however, the excitement felt in this erotogenic zone shifted to the thorax.

Furthermore, Freud was able to discern that the kissing episode produced disgust in Dora because of the reaction to the smell and sight of excrement. The genitals, he opines, are reminders of excremental functions.[45] Thus, he concluded that disgust is the avenue to expression of the sexual sphere of her life.[46]

Insight into the inner working of Dora's mind was afforded through dream interpretation. In one dream, a house was on fire. Dora relates that her father was standing beside her bed and woke her up. In addition, her mother wanted to stop and save a jewelry box (*Schmuckkästchen*). Freud's well-known position is that "every dream is a wish which is represented as fulfilled, that the representation acts as a disguise if the wish is a repressed one, belonging to the unconscious."[47] By questioning Dora, Freud was able to arrive at some answers in his quest to peel the layers off her hidden unconscious mentations. It turns out that Herr K had given Dora a jewelry box. According to Freud, it is appropriate to reciprocate, i.e., to give a jewelry box to him. Freud makes two interconnected interpretations: the jewelry box refers to her genitals (the colloquial "box"), and rather than accepting, she is giving herself to Herr K. But it was really her father who

was standing in for Herr K. Freud's grand summary is thus: Dora was sum-
moning up her old love for her father in order to protect herself from the
lustful desires directed toward Herr K.[48] Consciously, she couldn't admit
her true feelings for Herr K.

There is an addendum to the dream that allowed Freud to gain insight
into Dora's transference. She reported that she smelled smoke after experiencing the dream. Freud used the expression to Dora, "there can be no
smoke without fire" to suggest that important information might be lurking
beneath her awareness. What Freud adduced, without Dora's help, was that
Dora was longing for a kiss and would of necessity take note of the smoker's
breath.[49] Since Freud was a smoker too, he concluded that Dora would like
to have a kiss from Sigmund Freud.

Lastly, Freud found that an etiological factor in her mental disorder was
masturbation. He suspected masturbation as the source of her difficulty
based on her playing with a piece of jewelry, a reticule that "comes apart at
the top in the usual way, was nothing but a representation of the genitals,
and her playing with, her opening and putting her finger in it, was an entirely yet unmistakable pantomimic announcement of what she would like
to do with them—namely, to masturbate."[50] Freud began to suspect masturbation as the main cause of hysteria in that there is often an association
of masturbation with gastric pains.

"It is well known that gastric pains occur especially often in those who
masturbate. According to a personal communication made to me by W.
Fliess, it is precisely gastralgias of this character which can be interrupted by
an application of cocaine to the 'gastric spot' discovered by him in the nose,
and which can be cured by cauterization of the same spot."[51]

CRITIQUE OF THE DORA CASE

The first important issue is whether the diagnosis of hysteria was accurate
in that the alleged causative factors as well as treatment are hinged upon an
appropriate and relevant diagnosis. The DSM format no longer contains the
diagnosis conversion hysteria or hysterical neurosis, but it does contain conversion disorder.[52] This is not to cast a sexist light on this original diagnosis,
but the term hysteria is derived from the Greek work for "uterus."

The DSM-IV lists six diagnostic criteria:

A. One or more symptoms or deficits affecting voluntary motor or sensory function
suggest a neurological or other general medical condition.

B. Psychological factors are judged to be associated with the symptoms or deficit
because the initiation or exacerbation of the symptom or deficit is preceded by
conflicts or other stressors.

C. The symptom or deficit is not intentionally produced or feigned (as in factitious
disorder).

D. The symptom or deficit cannot, after appropriate investigation, be fully explained by a general medical condition, or by the direct effects of a substance, or as a culturally sanctioned behavior or experience.

E. The symptom or deficit causes clinically significant distress or impairment in social, occupational or other important areas of functioning or warrants medical evaluation.

F. The symptom or deficit is not limited to pain or sexual dysfunction, does not occur exclusively during the course of somaticization disorder and is not better accounted for by another mental disorder.

There are some changes in the diagnostic scheme from one DSM to another, but essentially this disorder refers to a patient displaying what purports to be neurological or physical symptoms for which there is no underlying anatomical or physiological basis. For example, a person may claim suddenly to be blind, but under hypnosis, the individual can see.

First, a thorough medical evaluation must be performed to rule out neurological etiologies. "In early studies, general medical etiologies were later found in from one-quarter to one-half of persons initially diagnosed with conversion symptoms."[53] In Dora's case, it did not appear that there was a concurrent medical evaluation.

Second, it appears that the DSM-IV is theoretically agnostic, at least with respect to repressed infantile sexuality as an etiology of a conversion disorder. Rather, it appears that the concept of conversion relates to a recent stressor that precipitates the conversion from the body to the mind. Not excluded from consideration is the concept of secondary gain, i.e., external benefits are obtained or noxious responsibilities avoided.[54] For example, an individual who can no longer see might gain sympathy or would not be required to work.

What were Dora's physical symptoms? At the age of eight, she had a bout of "over-exertion," which was diagnosed as chronic dyspnea. First, it should be noted that the DSM-IV states that conversion symptoms in children under ten years of age are usually limited to gait problems or seizures.[55] At this age in Dora's life, there were no such complaints. Her presenting problem ten years later did not include tiredness or over-exertion. Nevertheless, Freud concludes that her asthma-like condition is related to a "detached fragment of the act of copulation," in that he was able in Dora's case to trace her nervous asthma back to overhearing sexual intercourse taking place between adults.[56] Since there is no proof that Dora overheard anything along these lines, this is at best only a Freudian hypothesis. Furthermore, since there were no adequate medical exams, he really could not rule out an actual organic basis to her asthma or overexertion. Lastly, no data are presented as to whether the so-called asthma was a daily problem or occurred only when she went mountain climbing. Freud notes that Dora's first attack came after she was mountain climbing and that she had really been out of breath.[57] Since such a straightforward explanation would be of no avail to psychoanalytic theory, it was essentially negated. Tracing her "hysteria" back to real events, consciously experienced, does not accord with Freud's theory of repressed infantile sexuality.

The alleged symptoms of hysteria, such as a cough, preceded the incidents with Herr K. Thus, "if the trauma theory is not to be abandoned, we must go back to her childhood and look for any influences or impressions which might have had an effect analogous to that of the trauma."[58] At this point, it should be noted that there is a severe question as to whether, under the DSM-IV, Dora could be accurately diagnosed as suffering from conversion hysteria; i.e., there does not appear to be a temporal relationship between the onset or exacerbation of symptoms and a conflict or stressor (Criterion B).

Regarding her seizure and convulsions, all that is definitively stated is that apparently Dora's father reports a loss of consciousness after a heated discussion subsequent to her so-called suicide letter. Freud states in a footnote that the attack was, "I believe accompanied by convulsions and delirious states."[59] He offers no confirmation; only somehow he surmises that, during the loss of consciousness, seizure-like symptoms occurred. What is a loss of consciousness? Since Freud was not there and only has a very biased historian to inform, much more data is needed before concluding that the seizure was non-organic. Furthermore, it is doubtful that one fainting spell, even if true, is enough to warrant a diagnosis of a neurosis. Finally, was this alleged fainting spell related to prior developmental gremlins hidden in her unconscious or rather to a somewhat stressful argument with her father about the untenable position between herself, her father, Herr K, and others?

What about aphonia, a condition in which the patient speaks in a whisper or is even mute? The aphonia may have been related to a cough, which, interestingly, disappeared spontaneously.[60] First, there is little information surrounding the extent and nature of her aphonia except that it appeared to last as long as Herr K was absent, i.e., three to six weeks. But it cannot be determined whether the aphonia, let alone the cough, occurred in or out of Herr K's presence. The cough apparently was not occurring in Freud's presence, nor was it a presenting problem. Fascinatingly, the cough spontaneously disappeared when Freud told her the cough was an excitation in her throat that was really reflecting a sexual gratification.[61]

What is interesting is how Freud presents the conclusion that there is a causal connection between Dora's cough and her unconscious visualization of oral sex. "The conclusion was inevitable that . . . she pictured to herself a scene of sexual gratification."[62] That it is Freud's speculation is not immediately clear, perhaps in part because of the long and flowery sentence structure. The inevitable conclusion is that Freud pictured for Dora the scene of sexual gratification. There is no apparent confirmation on Dora's part. Freud does not take much credit for his insightful interpretation because he astonishingly notes that "her cough had so often before sponta-neously disappeared."[63] Not only did the cough precede the alleged stress, i.e., Herr K's advances, but psychoanalysis was not needed to clear up her prior alleged "hysterical" cough. So Freud is not going to take credit for his instant "cure."

Her alleged symptoms did not seem to affect her ability to function in school or attend lectures. The so-called organic symptoms, i.e., coughing, tiredness, aphonia, were not even the presenting problems. Rather, it was Dora's, or perhaps more accurately her father's, distress at the mess their family was in, along with an independent daughter who refused to accept the insupportable dictates of her father. Thus, under Criterion E, the di-agnosis of conversion disorder cannot be made. Furthermore, there is little or no evidence of secondary gain. Freud discusses this issue in general terms and may erroneously imply that Dora was avoiding something through her symptoms. Recall that Dora's symptoms as seen first through her father's eyes were "low spirits" and false beliefs about Herr K. It does not appear that Dora was playing the sick role but rather was trying to point out to her father the inequities of her current life situation.

Another issue relates to the presenting problem: low spirits and a change in her character. The latter seems to refer to Dora allegedly imagining the romantic overtures of Herr K. Could a diagnosis of depression be warranted? First, there are no indications of poor appetite, only that she was a poor eater and had some disinclination for food.[64] This statement by itself is too vague to qualify as a symptom of depression. The other criteria were not present: sleep problems, low self-esteem, poor concentration or feelings of hopelessness.[65] (There may be an indication of low energy or fatigue but only after mountain climbing or talking to Freud.) Furthermore, it appears that the original German word, *Verstimmung*, was somewhat colloquial, i.e., "low spirits" in the translation.[66] Although Masson translated *Verstimmung* to mean "depression," nothing in the case history warrants a conclusion of this diagnosis.[67] Thus, she does not meet or really come close to the DSM-IV diagnosis of dysthymia (neurotic depression). The so-called suicide note is quite ambiguous; it could mean Dora wanted to get away from the family. That is exactly what she did several months after finishing her analysis with Freud.[68]

In the infinite expansion of diagnostic categories, there may be one that applies to Dora, namely, V61.20,[69] which is a condition that may be a focus of clinical attention—parent/child relational problems in which there is clin-ically significant impairment in individual or family functioning or the de-velopment of clinically significant symptoms in parent or child. Dora's father showed little concern for Dora's true feelings but attempted to use Freud to talk some sense into her.

In summary, regarding Dora's psychodiagnosis, there seems to be little or no justification for labeling her as suffering from a conversion disorder.

Dora wasn't even referred for the alleged condition in the first place, but rather for situation difficulties with her family and friends. She carried out her daily activities and was able to attend school and further her education. There is even less indication of a depressive disorder. A strong argument can be made that Dora was only suffering from a culturally biased diagnostic schema that is tilted against independent, free-spirited young adult females.

A major issue relates to Freud's interpretation of Dora's dreams. Freud's hypothesis as derived from her dreams may have been entirely incorrect. Dora may have really wanted her father to protect her from Herr K and hoped both in the dream and in reality that this would happen. Freud interpreted Dora's dream in ways that offer no consideration to what were her real-life conscious concerns and observations, namely, emotional abandonment and lack of protection on the part of her father. On the contrary, Freud "took every opportunity to use Dora's dreams against her, and to interpret them in directions he wished."[70] Whatever was in her dreams would wind its way in the web of Freud's repressed infantile sexuality theory. At best this may have been an exercise in great superfluousness because Freud was grafting his evolving theory into the history of a patient who arguably didn't have a conversion disorder! At worst, Freud is constructing a phony lattice that will not have any empirical or clinical support. His theory of wish-fulfillment gains no support from Dora.

Apparently, Dora's independence immunized her to Freud's psychoanalytic interpretations of her dreams. At the end she commented that nothing remarkable seems to come from the interpretation.[71] This young adult totally rejected what she may have perceived as inapplicable or irrelevant commentary on her dreams.

In order to gain insight into what was happening with a patient, Freud relied on clinical intuition or what might be more accurately termed his mental telepathy. In 1925 Freud stated his view on thought transference via extrasensory means: "I have often had an impression in the course of experiments in my private circle, that strongly emotionally colored recollections can be successfully transferred without much difficulty."[72]

A propitious time for thought transference is especially when a thought emerges from the unconscious.[73] Can this be the reason Freud could deduce information from the unknown and unseen unconscious of Dora? Freud may also have been able to time travel and observe Herr K's erection upon Dora. "I have formed in my own mind the following reconstruction of the scene."[74] It was Freud who visualized this scene, not Dora. Furthermore, how did Freud divine that Dora was sexually aroused in her clitoral area?[75] Did he project himself into the bowels of her unconscious and see that unsavory things were going on? How did he know she masturbated? One explanation for Freud being able to prove Dora's hidden agenda is based on mental telepathy.

Another explanation relies on Freud's alleged clinical ability. In some instances, Freud would not take no for an answer. Thus, he claimed that there is no such thing as a "no" in the unconscious.[76] Thus, Dora didn't remember being completely in love with her father as a youngster. An emphatic "no" that is given after a repressed thought is presented by way of an interpretation means that the analyst has struck pay dirt. The "no" must be "yes." It is quite simple: if the client agrees with the analyst's position, he or she confirms the data. If the patient disagrees with the analyst, he or she confirms the data. There has been no scientific, logical or empirical data yet to show when and how what someone says may or may not reflect the opposite of what they say, let alone reveal a primary route to unconscious.

There has been no clinical verification by Freud or any of his followers that rubbing a piece of clothing relates to symbolic masturbation. Actually, Freud did know the distinction between an emotionally charged event and an everyday one when he allegedly commented that sometimes a cigar is just a cigar. Assuming for the moment that Dora was an early-age masturbator, did that lead to her alleged "hysterical" symptoms or a repressed desire to have a romantic relationship with Herr K? The problem for Freud was that he had a theory in search of data and would try to fit the data to his theory regardless of the presenting problems and clinical diagnosis.

Freud insisted that the revenge motive underlay Dora's resistance to Herr K's affections.[77] A simpler possibility is that Dora was rightly fed up by the deceits of her father and Herr K. Dora had correctly discerned that her father was having an affair with Frau K.[78] So rather than deal with a real issue, Freud asserts that Dora has a sexualized interest in her father, which warded off her temptation in Herr K's direction.[79] In this entire morass, which includes Herr K, Frau K, Dora's parents and other significant environmental details (a governess who was also the object of Herr K's romantic inclinations), only Dora, who was dragged into therapy, was the focus of attention. The solution was to marry Herr K![80]

OTHER CASE REPORTS: RAT-MAN AND WOLF-MAN

Rat-Man

Apparently as late as 1908, Freud had not published a psychoanalytic success story. Thereupon, he pressed the Rat-Man case into service to demonstrate a successful analysis. Rat-Man suffered from obsessive thoughts that something horrible would happen to his father and lady friend. Freud was able to deduce a number of hitherto repressed conflicts based in part on Rat-Man's dreams and free association. Starting with the German word for rat (*Ratte*), Freud easily glided to *Spielratte* (gambling rat). Rat-Man's father was a gambler. The word "rat" was also associated to money in that the translation for installments in German is the plural "*Raten*"—almost the same as *Ratten*. With respect to Rat-Man's girlfriend, a further connection was uncovered by the association to *hieraten*, which means "to marry" in German.[81] Furthermore in childhood, the Rat-Man was punished by his father for allegedly biting someone.

Freud put the causes of Rat-Man's obsession into perspective: He was unconsciously fantasizing that he was a rat and a biter, and was having anal intercourse with his female friend.[82] Furthermore, Freud was able to determine that Rat-Man's father had, as a child, threatened him with castration. When this interpretation was communicated, Rat-Man's obsessions disappeared.

It appears that Freud not only kept progress notes on the Rat-Man, but there were significant discrepancies between the published case and the notes.[83] Thus, there may be fictionalized reconstructions of what and when things were said. Grünbaum, a Freudian scholar and critic, contends that the case history may have been altered for purposes of publication in order to prove the etiological significance of the oedipal fantasies rather than pointing to real physical abuse as a causative factor.[84] Citing the Freud/Jung letters, Sulloway demonstrates that Rat-Man was not necessarily improved but rather broke off his analysis after a short period and before his transference had been fully resolved.[85] Apparently, Freud confessed to Jung that Rat-Man was still having ongoing problems. It may be that there was some symptomatic relief of some of his obsessions, but the core of his transference issues with his father was still troublesome.[86]

Finally, with respect to the associational zeal with which Freud penetrated the exterior of Rat-Man's defenses, it can only be reiterated that, to some extent, there is a feeling that a word game is being played. Freud offers no data that puns are a guiding light to the inner mechanisms of the mind. Since Freud did not invent a real time machine, there is no easy way to check his theoretical formulations regarding the etiology of Rat-Man's obsessions.

Wolf-Man

The Wolf-Man was seen by Freud from 1910 to 1914 and briefly thereafter. He was re-analyzed by a number of different analysts until his death in 1978. He was, therefore, in and out of analysis for over 60 years.[87] The Wolf-Man, too, was suffering from an obsessional neurosis that, according to Freud, stemmed from the age of 18 months when he witnessed his parents having intercourse.

Wolf-Man's famous dream involved white wolves sitting on a big walnut tree. Fearful of being eaten up by the wolves, he screamed and woke up.[88] Freud's interpretation was as follows: The white wolves stand for the parents' white underwear, whereas castration fears emanate from witnessing parental intercourse, which enabled Wolf-Man to note that his mother lacked a penis.[89] As it turned out, Wolf-Man was interviewed near the end of his life and offered some commentary on his famous analysis: the dream interpretation was improbable and farfetched.[90] Wolf-Man disputed that he was helped by Freud, and he also disputed some of the basic underlying "facts" used to formulate dream interpretation; i.e., in Russia, where Wolf-Man grew up, children sleep with their nanny and not in their parents' bedroom.

CLINICAL RESEARCH

Because of the breadth and complexity of the psychoanalytic method, little in the way of experimental research has been done on the basic theoretical tenets. Interestingly enough, it appears that Freud himself, as well as other clinicians, is not particularly concerned with experimental confirmation of his clinical findings. In a well-known letter from Dr. Saul Rosenzweig to Sigmund Freud, Rosenzweig reported experimental validation of repression. Freud seemed to have a "so what" attitude.[91] Psychoanalysis was so strong and so self-confirming that apparently there was no need for any experimental confirmation. For Freud, the verification of his clinical techniques and theories sprang from the case study method.

A number of studies have been launched in an attempt to show relationships between early toilet training and the influence on adult personality. Torrey reviewed a total of 26 reports.[92] Most of the studies, however, either did not test the theory or had methodological flaws, i.e., no control groups. Of the four studies that had some minimal controls, none showed any relationship between toilet training experiences and adult personality.[93]

The other stages of psychosexual development fare no better. Thus, there are no studies that support Freud's theory regarding the oral, anal or phallic stages. Furthermore, there appears to be no clinical documentation that a boy's identification is related to castration anxiety.[94] The research in this area suffers from the difficulty in trying to extract unconscious motivation of infants from adult clients. There are likely to be severe problems with memory and accuracy, let alone the contamination effect of the analyst's interpretative authority.

Several large-scale clinical research projects have been initiated over the past several decades to assess whether psychoanalytic patients improve upon receiving therapy.[95] The review by Bachrach et al. in a psychoanalytic journal appears not to have pulled any punches. The research was conducted at major centers such as the Menninger Foundation, Boston Psychoanalytic Institute, the New York Psychoanalytic Institute and the Columbia Psychoanalytic Center. There were massive amounts of documentation and statistical analyses. Two major problems deserve attention.

Although undoubtedly some people improved as a result of the psychoanalytic therapy, not only did the projects not demonstrate superiority of psychoanalysis, but there were no indications of the underlying psychoanalytic process at work. In essence, these were impressionistic studies. As the authors note, these studies have not "contributed fresh insights into psychoanalysis,"[96] nor have the investigations added to the knowledge base of psychoanalysis. In the Menninger Project, there were a "number of cases with insoluble transference reactions . . . sometimes associated with countertransference."[97] Some analysts were found to be defensive to transference issues and to unduly foster positive transference and even collude in avoiding central issues.

A second area of concern is that virtually all of the attending or primary therapists were students. Generally, interns or graduate students in training are not directly observed but rather report their findings to supervisors. Based on these supervisory sessions and progress notes or case conferences, the supervisor makes recommendations. Considering the rapidly increasing number of psychoanalytic schools where there is no agreement on terms or basic processes, how can anyone guarantee that a student is providing the prescribed therapy? As Bachrach et al. note, there were differences in the Menninger Project between what the analysts believe they say and what others observe in the actual tape recordings of the sessions.[98] Thus, there is no assurance of quality control. Moreover, in a comprehensive review of negative outcomes in psychotherapy, including psychoanalysis, it was found that therapists underestimated psychopathology.[99] Thus, even trained psychotherapists, who may be working independently, do not at times have accurate perceptions of the seriousness of the emotional problems in the patients they are treating.

An initial attempt has been made to confirm the theoretical concept of transference from within the psychoanalytic framework. In a series of research investigations, Luborsky announced that "the transference has been verified."[100] Although the authors announce a major breakthrough in confirming "the transference," there is a great deal of room to doubt this declaration. First and foremost, these studies offer no support to the notion that transference involves unconscious processes, or if it does, how to distinguish between unconscious and conscious perceptions. For example, it appears that the statement, "I have to prove myself—to come across to people and impress them—I think it is happening right now in here," could be a very accurate perception.[101] What is interpreted as transference could actually be the therapist's countertransference. This issue is not dealt with here.

There appear to be no unambiguous data that support the notion of transference.[102] The multitudes of therapies that have emerged in the psychoanalytic camp itself have not universally agreed on how to deal with transference issues. The announcement in a professional journal that the Freudian concept of transference has been confirmed or validated is a bit premature.

CRITIQUE AND ANALYSIS

The past 100 years of psychoanalysis have perpetuated at least five fictions: that psychoanalysis is superior to other forms of therapy; that analyzing the transference relationships is necessary for a successful analysis and can be accurately measured; that dream interpretation and free association are valid investigatory tools that chip away at and reveal the unconscious; that at the root of neurosis is repressed sexual infantile conflicts; and lastly, that psychoanalysts have identified the active therapeutic ingredients that are responsible for producing change in behavior.

Absolutely no evidence has ever been produced that demonstrates the alleged superiority of psychoanalysis over other forms of therapy. A statement that psychotherapy is more effective than other forms of therapy is illusory.[103] Over the years, comparisons between psychoanalysis, Behavior Therapy and Humanistic Therapy have revealed few or no differences in outcome. In the consumer survey, no modality of therapy rated better than any other types of therapy for any particular problem.[104] Comprehensive reviews have not revealed any superiority of psychoanalysis.[105]

Since analyzing the transference relationship is at the heart of psychoanalysis, it is instructive to describe how a student learns to deal with this phenomenon in his own practice. In a training institute, a potential analyst is seen by a so-called training analyst. The first issue that emerges is how free the student will be in discussing intimate details with a future colleague. Second, how generalizable are the results of analyzing a student's transference? Since the student or trainee is not exactly a "real" patient, the student is in a double role as both trainee and patient.

In a training analysis, there is no assurance that the analyst is correctly dealing with the student's transference. The first psychoanalyst, Freud, did not have a supervisor, but rather relied on self-analysis and peer consultation. As Masson makes clear, however, in a training setting, the analyst can misperceive the alleged transference. At times, Masson believed the analyst was free-associating to his comments and ignoring transference material.[106] There appear to be no reports or verification that the training analysts are correctly dealing with transference issues with their trainees.

On the contrary, the subjective nature of transference perceptions was revealed by the differing interpretations that are offered among a therapist, supervisor and outside consultant.[107] If, assuming for the moment, all three were classic psychoanalysts, each analyst could interpret the data from his own vantage point.

With the revision and extension of psychoanalysis, however, there are varying and, at times, conflicting approaches to the interpretation of transference. Each therapist might examine the data from a slightly different perspective and assume that what is presented in the clinical hour are representations of pristine earlier developmental phenomena.

This example makes clear that any given observer of the same clinical data may have a quite different perspective. Not only a therapist's role but also his psychoanalytic orientation colors the interpretation of psychoanalytic events. It seems that each observer can cultivate data to support his own idea of the transference relationship. What is disturbing to this psychoanalytic author is "not only that each observer has a new theory, but each adduces a unique set of data in support of it."[108]

Without studies to validate the nature of transference, no one can be sure that the analyst is correct. There are no guidelines to confirm the validity of any interpretation of the transference relationship. The therapist not only lacks an accurate pipeline into the current unconscious of the patient but has no way to know whether the alleged transferential events of infancy or childhood are accurate. Furthermore, 40 different brands of psychoanalysis might lead to 40 different interpretations. There is no clinical tool to document whether 1 or 40 of the interpretations are correct. Use of clinical intuition as apparently espoused by Freud does not meet the rigors of a scientific enterprise.

In the final analysis, investigating transference may be beyond the capacity of present-day scientific methods. Because of the subjectivity involved in the interpersonal interaction between patient and analyst, there is no way at present to ascertain the clinical accuracy of the alleged correctness of the presence of transference. Furthermore, as shown by the other therapeutic modalities, analyzing transference does not necessarily seem critical to the outcome in terms of reported improvement in mental functioning.

Dream interpretation and free association as roads to the unconscious are greatly flawed and are contaminated by the therapist's own idiosyncratic input. Dream interpretations could as easily flow from the associations of the therapist. For example, a psychoanalytic patient had a dream about a blob.[109] Freud might interpret the blob as an expression of anal sadism. An object relations analyst might interpret the blob as the person's true self, which represents an inchoate unformed mass looking for possible growth. An ego analyst might interpret the blob as representing a structure-less malformed interior without stable identifications. Another view is that the blob reflects that actual self but also portrays aborted development of a person's sense of subjectivity or personhood.[110]

Therefore, it appears virtually impossible for one therapist to provide the correct interpretation and the appropriate linkage to the unconscious. The meaning of a dream has more to do with the school of thought than any scientific reality. Any dream could have 10 or 100 meanings.

The myth of sexual conflicts and fantasies as causative factors in mental disorders is clear from the misdiagnosis of Dora. First, there was no apparent underlying mental disorder, so there can be no rational connection to hidden childhood conflicts. Freud seemed to be in search of new data to support his evolving theory and simply contoured Dora's story to match his theory. There are no data that remotely support any of the psychoanalytic processes.[111] "Clinical psychoanalysis, in any of its forms, has virtually no basis in systematically validated research.[112]

The patient's account may be fiction or the truth. The therapist has no tools to decipher whether the patient's narrative is real or imagined, or even encouraged by the therapist. The therapist, meanwhile, readily accepts the narrative as being relevant to the patient's psychopathology. It appears that Freud and many of the next generations of followers do not distinguish which are actual toxigenic events and which are mythical ones.[113] It is enough that the patient comes to believe in the authenticity of the therapist-assisted revelation. Insight is blended with pseudo-insight. Amazingly, there appears to be no clinical research to support the notion that believing a possibly erroneous or fantasy incident is a necessary element in improving emotional functioning.[114]

Because of the demand characteristics inherent in psychotherapy, there is no way at present to show that analytic insight or techniques are the active ingredients responsible for altering behavior.[115] A major conclusion in a large-scale review of studies with placebo controls was that there were insignificant differences between the so-called active psychotherapy and the inert control groups.[116] If individuals recover spontaneously at a rate similar to control groups, then it is poor reasoning to conclude that an analysis of transference, for example, is critical to improvement. Suggestion, expectancy and the passage of time need to be taken into consideration. The contention that something in psychoanalysis is necessary to provide change in emotional functioning is on shaky ground.

In the private cubicle of the therapy office, the patient may experience new thoughts or perceptions. Some of the ideas may be facilitated by the therapist's beliefs. The patient may enter therapy with an expectation of change and be more susceptible to the therapist's interpretations. In the case of Dora, Freud tried mightily to influence the patient to fit her beliefs into his evolving theory of adult psychopathology. Dora resisted Freud's interpretations and left therapy after a short time. Over the course of the twentieth century, however, hundreds of thousands of patients may have been convinced by their therapists to believe in perhaps a fictional account of their unconscious or repressed motivation.

There are no independent data that can confirm any of Freud's contentions in his case histories. There appears to be no credible evidence that supports the validity of his intrapsychic excursions into the depths of the minds of the mentally ill. The Wolf-Man case may have been such a fiasco that efforts may have been made to keep the Wolf-Man from going public. He wanted to emigrate to America, but the psychoanalytic establishment at that time apparently discouraged him.[117] Although he may have been a disgruntled ex-patient, he did not appear to show any signs of a successful psychoanalysis.

In the final analysis, based on what is known 100 years later, there appears to be no empirical support for psychoanalytic formulations. Not one of the grand psychoanalytic concepts, such as the oedipal complex, castration anxiety or adult correlates of childhood personality, has received experimental support.[118] Psychoanalysis has survived over 100 years as a model of a psychotherapeutic endeavor that relies more on fiction than science. As such, it may be one of the greatest scientific hoaxes of the twentieth century. From a scientific perspective, psychoanalysis should be declared dead.

NOTES

1. Grünbaum, A. (1993). *Validation in the clinical theory of psychoanalysis: A study in the philosophy of psychoanalysis* (p. 10). Madison, Conn.: International Universities Press.

2. Hall, C. S. & Lindzey, G. (1970). *Theories of personality* (2nd ed.) (p. 32). New York: John Wiley & Sons.

3. Hall & Lindzey, *Theories of personality* (p. 34).

4. Arlow, J. A. (1995). Psychoanalysis. In Corsini, R. J. & Wedding, D. (Eds.), *Current psychotherapies* (5th ed.) (p. 25). Itasca, Ill.: Peacock Publishers.

5. Hall & Lindzey, *Theories of personality* (p. 50).

6. Prochaska, J. O. & Norcross, J. C. (1994). *Systems of psychotherapy: A transtheoretical analysis* (3rd ed.) (p. 30). Pacific Grove, Calif.: Brooks/Cole.

7. Mitchell, S. A. & Black, M. J. (1994). *Freud and beyond: A history of modern psychoanalytic thought* (p. 15). New York: Basic Books.

8. Hall & Lindzey, *Theories of personality* (p. 53).

9. Prochaska & Norcross, *Systems of psychotherapy* (p. 32).

10. Erikson, E. (1950). *Childhood and society.* New York: Norton.

11. Sullivan, H. S. (1953). *The interpersonal theory of psychiatry.* New York: Norton.

12. Mitchell & Black, *Freud and beyond.*

13. Greenberg, J. R. & Mitchell, S. A. (1983). *Object relations in psychoanalytic theory* (p. 12). Cambridge, Mass.: Harvard University Press.

14. Arlow, Psychoanalysis (p. 32).

15. Grünbaum, *Validation in the clinical theory* (p. 172).

16. Grünbaum, *Validation in the clinical theory* (p. 172).

17. Masson, J. M. (1994). *Against therapy* (p. 84). Monroe, Maine: Common Courage Press.

18. Mitchell & Black, *Freud and beyond* (p. 249).

19. Grünbaum, *Validation in the clinical theory* (p. 176).

20. Grünbaum, *Validation in the clinical theory* (p. 176).

21. Mitchell & Black, *Freud and beyond* (p. 207).

22. Spence, D. P. (1982). *Narrative truth and historical truth.* New York: Norton.

23. Mitchell & Black, *Freud and beyond* (p. 5).

24. Arlow, Psychoanalysis (p. 28).

25. Mitchell & Black, *Freud and beyond* (p. 6).

26. Mitchell & Black, *Freud and beyond* (p. 6).

27. Grünbaum, *Validation in the clinical theory* (p. 24).
28. Freud, S. (1953–1974). The interpretation of dreams. In *The Standard edition of the complete psychological works of Sigmund Freud* (J. Strachey, Trans.), Vols. 4 and 5 (pp. 1–626). London: Hogarth Press and the Institute of Psycho-Analysis. (Originally published in 1900–1901.)
29. Mitchell & Black, *Freud and beyond* (p. 9).
30. Mitchell & Black, *Freud and beyond* (p. 9).
31. Mitchell & Black, *Freud and beyond* (p. 9).
32. Mitchell & Black, *Freud and beyond* (p. 9).
33. Mitchell & Black. *Freud and beyond* (p. 10).
34. Freud, S. (1959). Fragment of an analysis of a case of hysteria. In *Collected papers*, Vol. 3 (A. & J. Strachey, Trans.) (pp. 13–146). New York: Basic Books. (Originally published in 1905.)
35. Masson. *Against therapy* (p. 85).
36. Spence, D. (1990). The rhetorical voice of psychoanalysis. *Journal of the American Psychoanalytic Association, 38* (pp. 579–603).
37. Freud, Fragment of analysis (p. 17).
38. Freud, Fragment of analysis (pp. 26, 31).
39. Freud, Fragment of analysis (p. 28).
40. Freud, Fragment of analysis (p. 28).
41. Freud, Fragment of analysis (p. 38).
42. Freud, Fragment of analysis (p. 39).
43. Freud, Fragment of analysis (p. 64).
44. Freud, Fragment of analysis (p. 39).
45. Freud, Fragment of analysis (p. 40).
46. Freud, Fragment of analysis (p. 40).
47. Freud, Fragment of analysis (p. 82).
48. Freud, Fragment of analysis (p. 85).
49. Freud, Fragment of analysis (p. 89).
50. Freud, Fragment of analysis (p. 93).
51. Freud, Fragment of analysis (p. 95).
52. *Diagnostic and statistical manual of mental disorders* (4th ed.) (p. 452). Washington, D.C.: American Psychiatric Association.
53. *Diagnostic and statistical manual IV* (p. 453).
54. *Diagnostic and statistical manual IV* (p. 453).
55. *Diagnostic and statistical manual IV* (p. 455).
56. Freud, Fragment of analysis (p. 96).
57. Freud, Fragment of analysis (p. 96).
58. Freud, Fragment of analysis (p. 36).
59. Freud, Fragment of analysis (p. 31).
60. Freud, Fragment of analysis (p. 30).
61. Freud, Fragment of analysis (p. 59).
62. Freud, Fragment of analysis (p. 59).
63. Freud, Fragment of analysis (p. 59).
64. Freud, Fragment of analysis (p. 38).
65. *Diagnostic and statistical manual IV* (p. 349).
66. Freud, Fragment of analysis (p. 35).
67. Masson, *Against therapy* (p. 87).

68. Freud, Fragment of analysis (p. 144).

69. *Diagnostic and statistical manual IV* (p. 681).

70. Masson, *Against therapy* (p. 101).

71. Masson, *Against therapy* (p. 127).

72. Freud, S. (1959). Occult significance of dreams. In *Collected papers*, Vol. V (A. & J. Strachey, Trans.) (pp. 158–162). New York: Basic Books. (Originally published in 1925.)

73. Freud, *Occult significance of dreams* (p. 160).

74. Freud, Fragment of analysis (p. 38).

75. Freud, Fragment of analysis (p. 39).

76. Freud, Fragment of analysis (p. 70).

77. Freud, Fragment of analysis (p. 115).

78. Masson, *Against therapy* (p. 95).

79. Masson, *Against therapy* (p. 95).

80. Masson, *Against therapy* (pp. 94–95).

81. Freud, S. (1959). Notes upon a case of obsessional neurosis. In *Collected papers*, Vol. 3 (A. & J. Strachey, Trans.) (pp. 293–383). New York: Basic Books. (Originally published in 1909.)

82. Sulloway, F. (1991). Reassessing Freud's case histories: The social construction of psychoanalysis. *ISIS*, *82* (pp. 245–275).

83. Sulloway, Reassessing Freud's case histories (pp. 245–275).

84. Grünbaum, *Validation in the clinical theory* (p. 150).

85. Sulloway, Reassessing Freud's case histories (pp. 245–275).

86. Sulloway, Reassessing Freud's case histories (pp. 245–275).

87. Sulloway, Reassessing Freud's case histories (pp. 245–275).

88. Freud, S. (1959). The dream and the primal scene. In *Collected papers*, Vol. 3 (A. & J. Strachey, Trans.) (p. 498). New York: Basic Books. (Originally published in 1913.)

89. Sulloway, Reassessing Freud's case histories (pp. 245–275).

90. Obholzer, K. (1982). *The Wolf-Man sixty years later: Conversations with Freud's controversial patient.* London: Routledge & Keagan Paul.

91. Grünbaum, *Validation in the clinical theory* (p. 352).

92. Torrey, E. F. (1992). *Freudian fraud: The malignant effect of Freud's theory on American thought and culture* (pp. 219–222). New York: HarperCollins.

93. Torrey, *Freudian fraud* (p. 220).

94. Torrey, *Freudian fraud* (p. 221).

95. Bachrach, H. M., Galatzer-Levy, R., Skolnikoff, A. & Waldron, S., Jr. (1991). On the efficacy of psychoanalysis. *Journal of the American Psychoanalytic Association, 39* (pp. 871–916).

96. Bachrach et al., On the efficacy of psychoanalysis (pp. 871–916).

97. Bachrach et al., On the efficacy of psychoanalysis (pp. 871–916).

98. Bachrach et al., On the efficacy of psychoanalysis (pp. 871–916).

99. Mohr, David C. (1995). Negative outcomes in psychotherapy: A critical review. *Clinical Psychology: Science and Practice, 2* (p. 23).

100. Luborsky, L. et al. (1985). A verification of Freud's grandest critical hypothesis: The transference. *Clinical Psychology Review, 5* (pp. 231–246); Fried, D., Crits-Christoph, P., & Luborsky, L. (1992). The first empirical demonstration of

transference in psychotherapy. *Journal of Nervous and Mental Disease, 180* (pp. 326–331).

101. Luborsky et al., The transference (pp. 231–246).

102. Weinberger, J. (1995). Common factors aren't so common: The common factors dilemma. *Clinical Psychology: Science & Practice, 2* (pp. 45–69).

103. Arlow, Psychoanalysis (pp. 15–50).

104. Seligman, M.E.P. (1995). The effectiveness of psychotherapy: The Consumer Reports study. *American Psychologist, 50* (pp. 965–975).

105. Weinberger, Common factors aren't so common (pp. 45–69).

106. Masson, J. M. (1991). *Final analysis: The making and unmaking of a psychoanalyst* (p. 25). New York: HarperPerennial.

107. Greenberg, J. (1994). Psychotherapy research: A clinician's view. In Talley, P. F., Strupp, H. H. & Butler, S. F. (Eds.), *Psychotherapy research & practice: Bridging the gap* (pp. 3–7). New York: Basic Books.

108. Greenberg, Psychotherapy research (p. 7).

109. Mitchell & Black, *Freud and beyond* (p. 185).

110. Mitchell & Black, *Freud and beyond* (p. 185).

111. Bachrach et al., On the efficacy of psychoanalysis (pp. 871–916).

112. Orlinsky, D. E. (1994). Research-based knowledge as the emergent foundation for clinical practice in psychotherapy. In Talley et al. (Eds.), *Psychotherapy research & practice* (pp. 99–123).

113. Grünbaum, *Validation in the clinical theory* (p. 182).

114. Grünbaum, *Validation in the clinical theory* (p. 177).

115. Grünbaum, *Validation in the clinical theory* (p. 199).

116. Prioleau, L., Murdock, M. & Brody, N. (1983). An analysis of psychotherapy versus placebo studies. *Behavioral and Brain Sciences 6* (pp. 275–310).

117. Sulloway, Reassessing Freud's case histories (pp. 245–275).

118. Crews, F. (1995). *The memory wars: Freud's legacy in dispute* (p. 298). New York: New York Review.

Chapter 3

Cathartic Therapies: From Primal to *est*

According to several theorists, the cause of mental illness can be found in early life trauma. The experiences may be embedded in the unconscious mental tissue or in the physical body tissue. Cathartic therapists require that their patients re-experience the alleged trauma in order to bring what was once repressed out into the open. A *catharsis* refers to a type of emotional ventilation in which pent-up feelings are discharged.

Although these approaches owe their origin to classic psychoanalysis, the specific techniques for uncovering the hitherto repressed trauma sharply diverge from Freud's theory. Although Implosion Therapy has cathartic elements, it is covered in the behavioral chapter. The distinction is that implosion relies on having the patient fantasize trauma, whereas the cathartic approaches, Primal Therapy and Bioenergetics, assume that the patient is re-experiencing actual trauma. Attack Therapy attempts to tear down the patient's defenses by extreme verbal or physical measures.

PRIMAL THERAPY

In every decade since the 1960s, there has been a therapy or two that has had a meteoric and immediate success. One of those therapies was Primal Therapy, which, in the early 1970s, was almost a household term. Some mental health professionals were quite impressed with Primal Therapy; e.g., "Janov's Primal Therapy represents an ingenious innovation in the new field of body psychotherapies."[1] Primal Therapy was dramatic, bold and different. Where Freud feared to tread, Primal Therapy eagerly went. The source of psychopathology was not just unmet needs and conflicts from early childhood, but intrauterine and birth trauma. It was a universal cure for neurosis and with virtually unlimited success. By 1996, however, Primal Therapy was included in a book entitled *Crazy Therapies*.[2]

At the base of psychopathology are unconscious wounds.[3] As a result of treating thousands of patients, Janov claims that Primal Therapy can reduce or eliminate many psychological and physical ailments. According to Janov, there is scientific research to back up his assertions. "It is a therapy that has been investigated for over 15 years by independent scientists, and the findings are consistent."[4]

An eerie scream from one of his earlier patients led to the development of Primal Therapy. This was the "product of some unconscious, universal, intangible wounds."[5] The pain underlying the scream is called "primal pain." These primal pains may emanate from surgery, physical or sexual abuse, or neglect, and lack of love. Due to the horrendous nature of these events, the conscious mind does not integrate these memories but stores the experience in the unconscious.

Because of repression, the patient has no conscious awareness of the early traumatic events and how they impact on his adult life. Repression works by a way of *gating*. Not only pain, but the perception of pain, is blocked via gating. According to Janov, both physical and psychological pain stimulates or produces repression. Once gating begins, "neural circuits are functionally disconnected."[6] The patient's thoughts are disconnected from feelings and have a life of their own. Janov mentions the classic studies of Melzack and Wall on pain inhibition as support of gating.[7] Janov suggests that emotional pain is repressed or blocked in a similar manner to that of physical pain.

A patient in Primal Therapy is able to reconnect with the primal pain, and the repression is dissipated when reliving a birth sequence. The trauma is impressed or imprinted into the nervous system but remains unknown due to repression. Relying on other classic works by Penfield, Janov points out that when the temporal lobe of an epileptic's brain was directly stimulated with electrodes, the patient would report a type of reliving of past events.[8] Thus, all memory is duly recorded, and, when the patient re-connects with the developmental trauma, then physical changes occur. For example, when reliving the birth sequence, the patient will again show the forceps mark on the head.[9] In essence, neurosis is a natural process of shutting out the overwhelming amount of stimulation so as to protect a person from the overload.[10]

The sensory, cognitive and physical overload begins in the womb. A patient who underwent a birth primal, i.e., a reliving of the birth process, reports feeling the steel forceps used in her delivery.[11] In the following case vignettes, birth trauma leads to a panoply of neurotic conditions. Later trauma may be important and additive, but at the crux of Janov's position is the idea that actual veridical negative experience in the womb and just after birth forms the basis of adult neurosis. For example, manic depression (now called bipolar disorder) emanates from a birth struggle followed by near success.[12] Janov describes several scenarios of how a cyclic personality is formed: struggling to get out of the birth canal "against a tumor," and the resultant cesarian section, or being held back in labor while waiting for the doctor to arrive. When adult life is difficult and stressful, the cyclic pattern repeats itself. Another example is a migraine headache, which often has its origin in oxygen starvation at birth, when there is vasoconstriction followed by dilation and a throbbing of the head.[13]

Psychotherapeutic Techniques

Within the unconscious, there are no id forces or other mysteries. For Janov, the unconscious contains the heavy trauma. The therapist is to make the unconscious conscious. Psychodiagnosis is not important. Inculcating insights is irrelevant. Getting to the early trauma is the only job of the primal therapist. As shown below, the veridicality of the experiences is accepted.

What the primal patient does is to revert to the early developmental point and relive the pain until it is finally resolved and out of the system.[14] The screams assist in expunging the pain, allowing the unconscious to be contacted and dealt with. According to Janov, measures of physiological changes accompany the primal sessions: Along with brain function and structure and immunological changes, blood pressure and heart rate drop.

Primal Therapy has been applied to a wide variety of mental disorders including eating disorders, sexual perversions, alcoholism, depression, manic depression and anxiety.[15] The therapy in each case is essentially the same.

A full description of the therapy technique cannot be given since no full published account exists. Janov demurs from revealing his procedures due to "charlatans" ripping him off as well as concerns about untrained practitioners using his methods. On the other hand, Janov contends that Primal Therapy uses a "precise scientific methodology which requires years of training for its correct employment."[16]

A few nuggets of information can be gleaned from Janov directly and from some of the case histories. An initial patient is not given extensive psychological screening, but it appears rather that it is the patient's willingness to undergo the rigors of Primal Therapy that determines whether he or she is an appropriate candidate. There is no specific time limit for the individual session, which could last many hours. After the initial sessions, group therapy is scheduled. In order to prime the patient, the individual stays in a hotel room and abstains from TV or radio, smoking, alcohol or illicit drugs and sex. The prospective patient spends 24 hours in virtual isolation.[17]

Primal Therapy stimulates a regression to early developmental levels. The patient is primed to do so by reading a book or hearing about Primal Therapy in the news media. Most, if not all, patients understand that they will be asked to undergo a rigorous procedure, i.e., to have primals where they let out their emotions and feelings. Patients who have primals begin to yell, scream, kick and verbally reflect the abandonment and hurt of yesteryear. Thus, the patient may proclaim that no one loves him or cares for him; he is not heard but is ignored and abandoned by his parents. The crying can go on for hours. The therapist may interject questions from time to time for clarification, but mainly the primal process appears to take on a life of its own with spontaneous regression and apparent re-experiencing of both early life experience and even intrauterine trauma. The intensity of this experience opens the floodgates of the hitherto repressed unconscious sources of pain.

Case Reports

"Alieta" appears to be the most recent and extensive case presentation.[18] The story is told in her own words from the diary of her three-week Primal Therapy. Her mental state is one of unhappiness. She begins at the motel where the required restrictions on alcohol, watching TV, and so on, are in place. Before meeting her therapist, Alieta muses about what it is like to feel and even attempts to force herself into feeling.[19]

As she is lying on the floor in the therapy room, a memory is about to emerge. The therapist urges her to let it out. Alieta sees her father at work, but he is ignoring her. Later in the group, she observes other patients sitting or crying while on the floor. There are huge screams and "a body swirls in agony" with people yelling things like "I am going to kill you" or "I hate you." In subsequent sessions as Alieta gets angry, she begins to regress into a fetal position and yells like a child.[20] Her head is pushing something, her legs have feelings, but she is in a strange black place. As she keeps on pushing, Alieta writes "I am in the womb," and she wants to get out.

Five years later, Alieta reports feeling unexpected agony and great joy. She writes her thoughts from her prior primals and how she now conceives that her mother might not want her. "When the signal of birth was given, . . . I started going down the canal and all was fine. I should have gone out but I couldn't, and started suffocating."[21] When she was eventually born, it was with a bar across her forehead; she was purple with rage. After 15 years, she occasionally has primals, but the pain has subsided. She is happy, and her life is in order. There is no indication of what took place, therapy-wise, in the subsequent 15 years.

Clinical Research

Janov references no research on the ability of infants to recall significant events whether traumatic or trivial. Rather, Janov relies on the above-mentioned Penfield study, which shows that electrodes may stimulate and retrieve nontraumatic memory. Janov infers that traumatic memories are imprinted and thus are retained in the temporal lobes on an indefinite basis. However, no research has demonstrated that currently forgotten memories of infancy can be revived from electrodes placed on brain structures.

In the prior 15 years, Janov reports that he has conducted three separate studies indicating the role of repression in disease.[22] Body temperature, blood pressure and pulse were monitored. After eight months of therapy, all three measures decreased. Almost two-thirds of all patients displayed a drop in body temperature. In the hypertensive patients in the study, blood pressure dropped 24 points, and heart rate slowed by 10 beats on average.

Janov states that two studies "on our patients" done by researchers in Copenhagen "found a significant change in brain function as a result of reliving experiences."[23] A related study was conducted on primal patients at the UCLA Brain Research Institute.[24] An index of repression was obtained by examining various parameters, including the above-mentioned vital signs along with brainwave functioning. "In several studies, we have found that repressed individuals have a lower resting EEG (alpha band) than those who have access to their feelings, including those who have frequent anxiety attacks."[25] Thus, after one year of therapy, according to Janov, there is less repression as reflected by the lower amount of neuronal activity. Indeed those with the lower alpha readings take longer to cry and to get into their feelings.[26]

A study by Karle et al.[27] attempted to demonstrate the physiological changes associated with Primal Therapy. The experimental group of 29 patients was given pre- and post-therapy measurements of blood pressure, pulse, rectal temperature and EEGs. The active control group performed exercises during the week-long study, and the inactive control group read and talked for 1.5 hours. The results showed modest support for the notion that, after Primal Therapy, there were reduced vital signs and slowing of brainwave functioning. These physiological changes are not necessarily restricted to Primal Therapy. Hart and Corriere defected from Primal Therapy and developed feeling therapy, which involves patients moving through different cycles of feeling. Thus, the extreme catharsis employed by Primal Therapy may not be necessary for physiological change.[28]

The interrelationship between repression and the immune system is reported by Janov.[29] Janov's hormone studies show, among other things, that "stress hormone levels are reduced as pain is reduced in the human system."[30] Soft tissue growth has been found in female patients, including breast growth. Extensive neurophysiological research allegedly supporting Janov's position is presented. No data or retrievable references are listed that provide any specific detail of any of his claims. No research authored by Janov is cited in his 1994 book.

Critique and Analysis

One of the difficulties in assessing the research mentioned in Janov's[31] book is the quality of the references or, more precisely, the lack of specific citable publications. In many instances, the reader has to guess where the studies are published. The study by the UCLA Brain Research Institute was apparently reported at a conference. The Copenhagen studies were reported either at a conference in 1991 or in the *Acta Psychiatrica Scandinavica*. A check of *Acta Psychiatrica Scandinavica* for 1980 does not list the authors or the study on brainwave functioning and emotional reactions. Thus, there are no published or peer-reviewed investigations directly supporting the effectiveness of Primal Therapy. By conducting in-house studies, there is little chance of refutation or disconfirmation or even illumination. The few meager studies that are published offer little to no support for the notion that intense regression and catharsis lead to improved mental health. Janov hides not only his therapeutic techniques but also the alleged studies supposedly supporting the amazing results.

Someday in the distant future, the work of Penfield, Sperry, Melzack and psychoneuroimmunological studies may relate to Primal Therapy. That day is not now. By latching onto famous neurological investigations, Janov is attempting to appropriate for his theory what Freud only dreamed of in his great scheme: that there would be a neuronal substrate to psychological behavior. One of Freud's early pronouncements but one he later abandoned was that there was a neurological basis for psychological processes.[32]

Reliance on Penfield, for example, is quite misplaced.[33] First, there are no studies showing that early infancy, let alone birth memories, can be retrieved by means of electrode placement in the brain of an epileptic, for example. Second, Janov assumes that the memory of Penfield's patient was historically true. There is no research that demonstrates the accuracy of birth, let alone prebirth, memories. Third, taking a person back to a particular place through hypnosis or showing a photograph may prompt some recall, but such efforts can also be contaminated by a variety of cues. At best, this line of research is tangentially relevant to Janov's thesis. At worst, he is blithely quasi-citing famous studies, which he imagines support his point of view. Most significantly, even if direct stimulation of brain tissue produced accurate memories, how does that relate to the production of accurate memories by way of placing "psychological" electrodes into the mind? Janov extrapolates over a chasm that causes many of his ideas to fall into the science fiction realm.

The neurobiological studies have little to do with supporting the notion that regression to infancy or birth can yield reliable or historically accurate memories, let alone demonstrating how catharting for hours and months on a narrow set of issues brings emotional relief.

There is little support for the notion that a measure of repression has been discovered. The concept of repression is difficult to validate even in innocuous laboratory studies.[34] Use of fancy brain-behavior terms and random allusions to published studies do nothing to shore up one of Janov's contentions that, not only is material residing in the brain tissue, but it is possible to assess the degree of blockage by psychophysiological measures such as body temperature.

Primal Therapy rests on a fundamental and primary fiction, namely, that undergoing Primal Therapy and experiencing primals will alleviate one's pain and produce therapeutic change. As Rosen notes in *Psychobabble*, a patient may be reliving, at least in part, a fantasy mixed up with present-day needs and concerns.[35] Furthermore, there is no way to know if the patient is re-experiencing an actual event or "just doing a good hysterical imitation of being there."[36]

Primal Therapy does not involve patient input. It is extremely dictatorial in that the therapist is always right and omnipotent. There is emotional tyranny in that patients are made to feel they don't know much "by therapists eager to anchor *all* of a patient's utterances securely in the infantile past."[37] Patients in this type of therapy regress, are made dependent on the therapist, may suffer a loss of self-esteem and feel diminished.[38] Furthermore, based on the excessive cost for the short-term therapy in particular, a patient may simply convince him or herself that the new person is the way he or she wants to be.[39] So Primal Therapy leaves some people in a worse condition than when they began.

Since there is no psychological testing, psychodiagnosis or formal follow-up, it is difficult to know what types of patients might be helped. It may be counterproductive for patients with poor reality testing and "defective egos" to undergo Primal Therapy.[40] Regarding "Alieta," one wonders if she was really cured of her neurosis. Did she really have the birth memories, or did Primal Therapy induce a psycho-historical fiction? If it is Janov's position that any patient can be cured, his recent publications should be regarded as anecdotal and closer to fiction than science.

How does the therapist evaluate the progress of ongoing therapy? Is there a simple distinction between the real and the unreal self?[41] There appears to be no determination other than what the therapist says. Thus, it is the therapist who determines if the patient has excavated the hidden roots of the trauma and experienced the primal pain. Whether a patient is progressing is anyone's guess.

Since there is no relevant research, Primal Therapy could simply be chalked up as a placebo and the excessive demand characteristics of the extreme rituals and procedures as well as group pressures. But why should a person endure such intense and perhaps phony reliving of experiences when there may be less onerous and perhaps more effective techniques? For example, as shown by the NIMH study described in Chapter 6, cognitive behavior therapy, both with and without medication, apparently reduces depression in about 16 weeks.

BIOENERGETIC ANALYSIS

Several therapies including Primal, Gestalt and Reichian, have a psychoanalytic heritage, with an added emphasis on body awareness.[42] Thus, there is an interest in dream analysis, transference and the hidden terrain of the mind found in the unconscious. Bioenergetic Analysis, however, is a direct descendant of Reich's character-analytic vegetotherapy and involves direct physical touching of the patient. As a historical note, it is interesting that Wilhelm Reich treated both Lowen, the founder of Bioenergetics, and Fritz Perls (Chapter 5). At present, there are Reichians practicing in the Los Angeles area, and according to Lowen, over 40 centers worldwide offer formal training programs in Bioenergetic Analysis.[43]

Origins of Bioenergetic Analysis

The core of psychopathology for Reich was rooted in sexuality. He viewed sexuality and the orgasm as the source of energy regulators for the body.[44] The function of the orgasm is to discharge excess energy. Reich viewed energy as a literal force. In addition, Lowen viewed energy as a biological reality.[45] Working against a full general release is the pathological character structure, which is composed of muscular armor. The task of the therapist is to attack the sexual repression by chipping away at the armor. The person's armor serves as a protection against painful and threatening emotions.[46] In Reichian Therapy, the patient is nude and is physically massaged or manipulated so that the therapist has direct access to the rings of muscular armor. During the session, the patient can ventilate, scream or kick as the blockaded armors begin to be liberated.

Lowen's Modifications

Four major changes from Reich's theory form the basis of Bioenergetic Analysis:

1. There is an emphasis on pleasure rather than exclusive sexuality. The former includes the latter.

2. Rather than lie on a bed, patients can stand while being touched.

3. Patients can help to devise their own exercise, some of which can be done at home.

4. There is an equal balance between the physical work and the analytic.[47]

Bioenergetic analysts attempt to release the stored-up bodily emotions by directly working with the body and also using the analytic framework. One of the key elements in producing change is the analysis of oedipal conflicts and dealing with sexuality. There is no formal diagnosis or psychological testing. Rather, diagnostic assessment is made of the body, which is integrated within the analytic framework.

Character Structures

According to Bioenergetic analytic theory, there are five separate character structures: schizoid, oral, narcissistic, masochistic and rigid.[48] There are defensive strategies in both the psychological and muscular levels. The types are presented separately, but in actual cases there may be characteristics of several structures in the same person. The following evolved from Lowen's clinical practice and theory.

The *schizoid* character structure refers to the split between thinking and feeling. The person may be withdrawn and have experienced loss of contact with external reality.[49] From the body viewpoint, these patients demonstrate a lack of a good connection between the head and trunk. In some individuals, the neck is elongated, and in others the head tilts away from the line of the body. In the schizoid personality, there is also a split between the lower and upper half of the body in that there is a "severe contraction in the region of the waist or a lack of proportion . . . between the two halves of the body."[50] In addition, the face is mask-like, the eyes do not make contact with others, and the feet are in contraction and are cold.[51]

Developmental antecedents to the schizoid character are found in the mother's early rejection. In every case such rejection is accompanied by the mother's covert and overt hostility.[52]

The *oral* character structure originates in early infancy from a deprivation of parental nurturance. This causes a fear of abandonment, which is later manifested in lack of support in the legs and underdeveloped musculature. For reasons that are unclear, the oral person develops a long thin body along the lines of Sheldon's ectomorphic body configuration.[53] "The eyes are weak with a tendency to myopia, and the level of genital excitation is reduced."[54] There is difficulty standing on one's feet, both literally and figuratively. The oral person is dependent and clings to others, in part because of fear of being abandoned or left alone.[55] A sign of this oral character is a tendency toward depression.

The etiological factors in the oral character structure are thought to be due to an actual loss of a nurturing maternal figure by death, illness, absence or by way of a mother who herself is depressed. The developmental history is reflected in precocity in areas such as walking and talking.

The *narcissistic* character originates in early childhood and is based on parents making the child feel special by way of non-acted-out sexual seduction. The child develops a sense of superiority and grandiosity. To do so, the narcissistic person must view himself above others. This results in an overdeveloped upper half of the body in relation to a weaker lower half. Thus, strong tensions will be located in the back and legs.

Lowen identifies five increasing levels of narcissistic disorders, all of which involve a disturbance or loss of self: phallic-narcissism, narcissistic character, borderline personality, psychopathic personality and paranoid personality.[56]

Etiologically, all of Lowen's narcissistic patients have been humiliated by parents who use power as a way to control the child.[57] Such humiliation may take the form of physical abuse or extreme verbal criticism. The child is mocked or put down when trying to express his own feelings.

The *masochistic* character structure is found in adults who were forced to be submissive as children. These individuals tend to whine and complain. Although on the outside these individuals are submissive, inside on the "deeper emotional level" there are negative and hostile feelings.[58] These individuals hold tension in the muscles that "control the outlets at the upper and lower ends of the body." Viewed body-wide, these individuals are muscularly overdeveloped and show tension in their flexor muscles. The masochistic character structure is reflected by the patients' poor body posture. Physically, these individuals have short, thick body musculature and, for unknown reasons, have an increased growth of body hair.[59]

The masochistic character structure forms in a situation where nurturance and love are combined with severe pressure. In these families, the mother is dominant and the father is passive. There is also a strong focus on eating and defecation. The masochist is afraid to stick his neck or genitals out, for fear that the organ or the person will be cut off.[60]

The *rigid* character structure describes common factors in several personality types. It is referred to as the phallic-narcissistic in man and the hysterical in woman. The main features include an erect body that is carried with pride. But this erect posture is maintained by rigid back muscles that reflect an attitude of holding back. The rigid character "stems from early experiences of being humiliated by the parent of the opposite sex during the time in the oedipal period when the child felt a sexual interest in that parent."[61] The significant trauma is based on frustrated erotic gratification.[62]

Psychotherapeutic Techniques

Bioenergetic exercises and deep breathing are initially used to mobilize the body. The patient is partially clothed and may be standing on the "bioenergetic" stool. One position, called grounding, allows the patient to make contact with the floor by bending over and touching the ground with the tips of his fingers.[63] Limitation in body mobility is both a cause and an effect of unresolved infantile conflicts. In addition, restriction of natural respiration is both a cause and an effect of anxiety. A variety of special body movements allow the person to gain contact with his body and to "begin to understand the relation between the present physical state and the experiences of infancy and childhood that created it."[64] In order to release hitherto bound-up energy, the patient may yell, kick or scream. Once sobbing starts, the cries become involuntary, with the effect that suppressed feelings are released.[65]

Feelings can be brought to the conscious level by asking a patient with a tight jaw to bite on a towel. Having a person hit a bed may evoke feelings of anger. In an attempt to release repressed sexual feelings, the analyst may apply pressure directly to the patient's groin. The patient will feel pain in the pelvic area and will become aware of the tension and underlying fear of castration.[66] The patient is treated both on the bodily level and analytically. Thus, verbal analysis of dreams, slips of the tongue, early development and interpretations are included in the same sessions as the body work.[67]

Case Reports

Martha was a woman in her late thirties whose main problem was a lack of feeling.[68] She complained of an empty life with little interaction with others, especially outside of work. Outwardly, she appeared normal and seemed to cover up by her vivacious manner. Her mother was described as someone who rejected and humiliated her. The father seemed distant and uncaring.

She was given breathing, kicking and grounding exercises to increase the vibrations in her legs. Lowen broke through her constricted jaw muscles, and Martha was able to cry, but there still was an incomplete release of her hidden hostile feelings.

Lowen's goal was to release the pent-up hostility that was caused by the poor familial relationships. When Martha began to realize the actual source of her anger, she took the available tennis racket and began to beat the bed with it. As she did so, she exclaimed anger and hate at the people she believed were responsible for her lack of sexual feelings. Thus, Martha gained insight into the origin of her feelings.[69]

Clinical Research

Hendricks and Hendricks developed a body-centered therapy, which is an outgrowth of Reichian Therapy and Bioenergetics. In their book, they succinctly summarized their research protocol.[70] First, the therapists took notes on several thousand patients for whom there were positive results. Next, the therapists scrutinized the notes for common elements that "seemed to be connected to breakthroughs."[71] Hours of videotapes were viewed in order to document relief of symptoms of an "increase in aliveness." The next three years were spent eliminating the irrelevant aspects and retaining only the essential elements that produce change.

Lowen conducted no research. Not only did he not conduct any basic research on any of the Reichian techniques, but there is none on the modifications and alterations of Reich's approach. Thus, not a single research study anywhere documents the efficacy of Body-Centered Therapy or Bioenergetics.

Critique and Analysis

Despite the large volume of his written work, Lowen never presents any research to support the Bioenergetic analytic position. Thus, his case histories are all that exist as proof of the efficacy of his procedure. Once again, the alleged empirical support is based on self-authentication by the originators and followers of the therapeutic modality. The problem for Lowen is that he built his theory, not only upon the flawed Freudian edifice (Chapter 2), but upon the extreme and untested Reichian foundation. Lowen has borrowed the worst of both worlds.

Lowen borrows the unverified ideas from Freud on the oedipal conflict and transference, for example. He then implants the discredited and bizarre Reichian notions of muscular armor and the relationship to personalty and emotion. Lowen then develops and expands a procedure to release the trapped muscularized emotion by means of almost instantaneous body-personality diagnosis.

He has presented no documentation that persons with long or short necks have any particular type of character structure. Who does the measuring of bodily contractions and tension? Is it just visual? Who assesses the developmental antecedents of the various character types? Neither has he presented any data to support, nor has anyone ever tried to clinically confirm, the etiological significance of the character structures and their manifestation in body shapes or tensions.

Lowen uses the same flawed retrospective analysis of psychoanalysis. Do we really know much about Martha's mother or the true source of Martha's emotional difficulties? Furthermore, his definitions and assessments of "character structure" do not even fit with the framework of DSM-IV. He has proceeded to categorize people within his own parallel universe diagnostic system. It is unclear whether personality disorder is the same or different from character structures; e.g., especially confusing is his broad definition of narcissistic personality, which seems to overlap or conflict with the rigid character structure. Since much of his work involves character structure, it is surprising how brief the descriptions are. There are simply several pages where he pontificates on each different character type. There is no way to know exactly how he divines these five or so character structures.

None of the case studies shows how Lowen integrates the body with the mind. How is it that crying and blaming someone for your problems reduces the muscular tension and brings insight? In the Martha case, there is no follow-up history. One can find a plethora of exercises, some of which can apparently be used without a therapist. In *The Way to Vibrant Health*, Lowen and Lowen present over 100 different bioenergetic exercises to the public.[72] If a trained therapist is not needed, especially to integrate psychoanalysis with the bodily energy theory, how can he justify doing exercises alone? The implication is that the exercises are mechanical or random and not necessarily related to a root cause, and that any so-called improvement may be based on the extreme demand characteristic of the office setting and procedures.

Since touch is a new element that has been added to the therapy mix, it is imperative that the implications of the physical manipulations of the patient be examined. In the instance of treating adults who were victims of child abuse, for example, negative results may be engendered by the extreme physical contact between patient and therapist. Techniques such as Bioenergetics could, in these types of patients, "trigger anxiety, disorganization and dissociation."[73] Lowen provides no assurance that his techniques have no deleterious effects.

Finally, there is no meter that measures how energy is activated or mobilized in the body. How does anyone know if there are any biochemical or other changes during the energy exchanges? Can anyone but the athletically inclined really do these exercises, and if they are painful and noxious, might they not be counterproductive?[74] Without some clinical demonstration of effectiveness, should a patient endure the physically painful process which can provide no proof that the cause of their problem is a hidden emotion or feeling dating back to childhood or infancy? Lowen, like Freud and other psychic archivists, cannot confirm the accuracy or reality of early developmental memories, or whether his methods allow veridical, hitherto repressed material to erupt into consciousness.

PHYSICAL AND VERBAL ATTACK THERAPIES

It may be difficult to believe that some mental health professionals advocate the physical and verbal bashing of patients in an attempt to produce positive changes. This strange and sad legacy can be traced to so-called direct therapy[75] and Z-therapy.[76] The therapist is given full rein, including physical restraint and eliciting rage reactions, in order to obtain the desired results. The results may be silence or agreement with the therapist's views. A clear distinction is being made here between physically restraining someone who is about to kill him- or herself or otherwise engage in some violent act and purposefully and proactively restraining the person to preclude harm to the self and others.

RAGE REDUCTION THERAPY—BACKGROUND

For the past 50 years, several mental health professionals have advocated techniques that require physical confrontation with the patient. Beating and humiliating patients has been condoned in the name of psychotherapy.[77] Both with adult schizophrenics and children, the theory states that anything is acceptable if it helps the patient. Trickery, manipulation and agitating patients are routine. Both Zaslow and Rosen lost their licenses to practice for engaging in these techniques. Although the mental health profession apparently was well aware of Rosen's procedures, he was able to practice with little or no criticism of his brutal techniques.[78]

Feeling therapy became quite popular in the 1970s.[79] The innovators were defectors from Primal Therapy and were seen regularly on national television as psychotherapy experts. What happened in actual practice was that patients were shoved, humiliated and told to live together.[80] In one instance, a patient was told to take off her blouse, crawl on the floor and moo like a cow.[81] This therapy was brought to a halt by a multitude of malpractice lawsuits.

The underlying rationale in several approaches is that antisocial children must express rage in order to be helped.[82] The antecedents of high-risk emotionally disturbed children are breaks in attachment behavior to a stable adult figure (usually the mother) in the first or second year of life.[83] There is a lack of trust that leads to the acting-out conduct disorders of children. Magid and McKelvey cite the "eminent therapist" Zaslow as someone who originated a technique for treating psychopaths.[84] The origin of distrust is found in perceiving parents as the cause of their problems and building a protective wall around themselves. The essence of therapy is to destroy the walls.

"Avant-garde clinics" around the world endorse the innovative approach called Rage Reduction Therapy.[85] The therapy involves physically holding and controlling a young child who is confronted with extreme resistance to his efforts to escape the clutches of the adults. It is contended that the patient is resistant to acting and loving responsibly. The therapy "contains explosive dialogue as the psychopathic patient is encouraged to work through his unbelievable rage and anger" while being forced to accept the absolute control of the adult caretakers or therapists.[86]

Psychotherapeutic Technique

When natural bonding fails, the only way to obtain normality is through a rebonding process. In Rage Reduction Therapy, this objective is accomplished by "asking" the child to lie down between a group of two to four adult-trained "body holders."[87] The idea behind this positioning is to reconstruct the face-to-face position of mother–infant contact during normal attachment. The therapy sessions may last up to eight hours and are orchestrated with the precision of a surgeon. Rage responses are provoked by tickling the child's rib cage. When the child becomes irritated, the therapist continues to provoke by shouting at the child.

The child who could not be previously restrained is now held irresistibly by the body holders. There is no escape. The child squirms and kicks but to no avail. As the session progresses, the child learns who is in control, i.e., the adults. "In this controlled loving situation, the unattached, untrusting child can explode into a more primordial rage and hate."[88] Magid and McKelvey liken the process to that of an exorcism in which the child begins with the "devil inside him and emerges at the end of therapy as a loving, tender, and responsible individual."[89] The bottled-up angry feeling, when vented under these controlled conditions, allows the patient to deal with the anger and with the long-simmering repressed pain.

Case Report

Jeremy's problems began at eleven weeks when he was placed for adoption. For the next 37 days, he bureaucratically bounced around before being placed in an adoptive home. Although there is no conscious memory of these painful events, it is the task of Rage Reduction Therapy to bring these memories into consciousness so that the inner rage can be expelled and dealt with. Lacking proper nurturance, this baby didn't receive love and attention and as a result was closed off from others. He shows signs of poor attachment or none at all.

Therapy begins with the mental health professional along with six others who are holding Jeremy down. The patient kicks and screams but is unable to get the professional away. A power struggle ensues, and Jeremy finally says that the therapist is the boss. Resistance is noted by "coughing, blinking and looking away from the therapist's eyes."[90] After rib stimulation and verbal prompts, Jeremy is able to express his rage at the therapist. "I hate you, I hate you, I hate you."[91] The shouting and expressing of hate now turn to his birth mother. Jeremy does report that he felt great at the end of the first session. There was no follow-up study on Jeremy's clinical status.

Critique and Analysis

Rage Reduction Therapy proactively provides physical restraint as well as taunting and teasing. At times an overly aggressive or suicidal patient may need to be restrained for his own and others' protection. In attack therapies, the therapist takes a patient who apparently has acted out in the past but at the moment may be quiet and still. The patient is then attacked by six or eight adults and physically and mentally beaten into submission. The session ends when the patient, whether accurately or not, says he is better and knows who is the boss. How does the therapist evaluate the validity of the patient's statements? If these are young psychopaths, maybe they are still playing a game.

Although maternal deprivation leads to emotional problems, is there any evidence that physically beating a child or a schizophrenic into submission produces any positive results? In 1994, the *American Journal of Orthopsychiatry* accepted an article that uncritically embraced the barbaric and brutal treatment of children.[92] The work of Zaslow and Cline, Magid and Mc-Kelvey was presented without much objection.

What should concern the general public as well the parents and guardians is the effect of therapists and staff and their actions on the children. The possibly horrendous effects of this incredible hostility on involuntary victims is overlooked. Also ignored is the possibility that the adult therapists are providing role models for aggression. It certainly would be helpful for the advocates of rage reduction to present clear short-term and long-term data to support their brutal techniques.

Another issue that deserves attention is how there can be informed consent when the child can't give it and the guardian may in effect be forced to give it. Thus, portions of the mental health community apparently ignore the degradation of the human spirit conducted under the guise of psychotherapy.

est AND LARGE-GROUP AWARENESS SEMINARS

Arising out of the human potential movement in the 1960s were a number of workshops, seminars and training programs.[93] The most famous human potential program was *erhard seminars training* known as *est*. *est* was an intensive 60-hour workshop designed to alter a person's life view. There are a number of *est* clones including Life Spring, Actualizations and Forum, which is a successor to *est*.[94] All of these workshops have several features in common. Participants are verbally attacked. The idea is to break down emotional defenses in order to allow new beliefs and attitudes to take over. There is a significant cathartic element in that emotional release is generated by the *est* techniques.

est borrows psychotherapeutic techniques from a wide variety of sources: spiritual aspects extracted from various eastern religions; and behavioral, psychoanalytic, gestalt techniques, as well as relaxation, guided imagery and psychodrama.[95] Therefore, there seems little doubt that large intensive seminars contain elements of both individual and group psychotherapy.

The seminars begin with a confrontational tone. An announcement is made that everyone is an "asshole."[96] The 250 participants are verbally assaulted.[97] The group leaders use an attack mode and have an authoritarian attitude. The leaders respond to criticism with intimidation, harassment and ridicule.[98] The participants are informed that they will be verbally attacked, insulted and angered. They are told they might "vomit, cry, get the shakes"[99] as well as have headaches or bellyaches.[100] During the training, the participants undergo the Truth Process. The participants are asked to focus on something that is bothering them, or on a problem or feeling that they are not handling very well. The participants are then asked to locate a space in a particular part of their body and then, as they go through their entire body and continue to relax, they are to become more aware of themselves. The leader then informs the group members that they are going to feel every feeling that there is to feel. The room becomes very noisy with the cacophonous sounds from the participants, who are now lying on their backs in a gigantic hotel ballroom. As they go into their spaces, 250 people are emoting, "giving free vent to vomiting, shaking, hysterical laughing, raging—re-creating experiences in a safe place."[101]

A number of *est*-like seminars have emerged over the last 20 years. Most borrow from *est*, Primal Therapy or other regression-inducing modalities. Life Spring was founded in 1974 by John P. Hanly and four other people in the human potential movement.[102] As of 1990, over 100,000 people have taken their training.[103] The seminar takes place over five days, lasting a total of 48 hours.[104] Life Spring, like *est*, makes the claim that it is providing an educational product and not psychotherapy. Although Life Spring uses a preliminary questionnaire to weed out people who are under psychiatric treatment, no significant psychosocial history is taken.

The group leaders in large group seminars generally are not licensed psychotherapists but may be sales managers, used car salesmen, or former disc jockeys. The leaders' backgrounds may be helpful at the introductory lectures in persuading a person to enroll in the full seminar. Quite noteworthy is the way the leaders or facilitators look and act. They are neatly dressed, clean-shaven and have an air of absolute authority. They might not display an emotion even when lambasting the trainees.[105]

Testimonials

Based on questionnaire data, most respondents indicated that *est* was helpful in a number of areas. This included improvement in physical health and work satisfaction, a more meaningful life, as well as decreased drug use and alcohol consumption. There was also reported improvement in various psychophysiological complaints such as headaches, insomnia, allergies and dysmenorrhea. When mental health professionals were surveyed, the results were also favorable. As many as 905 of the respondents reported some positive impact as a result of taking *est* training. Therefore, according to the self-reports, mental health professionals and the general public who participated in *est* training indicated significant improvement in their lives and in their mental status.[106]

Case Report

Dr. E was a 41-year-old physician who was referred for psychiatric evaluation because of "unusual persistence of angina symptoms in the presence of mild heart disease."[107] He had received five years of psychoanalysis 20 years prior to his *est* experience. At the time he enrolled in *est*, he had been in psychotherapy for about six months.

The *est* experience was quite favorable and positive. "In *est*, he gained an astonishingly clear view of his need to be a victim."[108] The participant was now able to integrate information from his earlier life with that of his current situation. He was able to achieve some far-reaching insights that went beyond his earlier psychoanalytic work. When the patient was seen two years later, his anxiety and depression had not returned and he had been without angina since shortly after completing *est*. The therapist has observed that this patient was doing better.[109]

Clinical Research

In a study in a federal prison, half of the subjects received *est* training and the other half received only a promise of future training.[110] There were dependent variable or outcome measures. The first was based on psychological tests such as the MMPI. The second outcome measure was physiological responses such as hand temperature, galvanic skin resistance and respiratory rate, which were thought to be sensitive measures of current anxiety level. The third dependent variable was behavioral measurements that included "inmate-initiated sick calls, self-reported drug usage, custody levels, merit awards, furloughs, rule infractions, and grievances."[111]

The subjects who completed *est* training showed significant positive changes on the psychological measures compared to the control group. What was also quite significant, however, was that there were no differences among the inmate groups on any of the physiological measures. The implication is that the improvement shown in the individuals who completed *est* training may have been influenced by the demand characteristics or placebo factor rather than any inherent active element of the *est* experience.

On the other side of the ledger, some limited research indicates that undergoing *est* may be a negative experience and can lead to significant psychiatric disturbances.[112] For example, Mr. A, a 39-year-old married executive, was involuntarily hospitalized midway through his *est* training. There was no history of mental illness in this patient; it was thought that any trauma he had previously experienced was resolved. But when the second day of training was completed, Mr. A experienced "a marked increase in energy, self-esteem and knowledge."[113] The patient became grandiose, manic and was subsequently involuntarily hospitalized. These results cannot necessarily be generalized to the wide array of patients who undergo intensive seminars such as *est*; however, some vulnerable persons may decompensate.

Critique and Analysis

First, an advertisement for a group leader or facilitator might be: "No training in psychotherapy needed." It appears that the major attribute required to conduct intensive group seminars is to be articulate, persuasive, have an authoritative appearance, and have completed the seminar. The argument that *est*, Life Spring or similar groups are not therapy cannot stand up to scrutiny. There can be little doubt that intensive seminars that alter one's perception of oneself and that change beliefs and behavior constitute psychotherapy. Clearly, a number of psychotherapeutic modalities are employed during these short-term seminars.

The psychotherapeutic approaches that are used can be described as a hodgepodge of conflicting approaches meshed together.[114] The result is a blending of unsubstantiated techniques, none of which has received any scientific support.

The seminars appear to produce a dependent, emotionally immature individual who is more likely to pledge allegiance to an authoritarian figure. Haken and Adams view Life Spring as a pathological experience in which "ego functions were systematically undermined and regression was promoted by environmental structuring, infantilizing of participants and repeated emphasis on submission and surrender."[115] Despite the passage of 20 years or so, there still is not one scintilla of evidence supporting the mental health efficacy of cathartic confrontive group seminars.

NOTES

1. Brown, M. (1973). The new body psychotherapies. *Psychotherapy: Theory, Research and Practice, 10* (pp. 98–116).

2. Singer, M. T. & Lalich, J. (1996). *Crazy therapies: What are they? Do they work?* San Francisco: Jossey-Bass.

3. Janov, A. (1991). *The new primal scream: Primal therapy twenty years on* (p. 3). Chicago: Enterprise.

4. Janov, *New primal scream* (p. 4).

5. Janov, *New primal scream* (p. 3).

6. Janov, *New primal scream* (p. 37).

7. Janov, *New primal scream* (p. 38).

8. Janov, *New primal scream* (p. 108).

9. Janov, *New primal scream* (p. 39).

10. Janov, *New primal scream* (p. 42).

11. Janov, *New primal scream* (p. 142).

12. Janov, *New primal scream* (p. 4).

13. Janov, *New primal scream* (p. 62).

14. Janov, *New primal scream* (p. 5).

15. Janov, *New primal scream* (p. 5).

16. Janov, *New primal scream* (p. 335).
17. Rosen, R. D. (1977). *Psychobabble* (p. 158). New York: Avon Books.
18. Janov, *New primal scream* (p. 81).
19. Janov, *New primal scream* (p. 82).
20. Janov, *New primal scream* (p. 93).
21. Janov, *New primal scream* (p. 100).
22. Janov, *New primal scream* (p. 240).
23. Janov, *New primal scream* (p. 245).
24. Janov, *New primal scream* (p. 245).
25. Janov, *New primal scream* (p. 245).
26. Janov, *New primal scream* (p. 246).
27. Karle, W., Correire, R., Hart, J., Gold, S., Maple, C. & Hopper, M. (1976). Maintenance of psychophysiological changes in feeling therapy. *Psychological Reports, 39* (pp. 1143–1147).
28. Karle et al., Maintenance of psychophysiological changes (pp. 1143–1147); Woldenberg, L., Karle, W., Gold, S., Corriere, R., Hart, J. & Hopper, M. (1976). Psychophysiological changes in feeling therapy. *Psychological Reports, 39* (pp. 1059–1062).
29. Janov, *New primal scream* (p. 248).
30. Janov, *New primal scream* (p. 249).
31. Janov, *New primal scream*.
32. Grünbaum, A. (1993). *Validation in the clinical theory of psychoanalysis: A study in the philosophy of psychoanalysis* (pp. 6–7). Madison, Conn.: International Universities Press.
33. Penfield, W. (1959). The interpretive cortex. *Science, 129* (pp. 1719–1725).
34. Silverman, L. H. (1985). Research on psychoanalytic psychodynamic propositions. *Clinical Psychology Review, 5* (pp. 247–257).
35. Rosen, *Psychobabble* (p. 213).
36. Rosen, *Psychobabble* (p. 237).
37. Rosen, *Psychobabble* (p. 210).
38. Singer & Lalich, *Crazy therapies* (p. 130).
39. Singer & Lalich, *Crazy therapies* (p. 130).
40. Yassky, A. D. (1979). Critique on primal therapy. *American Journal of Psychotherapy, 33* (pp. 119–127).
41. Brown, The new body psychotherapies (pp. 98–116).
42. Brown, The new body psychotherapies (pp. 98–116).
43. Lowen, A. (1994). Bioenergetic analysis. In Corsini & Wedding (Eds.), *Current psychotherapies* (5th ed.) (pp. 409–418). Itasca, Ill.: Peacock Publishers.
44. Lowen, Bioenergetic analysis (p. 411).
45. Lowen, Bioenergetic analysis (p. 412).
46. Lowen, A. (1975). *Bioenergetics* (p. 411). New York: Penguin Press.
47. Lowen, Bioenergetic analysis (p. 412).
48. Lowen, *Bioenergetics* (p. 151).
49. Lowen, *Bioenergetics* (p. 152).
50. Lowen, Bioenergetic analysis (p. 413).
51. Lowen, *Bioenergetics* (p. 153).
52. Lowen, *Bioenergetics* (p. 155).

53. Sheldon, W. H. (1954). *Atlas of man: A guide for somatotyping the adult male at all ages.* New York: Harper.

54. Lowen, *Bioenergetics* (p. 156).

55. Lowen, *Bioenergetics* (p. 157).

56. Lowen, A. (1984). *Narcissism: Denial of the true self* (p. 13). New York: Macmillan.

57. Lowen, *Narcissism* (p. 79).

58. Lowen, *Bioenergetics* (p. 163).

59. Lowen, *Bioenergetics* (p. 164).

60. Lowen, *Bioenergetics* (pp. 165–166).

61. Lowen, Bioenergetic analysis (p. 414).

62. Lowen, *Bioenergetics* (p. 169).

63. Lowen, A. & Lowen, L. (1992). *The way to vibrant health: A manual of bioenergetic exercises.* New York: Harper & Row.

64. Lowen, Bioenergetic analysis (p. 416).

65. Lowen, Bioenergetic analysis (pp. 416–417).

66. Lowen, A. (1984). *Narcissism: Denial of the true self* (p. 120). New York: Macmillan.

67. Lowen, Bioenergetic analysis (p. 409).

68. Lowen, *Narcissism* (p. 110).

69. Lowen, *Narcissism* (p. 116).

70. Hendricks, G. & Hendricks, K. (1993). *At the speed of light: A new approach to personal change through body-centered therapy* (p. 12). New York: Bantam Books.

71. Hendricks & Hendricks, *At the speed of light* (p. 12).

72. Lowen & Lowen, *The way to vibrant health.*

73. Cornell, W. F. & Olio, M. A. (1991). Integrating affect in treatment with adult survivors of physical and sexual abuse. *American Journal of Orthopsychiatry, 61* (pp. 59–69).

74. Brown, The new body psychotherapies (pp. 98–116).

75. Rosen, J. N. (1953). *Direct analysis: Selected papers.* New York: Grune & Stratton.

76. Zaslow, R. W. & Menta, M. (1975). *The psychology of the Z-process.* San Jose, Calif.: San Jose University Press.

77. Masson, J. M. (1994). *Against therapy* (Chapter 5). Monroe, Maine: Common Courage Press.

78. Masson, *Against therapy* (Chapter 5).

79. Woldenberg et al., Psychophysiological changes in feeling therapy (pp. 1059–1062).

80. Mithers, C. L. (1994). *Therapy gone mad: The true story of hundreds of patients and a generation betrayed.* New York: Addison-Wesley.

81. Singer & Lalich, *Crazy therapies* (p. 151).

82. Magid, K. & McKelvey, C. A. (1988). *High risk: Children without a conscience.* Lakewood, Colo.: Bantam Books.

83. Magid & McKelvey, *Children without a conscience* (pp. 60–61).

84. Magid & McKelvey, *Children without a conscience* (p. 194).

85. Magid & McKelvey, *Children without a conscience* (p. 205).

86. Magid & McKelvey, *Children without a conscience* (p. 205).

87. Magid & McKelvey, *Children without a conscience* (pp. 209–210).

88. Magid & McKelvey, *Children without a conscience* (p. 202).

89. Magid & McKelvey, *Children without a conscience* (p. 212).

90. Magid & McKelvey, *Children without a conscience* (p. 218).

91. Magid & McKelvey, *Children without a conscience* (p. 219).

92. Bath, H. (1994). The physical restraint of children: Is it therapeutic? *American Journal of Orthopsychiatry, 64* (pp. 40–49).

93. Finkelstein, P., Wenegrat, B. & Yalom, I. (1982). Large group awareness training. *Annual Review of Psychology, 33* (pp. 515–539).

94. Ankerberg, J. & Weldon, J. (1996). *Encyclopedia of new age beliefs* (pp. 259–308). Eugene, Ore.: Harvest House Publishers.

95. Finkelstein et al., Large group awareness training (pp. 515–539); Glass, L. L., Kirsch, M. A. & Parris, F. (1977). Psychiatric disturbances associated with erhard seminars training: 1. A report of cases. *American Journal of Psychiatry, 134* (pp. 245–247).

96. Bry, A. (1976). *est: Sixty hours that transform your life* (p. 72). New York: Avon.

97. Bry, *est: 60 hours* (p. 72).

98. Glass et al., Psychiatric disturbances associated with est (pp. 245–247).

99. Bry, *est: 60 hours* (p. 74).

100. Bry, *est: 60 hours* (p. 72).

101. Bry, *est: 60 hours* (p. 85).

102. Ankerberg & Weldon, *Encyclopedia of new age beliefs* (p. 299).

103. Ankerberg & Weldon, *Encyclopedia of new age beliefs* (p. 299).

104. Haken, J. & Adams, R. (1983). Pathology as "personal growth": A participant-observation study of Life Spring training. *Psychiatry, 46* (pp. 270–280).

105. Finkelstein et al., Large group awareness training (pp. 515–539).

106. Finkelstein et al., Large group awareness training (pp. 515–539).

107. Simon, J. (1978). Observation on 67 patients who took erhard seminars training. *American Journal of Psychiatry, 135* (pp. 686–691).

108. Simon, Observation on 67 patients (pp. 686–691).

109. Simon, Observation on 67 patients (pp. 686–691).

110. Hosford, R. E., Moss, C. S., Cavior, H. & Kerish, B. (1980). *Research on erhard seminars training in a correctional institution.* Lompoc, Calif.: Federal Correctional Institution (cited in Finkelstein et al., Large group awareness training [pp. 515–539]).

111. Hosford et al., *Research in a correctional institution.*

112. Glass et al., Psychiatric disturbances associated with est.

113. Glass et al., Psychiatric disturbances associated with est.

114. Finkelstein et al., Large group awareness training.

115. Haken & Adams, Pathology as "personal growth."

Chapter 4

Recovered Memory Therapy

One of the legacies of psychoanalysis is the tributary that flows to what may be called Recovered Memory Therapy. In contrast to the cognitive-behavioral approach (Chapter 6), those who provide Recovered Memory Therapy generally share the psychodynamic view. Thus, following Freud, it is assumed that the etiology of anxiety, depression and other mental disorders may be based on a forgotten trauma. If the trauma can be excavated, examined and dealt with, then the patient will be able to recover emotionally. This notion was first popularized on the world stage by Freud over 100 years ago and in a more recent and convoluted fashion (see Chapter 3) by Janov who postulated that even prenatal traumas may be a causative factor in adult psychopathology.

In the last ten years or so, Freud's ideas have been employed in the search for repressed memories of childhood abuse. Although there is no specific school of Recovered Memory Therapy, the therapist uses a number of techniques in dredging up memories. Hypnosis, sodium amytal and psychotropic medications, bibliotherapy and journaling, body work and dream analysis are methods used to extricate a forgotten trauma from the memory bank of yesteryear. Whether the recovered memories are true or false may not be a concern to some therapists. Because of the potential for harm to patients and their families, however, it is essential to be able to gauge the veridicality of the alleged retrieved memories.

A BRIEF HISTORY OF RECOVERED MEMORY THERAPY

In the space of 100 years, therapists have leapfrogged from Freudian techniques to the current-day attempts to uncover the historic archives in a person's unconscious. Perhaps the greatest impetus to the search for memories of forgotten childhood sexual abuse originated from the publication of *The Courage to Heal* by Bass and Davis in 1988.[1] There appeared to be an almost simultaneous and perhaps not coincidental explosion in the diagnosis of multiple personality disorder (now called dissociative identity disorder), especially in North America.[2]

Although Freud later abandoned his theory of the seduction of female patients in early childhood, the theory was resurrected by Masson,[3] who contends that the political climate of the 1890s in Vienna would not allow for such a claim. According to Masson, what is actually true is that sexual and physical abuse of infants is prevalent in the lives of many children.[4] Thus Masson's view, which is based on Freud's original position, is that the traumatic memories of childhood abuse, repressed and lodged in the unconscious, are the cause of adult psychopathology.

Herman relies heavily on Freud's original formulation. In *Trauma and Recovery*, Herman states that Freud's clinical description of the etiology of hysteria in 1896 rivals contemporary analyses.[5] "It is a brilliant, compassionate, eloquently argued, closely reasoned document."[6] Thus, by the late 1980s and early 1990s, Freud's original theory had made a major comeback and formed the basis for the assertion that actual forgotten sexual trauma is at the root of psychopathology.

In *The Courage to Heal*, Bass and Davis proposed that adult victims of childhood sexual abuse may have repressed the memory. This book is considered the "bible" of the recovery movement. One of the classic original statements in the first edition is, "If you think you were abused, and your life shows the symptoms, then you were."[7] *The Courage to Heal* is routinely recommended to patients who fit the profile of someone who may have been abused. It is not uncommon for this book to be part of the literature given to psychiatric in-patients.

A popular figure of the 1980s who also was not formally trained as a psychotherapist is John Bradshaw. His writings and tapes contain a clear implication that much of a person's unhappiness or emotional problems stems from the hidden past.[8] As Goldstein and Farmer note,[9] Bradshaw was influential in expanding the search for more survivors of childhood sexual abuse. Bradshaw reasons that many people have forgotten or buried their abuse, and if one wonders if they were abused, this may be a clue to the repression of the abuse. Pendergrast dubbed him the "Evangelist of Dysfunction."[10] Bradshaw's book presents no clinical research on uncovering hidden shame.[11]

One of the first major books to discuss specific techniques to recover memories was *Repressed Memories* by Fredrickson.[12] In a more authoritative and professional-appearing manner than *The Courage to Heal*, Fredrickson supports the contention of repression of childhood sexual trauma and how using the uncovering methods can lead to improved clinical functioning of the individual. A number of case vignettes are presented, but no clinical data are cited. Following the lead of Bass and Davis, a detailed checklist of symptoms of possible abuse is presented.

Several texts were published in the late 1980s covering the diagnosis and treatment of dissociative identity disorder (DID).[13] By the early 1990s, professional articles were published on how to deal with and treat victims of satanic ritual abuse (SRA), who were diagnosed as having dissociative identity disorder.[14] These authors state that cults create DID, and the challenge for the therapist is to neutralize cult mind-control programming.[15] One method to treat SRA victims is through mini-abreactions where the traumatic memory fragments are dealt with in a slow and gradual fashion. By the late 1980s and early 1990s, DID units were routine at psychiatric hospitals.

In 1992, Pamela Freyd formed the False Memory Syndrome Foundation after her daughter allegedly recovered a memory in adulthood of childhood sexual abuse. The Foundation was originated by adults who allege they were falsely accused of abusing their children. The false memory syndrome refers to patients who strongly believe illusory memories of recovered childhood sexual abuse. The Foundation's position is that the therapeutic crucible is responsible for the inception and maintenance of the false memory.

In *Memory and Abuse*, Whitfield[16] presents a method for healing the victim of sexual abuse and blasts the idea of false memories. In his opinion, false memories are extremely rare, although the exact extent is unknown.[17] He vitriolically and personally attacks the founders of the False Memory Syndrome Foundation and asserts that Pamela Freyd is unethical. Dr. Whitfield concludes there is evidence that her husband abused their daughter. It should be noted, however, that Dr. Whitfield apparently never performed a clinical or forensic evaluation on any of the Freyds.

Case reports from persons who suffered from childhood sexual and physical abuse are reported in Lenore Terr's *Unchained Memories: True Stories of Traumatic Memories Lost and Found*[18] and Feldman's *Lessons in Evil, Lessons from the Light—A True Story of Satanic Abuse and Spiritual Healing*.[19] First-hand accounts have also been published of former patients who have retracted or recanted their belief that they had recovered memories of abuse.[20]

Several books recount the history of recovered memories and question the validity of repressed memory. The most extensive coverage is in Pendergrast's *Victims of Memory*.[21] Pendergrast, a journalist, began his quest into this arena when his two daughters accused him of abuse. Loftus, who has done extensive work on eyewitness testimony, jumped into the fray with her article and a later book on *The Myth of Repressed Memory*.[22] The issue of the patient's vulnerability to the therapist's pronouncements is covered in Yapko's *Suggestions of Abuse*.[23] Vigorously attacking Recovered Memory Therapy are Ofshe and Watters, who contend that the recall of repressed memories and satanic ritual abuse is based on manipulation by therapists, who help to fabricate the so-called memories.[24]

Both Crews[25] and Webster[26] critically examine Freud's lineage in the battle regarding the validity of material emanating from the unrepressed unconscious. Their position is that, since Freud's theory is fundamentally flawed, particularly with respect to the notion that excavating childhood sexual abuse from the repressed portion of the mind will lead to insight and improvement, the recent approaches of recovered memory therapists are also flawed.

One of the first books that is research-oriented is *Recovered Memories of Abuse* by Pope and Brown.[27] The authors do not discount the possibility that some memories may be based on suggestion, nor do they contend that such retrieval is not possible. "In the light of the current state of scientific data and knowledge, each report of recovered memory of abuse must be carefully and fairly evaluated on an individual basis."[28]

SYMPTOMS AND DIAGNOSIS—CHECKLIST FOR RECOVERED MEMORY

Patients who present with a diagnosis of anxiety, depression, eating disorder and post-traumatic stress disorder (PTSD) may have an underlying cause of these disorders, a hitherto unrecognized and unrecalled childhood sexual trauma.[29] In order to assist the clinician with the extrication of this archival information, a set of symptom checklists and guidelines has been developed.

In 1988, Bass and Davis offered a number of questions, which, if answered "yes," suggest childhood sexual abuse. If a person notes some of these symptoms as an adult, it may be that for the first time he or she is realizing the devastating effects of childhood sexual abuse: "Do you have trouble expressing your feelings?" "Do you ever use alcohol, drugs, or food in a way that concerns you?" "Do you enjoy using your body in activities such as dance, sports or hiking?" "Are you satisfied with your family relationships?" "Are you afraid to succeed?" "Can you say no?"[30]

Several years later, Fredrickson provided a list of 63 symptoms. The checklist is designed to help the patients "start thinking about warning signals you may have or to validate signals that you feel may be clues to your abuse."

Seven areas of possible signs of childhood sexual abuse are singled out for attention:

1. Sexuality—e.g., "I seemed to know things about sex before they were explained to me."

2. Sleep—e.g., "I often have nightmares."

3. Fears and attractions—e.g., "I hate going to the dentist more than most people."

4. Eating disturbances—e.g., "I am seriously underweight or overweight."

5. Body problems—e.g., "Whenever I think of a person from my childhood, I get a sensation in my genitals."

6. Compulsive behaviors—e.g., "I have an addiction to drugs or alcohol."

7. Emotional signals—e.g., "I space out or daydream"; "I identify with abuse victims in the media, and often stories of abuse make me want to cry."

No formal psychological assessment can definitively determine whether a person has been sexually abused as a child. As Fredrickson notes, no single item is a "certain indicator of repressed memories." The reason is that some patients who were not sexually abused have some of the symptoms such as nightmares or eating problems. Fredrickson goes on to say, however, that if several items are checked in each category, "you will want to consider the possibility that you have repressed memories."[31]

In the case of Holly Ramona, expert witnesses testified at trial that this patient showed signs of childhood sexual abuse. Ms. Ramona was suffering from eating disorders and noticed that her father had acted differently toward her at a Christmas party. She informed her therapist that her father seemed to look at her sexually. At this point she began to have fragments of a memory of childhood molestation. Her memories of abuse extend up to the age of 16. Lenore Terr testified that there was corroborating evidence that supported the validity or veridicality of the retrieved memories. The evidence includes Ms. Ramona's continuing fear of her father, repulsion at eating a banana or pickle, having bulimia, PTSD, avoiding foods that reminded her of oral sex such as mayonnaise and white sauces, and constant and repetitive physical problems in her abdomen that were thought to simulate the pain of rape.[32]

DIAGNOSIS AND TREATMENT OF DISSOCIATIVE IDENTITY DISORDER

In 1996, the *Diagnostic and Statistical Manual IV* (DSM-IV) provided a newly expanded and updated version of multiple personality disorder, now called dissociative identity disorder (DID). The diagnostic criteria include the presence of two or more identities or personality states that are apparently separate from each other. The various identities or personalities are called "alters." Thus, each personality or alter has "its own enduring pattern of perceiving, relating to, and thinking about, the environment and self."[33] In addition, the identities or personality states must recurrently take control of the person's behavior. The next two symptoms appeared in the DSM-IV definition: "an inability to recall important personal information that is too extensive to be explained by ordinary forgetfulness." Last, the disorder is not due to the physiological effects of various substances or other medical problems.

According to Gould, dissociative identity disorder is cult-created, and most satanic ritual abuse victims suffer from DID.[34] The horrible trauma encountered by these victims produces a psychological wall, blocking the horrible memories. In 1992, a comprehensive checklist was presented that offers signs and symptoms of ritualistic abuse in children.[35] Ritual abuse, especially satanic ritual abuse, is viewed as a brutal form of abuse that involves torture and killing as well as sexual and emotional abuse. The victim is terrorized by mind-altering drugs, hypnosis and mind-control techniques.[36] There may be bloody sacrifices of the victim's own children and servitude as a prostitute.[37]

When examining children for signs of ritual abuse, the clinician should look for problems associated with the following: sexual beliefs and behaviors; toileting and the bathroom; the supernatural; small spaces or being tied up; death; doctor's office; fear of certain colors such as red or orange; emotional difficulties displayed with eating, speech, sleep or learning; family relationships; play and peer relationships; and strange beliefs.

As noted, treatment starts with the premise that the victims were involved in a mind-controlling cult as children and still remain under the domination and control of the cult. The cult creates alters, which can be re-contacted by the cult. For example, the cult can call out to the patient's alter through taps on his or her window or door, on the telephone or a special hand signal, or even a word or phrase.[38] The patient "must be helped to discover the cult functions that the cult-created alter serves."[39] The patient is helped by understanding the triggers that activate the cult cues used to access the particular alter.

TECHNIQUES USED IN RECOVERED MEMORY THERAPY

A variety of methods have been employed in an attempt to access repressed memories. None of the methods is unique to recovered memory technique. The focus, however, is narrow, with the aim being to zoom in on a blocked or repressed pathogenic experience. The various techniques can be used in various combinations but are presented separately here for ease of discussion.

Hypnosis

One way to uncover repressed memories, according to Fredrickson, is through hypnosis. Patients can be relaxed and asked to visualize important events in their past with a formal hypnotic induction or through less formal guided imagery. In some circumstances, the adult patient may be age-regressed to childhood. In this situation, the person is slowly and method-ically guided back to an earlier developmental stage. Fredrickson indicates that if abuse occurred in childhood, one can rely on the "unconscious to move toward revealing the trauma through imagery, feelings, and words."[40]

Images or flashes can be a prelude to a guided imagery tour during hyp-nosis. A patient named Dave had recurrent pictures of himself standing on a street corner halfway between his house and the bar owned by his father.[41] Under hypnosis, he imagined or viewed himself walking home and feeling sad. Although this memory was worked with, he still had the persistent image. Another hypnosis session brought Dave back to the bar. At that point while in hypnosis, "he got a clear image of having been sexually abused by one of the bar patrons in the back store room."[42]

Dreams

As viewed by Freud, dreams are the royal road to the unconscious. For therapists who are attempting to unclog the layers of the unconscious mind, dreams are one of the main royal roads that lead to repressed childhood sexual abuse. Repressed memory of abuse may be accessed by memory frag-ments in several types of dreams: nightmares, which may contain places where the abuse occurred, such as bedrooms, bathrooms, closets or attics. Indicators of abuse may be dreams that contain "penises, breasts, bottles, broomhandles or sticks."[43]

Nightmares can also contain memories of ritual abuse. Thus, blood, an-imal or human sacrifices, torture, chanting, robed figures or cannibalism can be dream reflections of repressed ritual cult abuse.

Both innocuous dreams and those that elicit strong feelings may be clues to repressed sexual abuse. According to Fredrickson, dreams containing ex-plicit sexual abuse are always repressed memory dreams.[44]

Body Work

Repressed memories of abuse may emerge from feelings and emotions that are triggered through massage, Rolfing or Bioenergetics. A tingling in the genitals, for example, or a muscle cramp in the thigh may be an im-portant message from the body memory. The memory so produced is thought to reflect trauma from an earlier developmental period that has been blocked and stored in the body tissue.

According to Fredrickson, "whenever a part of your body is touched that was hurt, the stored or blocked energy can be accessed."[45] An example of an emerging memory was "Sarah," who was quite sensitive to having her toes touched. As this occurred, she felt pain and anguish, which related back to her grandfather shoving wood chips under her toenails.

Pendergrast presents a brief case report of a body worker. It was reported that when the patient's arm was pulled, there was consistent resistance. "It turns out that during ritual abuse, she had witnessed another victim's arm being lifted in a similar fashion and severed at the shoulder."[46]

Bibliotherapy and Journaling

The person who begins to suspect that he or she may have been abused may be given two types of assignments: In one, the patient keeps a running narrative indicating any signs or clues regarding the abuse. With journal-writing, the person writes down his or her thoughts and ideas without stopping to analyze or censor those thoughts as if doing his or her own free association.

Journal-writing can begin by way of a symbol from a dream, a memory fragment, a bodily sensation or a sense that an abusive memory is trying to bubble up from the unconscious.[47] A special journaling technique is called storytelling, in which the patient tries to write a story about a child abuse scene, for example, "When I was younger, I was abused by . . .".[48] A second method is to quickly write down one's responses to a specific question. For example, when Ann was asked to quickly list five things her grandmother did, a total of eight items emerged. Ann listed hanging of a cat in front of her, nearly being suffocated, sexual abuse and other physical abuse.

The case of "Jane" (the patient's name is changed for reasons of privacy) illustrates the struggle to retrieve and validate memories by means of journal-writing. Jane entered therapy and embarked on a journey into the world of dissociative identity disorder. Jane contacted this writer and initiated litigation after coming to the belief that the memories of ritual abuse she retrieved were false. Her entries include:

A burning sensation in my vagina. Did it happen as a child, or maybe during the birth of my children. (March 23, 1990)

What's going on. I've had terrible feelings ever since I read that story in *The Courage to Heal*. Am I exaggerating or did someone stick their penis in my mouth? (April 24, 1990)

I'm sitting here listening to a Bradshaw tape and my thoughts drift. . . . I closed my eyes. I see my father embracing me, totally encompassing me. I'm very small, maybe four or five. Then I feel him inside me. . . . Am I making this up? (May 24, 1990)

The second assignment is to read books that relate to the retrieval of childhood memories of abuse. In *The Courage to Heal*, the authors offer advice for retrieving memories of abuse and how to deal with the emergence of the new material. Recovery therapists recommend books and tapes by

John Bradshaw, which focus on finding the secrets and toxins from early childhood. In *Healing the Shame That Binds You,* a twelve-step program is presented that can transform toxic shame into healthy shame. Part of the philosophy appears to be based on repression and dissociation; that is, some parts of the person may be unknown.[49]

Pharmacologically Assisted Interviews

A person who is uncertain as to whether abuse occurred as a child may be prompted to retrieve blocked material through the use of drug-assisted interviews. One of the major medications used is sodium amytal. Although sodium amytal was used in the past in military combat trauma situations, currently it is more often used in assisting people to retrieve memories of childhood abuse.[50]

The patient may harbor suspicions that abuse has occurred but has no direct memory or just a hazy memory for the events. After being given an intravenous injection of sodium amytal, which is a barbiturate, the patient becomes somewhat drowsy. The therapist guides the patient in a nondirective fashion to earlier critical scenes similarly to hypnotic age regression. It is surmised that, at this point, the ego defense guards are penetrated and veritable truth will emerge from the now opening unconscious.

CASE STUDIES

The first case report concerns a woman who recovered memories of satanic ritual while undergoing hypnosis. In the first example, the client continued to believe in the validity of her recovered memories. In the next example, the patient first learned of childhood sexual abuse while in therapy but later retracted the belief in the truthfulness or accuracy of the recovered memories.

"A True Story of Satanic Abuse . . ."

As the title implies, this is a case report of an adult woman who first discovered by means of hypnotically enhanced retrieval that she had been ritualistically abused. The patient, Barbara, presented with problems related to sexual functioning. "I'm afraid my husband will leave because I have so many problems."[51]

In order to determine what might be at the root of her sexual problems, the patient consented to undergo hypnosis. She was able to easily regress under hypnosis to earlier childhood scenes. During the first hypnotic session, Barbara viewed her grandfather cutting up and killing a cat.[52] After hearing about the ritualistic killing of a cat, Feldman "had a hunch" that the images in her dreams were not just symbols but were flashbacks of real memories. She then proceeded to inform Barbara of her opinion.[53]

The therapist reported that, from the beginning of the sessions, everything the patient stated was the truth. The basic reason was that the patient had no motive to make up or fabricate the incredible details.[54]

Over the course of the hypnosis sessions, a wide array of indescribable torture and abuse emerged. When Barbara was a child, she was subjected to multiple incidents of sexual and physical abuse. At six years of age, she reported under hypnosis that, in a doctor's office, an adult female performed oral sex to get rid of "all the bad stuff" and to "purify" her. The next episode that emerged was when Barbara was forced to cut off the penis of a young boy.[55]

Under hypnosis, she recalled giving birth to a baby at the age of 11. Barbara wondered how she was physiologically capable of giving birth at such a young age.[56] Apparently, this patient recalled menstruating at an early age. In a ritual, her grandfather cut her stomach open, and then a doctor completed the delivery.[57] Based on the cult's belief system, the baby was to be sacrificed. At first, snakes were allowed to roam on the newborn, then her grandfather impaled the newborn heart on the end of a knife and extricated it from the body. The heart was then eaten, and the body cut for later ceremonies.

Barbara has a scar across her lower abdomen, but she believes it is too tiny to be from a cesarean section.[58] In order to try to confirm the events that were retrieved under hypnosis, Barbara underwent a physical exam. The doctor confirmed that the scars in her abdomen were not from a cesarean section. There were burn marks on her arm that Barbara related to the hot pokers inflicted on her. Also a W or M was carved between her thumb and forefinger. The M might be her clan name, and the W might stand for witch. The pelvic exam indicated vaginal scarring. Based on this exam, the therapist concluded that "there was now some possible medical evidence" regarding the horrendous tortures inflicted on Barbara.[59]

When an impasse developed, Feldman's "mind was racing trying to think of what to do."[60] She had read several books on Past-Lives Therapy and said to Barbara, "I am willing to try if you're willing to be my first case."[61] Thus, Barbara's final sessions included Past-Lives Therapy (see Chapter 8) as an additional tool to unearth hidden trauma. At the conclusion of her therapy, Barbara's sexual problems had diminished or disappeared. One year later, Barbara was able to report the positive effects of therapy: She knew who she was, accepted herself and could express her feelings.[62]

A True Story of a Recanted Recovered Memory

Recent books, as well as countless lawsuits, relate to a patient first learning of childhood sexual abuse in therapy, only later to believe that the disengorged memory was not true.[63] The following case report contains the story told by a patient named Lynn.

In the mid-1980s Lynn had a long-standing eating disorder. Because of a distant relationship with her parents, her therapist told Lynn this meant her parents didn't love her or even neglected her. Lynn was able to disclose early that she had apparently always remembered being abused by her uncle. This was not a secret, and thus her family was aware of the molestation.

In Lynn's psychosocial history, there was a known history of abuse. According to Lynn, however, her two current therapists thought Lynn was not showing enough affect in relation to the abuse by the uncle.[64] Lynn was told that "since you feel uncomfortable hugging your father, he must have sexually abused you." In Lynn's view, her family was "sexually conservative," and she does not view this therapist's observation as having clinical credence.

Lynn reports that she didn't like her mother washing her hair in the bathtub. The therapist took this to mean that more than just hair washing went on. Also, the fact that Lynn moved frequently was taken as a sign of abuse in that abusers often move in order to avoid being caught.

After hearing the interpretation, Lynn began to believe in the possible validity of parental abuse and to visualize the events.[65] After admission to an in-patient psychiatric unit, she was given seven diagnoses, including dissociative identity disorder. As Lynn described it, there was an "ambush" of her father during a family interview while in the hospital. A guilt trip was laid on him for the actual or possible abuse. She didn't see him again for more than two years.[66]

In group therapy, there appeared to be a contagion effect. First, the participants were given books such as *The Courage to Heal* to read. Second, if one patient reported a flashback of a recovered memory regarding snakes or cannibalism, "a few days later . . . someone else has a similar flashback."[67] In occupational therapy, when Lynn preferred the color red, it was given a ritual abuse connotation; that is, she was drawing the blood that her father made her drink after he cut her with a knife.

With regard to body memories, while Lynn was hospitalized she experienced numbness in her hands. Her therapists told her that this was due to holding her father's penis. Lynn, however, attributed the numbness to taking 900 milligrams of lithium and a large dose of Xanax and Mellaril. Lynn does not now believe that she wanted to cut off her hands because she touched her father's penis.[68]

According to Lynn, during the course of her therapy she began to tell her therapists what they wanted to hear. Having no one else to turn to, she craved their attention. Lynn began to buy into the therapists' belief system and, despite her doubts, thought that the abuse might have actually happened. Lynn was one of five Dallas women in the same group that originally reclaimed memories of sexual abuse. Time away from the therapy group was the main reason Lynn was able to understand that the recovered memories of abuse were not veridical. She indicates that the "group pressure to trust the memories and to believe was just too strong to resist."[69]

RESEARCH

Can Traumas Be Forgotten and Recalled at a Later Time?

At least seven studies between 1987 to 1995 have dealt with the adult memories of victims of childhood sexual abuse. The studies involved adults who retrieved memories of repressed traumatic memories. Based on a total of 1,039 individuals interviewed or seen in therapy, as reported in these published articles, between 16 and 64 percent were found to have delayed memories (traumatic forgetting) of having been sexually abused or traumatized in other ways."[70]

Herman and Schatzow[71] believe that confirmation of the memories is important because "in the absence of confirming evidence, such studies . . . might conceivably be dismissed as seriously distorted at best, and at worst as the ever more elaborate documentation of woman's fantasies by naive investigators."[72] A total of 53 women in weekly group therapy were observed for three months. The patients in an incest survivor group included a woman who had questions about the validity of childhood sexual abuse. Some of these patients had undergone hypnosis or been given sodium amytal to assist in determining the validity of the memories.

According to Herman and Schatzow, 15 of the 53 women (or 28 percent) had delayed memories of the abuse. It appears that the women with no prior recall of abuse had recent recall either in individual or group therapy. Thus, the person who recovered memories did so while in therapy. It is not clear, however, why some patients were in an incest survivor group if those patients were not aware of the abuse. Confirmation or corroboration of the retrieved memories was reportedly found in 74 percent of this sample. The corroboration was obtained from the perpetrators, other family members, physical evidence from diaries or photographs or discovering that another sibling had been abused.

Several critical methodological problems are apparent in the Herman and Schatzow report.[73] First, experimenter bias may exist in that the clinicians who are treating the patients apparently are affiliated with the persons conducting the research. The experimenter effect[74] is well known in the annals of social psychology. Experimenter bias can affect the results of an investigation through the unwanted influence of the experimenter.[75] Expectancies and bias are exacerbated when the investigator has a vested interest in the outcome of the study and is completely responsible for running the subjects in all aspects of the study.[76] Cues and demand characteristics can be unintentionally conveyed to the participants as demonstrated in the Orne and Scheibe study.[77]

The Herman and Schatzow report was not even a "single-blind" study in that both the patients and the experimenters, who may have had a vested interest in the outcome, knew the purpose of the study and the identity of the participants. This severely undercuts any claim for unbiased reporting both on the part of the participant and the clinician-experimenter.

Second, most of the participants had some memory of abuse prior to entering therapy. Twenty of the patients always remembered the abuse and had no new memories in the course of therapy. A total of 19 patients recovered some additional memories in treatment. Therefore, the claim that most of the patients retrieved memories is inconsistent with the reported figures. Thus, over 70 percent of this sample always had some memory of their abuse.

Third, participation in suggestive group techniques could have biased the participants to over-report retrieved memories of childhood abuse. This was a highly select sample that was vigorously questioning whether there had been prior forgotten abuse. Use of hypnosis or sodium amytal to retrieve repressed memories may lead some individuals to state that they were abused because of the group pressure and demand characteristics of the therapy situation. No data are presented regarding which subjects received these or other memory retrieval techniques.

Finally, the data on the so-called corroboration seems flimsy. As Pendergrast has noted, there were only second-hand accounts and no verifications.[78] Thus, there is only "the word of the accusers, eagerly and uncritically accepted by their therapists." Because of the methodological flaws, this oft-cited study adds virtually nothing to the debate regarding the accuracy or possibility of retrieving repressed memories.

Williams conducted a newer study that attempted first to authenticate sexual abuse via hospital records.[79] This study, which was funded by the National Center on Child Abuse and Neglect, overcomes at least one of the major obstacles—namely, corroborating whether sexual abuse occurred in the first place. It appears, however, that the interviewers were aware of the purpose of the study and thus knew that the subjects had medical records indicating sexual abuse. The 129 subjects were victims of sexual assault who had been treated in a hospital as children. Williams was also a researcher in a prior study and apparently retrieved the names of the former patients and was able to locate the subjects for this study.[80] The former patients were told that the current research involved "a follow-up study on the lives and health of women who during childhood received medical care at a city hospital."[81]

During the extensive interviews, the women were questioned about whether they had been sexually abused as children. Of the 129 women in the study, 38 percent failed to report the abuse that was previously documented by the hospital report. According to Williams, her study offers support for the notion of repression of childhood sexual abuse.

Since this study has significant implications for the treatment of the emotionally disturbed, it is important to critically analyze these findings. The Williams study would be the first significant evidence suggesting that repression of childhood sexual trauma occurs and that there may be an accurate resurfacing of the memories many years later.[82] This study has been presented in the premier journal that documents innovative psychological techniques and almost immediately has been widely cited as demonstrating that 38 percent of women do not recall being abused as children.[83]

The main problem with her data analysis is that about 12 percent actually forgot any incident of abuse. A decision was made to interpret recall of the abuse in a strict manner. If the patient did not recall the episode in the hospital, but rather described another event, this was classified as a miss. To be classified as a hit, the patient had to state the precise episode that was in her medical records. To construe the data in this manner is misleading. If the question is: Do patients recall being sexually abused after a period of 17 years, then at least 88 percent were able to do so. If subjects below the age of two are excluded from the analysis, the figures for some recall are slightly higher.

There are several possibilities for the 12 percent of the sample who did not disclose or recall any sexual abuse. One possibility involves the issue of nondisclosure to a stranger, particularly one of a different race.[84] Perhaps some blacks were reluctant to tell the white interviewer about the abuse, even though they had always recalled the episode.

With regard to retrieval of repressed memories, Williams reports another set of data suggesting that 16 percent of the sample (12 women out of 80) forgot the abuse but had subsequent recall.[85] These subjects were able to describe their sexual abuse episode to the interviewers at the Philadelphia General Hospital in the 1990s. The data were elicited by asking the subject-patients whether there ever was a time when they did not recall being abused, and the age when they first forgot the abuse and then remembered.

An alternative explanation is that most, if not all, of the subjects had recall of some abuse. In a few instances, however, subjects were reluctant and embarrassed to tell a stranger about a sensitive event. The conclusion that accurate memories are retrievable from the unconscious rests on flawed questioning and to some extent on flawed data analysis. The questions asked to probe whether the subjects forgot their abuse did not necessarily address whether the entire episode had been forgotten. There may have been a time when a person was not thinking about the abuse but actually would not deny that it happened if asked at that time. From this line of questioning alone, it would seem at the very least that it is difficult to reconstruct ten or so years later when and if someone blocked out and then had a memory resurface. Second, apparently at least six subjects were never questioned in this key area according to the tables in the article. At one point, at least 15 cases were missing.[86] The absence of such a significant amount of data is a bit disconcerting. The Williams study, therefore, is of little help in determining whether perceived traumatic events in childhood are forgotten.[87]

As Ofshe and Watters have pointed out,[88] the Williams study does not address the validity of so-called recovered memories. The most significant finding is that almost 90 percent of the sample actually admitted to a stranger that they had experienced childhood sexual abuse. There may be several other reasons for nondisclosure: simple or ordinary forgetting in part due to the young age of several of the patients, particularly if the event was not especially noteworthy to the patient at the time. In addition, there is the remote possibility that some of the initial hospital reports were not accurate. In summary, that a few persons did not recall memories of sexual abuse is hardly remarkable, and it sheds little light on the repression and later excavation of veridical memories of childhood sexual abuse.

ACCURACY OF RECOVERED MEMORIES

Assuming for the moment that some traumatic memories are repressed and forgotten, and further assuming that delayed recall occurs, is there research that points to the veridicality of the archivally retrieved memories? Several studies conducted by Loftus and Ceci assess the possibility of inducing false or fallacious memories in children.[89]

A total of 96 preschoolers aged 3 to 6 completed seven interviews with the investigators. The children were presented with actual events from their lives as well as with false experimenter-contrived events. The children were asked to state whether the events really happened. The results indicated that the true events were almost always accurately recalled. However, slightly over one-third of the children agreed that the made-up events actually happened. According to Ceci et al., the results suggest that children can be misled into believing non-events actually happened.[90] The reports of the children who believed in the non-events were credible and could not be detected as fabricated when viewed by mental health professionals.[91]

A series of studies by Loftus deals with suggestibility for observed events and for autobiographical memory.[92] The most relevant investigation involved what Loftus refers to as experimentally planted memories of childhood trauma. In one case, Chris, who was now 14, was convinced by his older brother that he had been lost in a shopping mall at the age of 5.[93] After learning from his brother about the episode, Chris was able to incorporate the events into his belief system.

In a controversial investigation, Ofshe attempted to induce a false memory in an adult by the name of Paul Ingram.[94] Mr. Ingram, who held a civilian position with the Sheriff's Office, became a Christian fundamentalist who experienced routine moments of religious ecstasy. When his daughter accused him of sexual abuse, he denied the crimes at the time of this first interrogation. Police officers, however, indicated that it is possible to repress the memory of such events.

As Ofshe reports, the police engaged in hypnosis-like interviews and preyed upon his religious fervor. Finally, Ingram not only came to believe that he had committed incest but he had a clear visualization of what had taken place.

When Ofshe was called in to assess the validity of Ingram's confession,[95] he attempted to do so by intentionally misleading Ingram into believing he had witnessed and encouraged his children to have sex with each other. This, in fact, did not happen according to the children. Ingram was asked to close his eyes, sit silently and attempt to recall the proffered scene. With this mild prompting from Ofshe, Ingram had a clear visualization of the purported sexual encounter. Even when debriefed, Ingram clung to his new-found belief that he had witnessed sexual activity among his children.

The Loftus and Ceci studies cannot necessarily be generalized to persons who were abused and later recall the abuse. Taken as a whole, however, these experimental investigations suggest that it is nearly impossible to detect whether a later recalled memory is true or false. The Ingram case doesn't necessarily prove that false memories can be implanted, but it seems to show that persons who are agitated and vulnerable, much as is a patient in psychotherapy, might wish to accede to the belief system of an authority figure. In this regard, a study conducted by Spanos is instructive.[96] Both hypnotic and nonhypnotic subjects were regressed to the day of their birth. The subjects were misinformed that under hypnotic and nonhypnotic regression adults can "successfully and accurately remember events as far back as birth."[97] Both groups reported many memories, including seeing bars on their cribs, as well as the doctors and nurses. Almost half of the subjects described the memories as real rather than as fantasies.[98] The most logical explanation for this finding is that the subjects were producing false memories based on what the experimenter told them.

MEMORY RETRIEVAL ENHANCEMENT TECHNIQUES

Can hypnosis or sodium amytal lead to enhanced recall of forgotten memories? An additional question that needs to be asked is whether the previously blocked memories that are allegedly retrieved are actually veridical. This section examines whether techniques such as hypnosis or sodium amytal can reliably delve into a person's memory bank and extract historically accurate memories.

In a difficult investigation, police called upon a psychologist to use hypnosis to help uncover potential evidence and clear up inconsistencies in statements of a witness named "DD." DD apparently saw the victim as she drove by near his car. The woman was abducted and was never seen again.[99] By using hypnosis, it was hoped that new leads might develop by "returning" the subject, DD, to the crime scene, which allowed him to retrieve presumably forgotten material.

Prior to hypnosis, DD's statement to the police was three pages long; after hypnosis, it was eleven pages long. The new statement strongly suggests that DD began a whole new story and evidenced a desire to please. Furthermore, "there were florid signs of elaboration of events, substitution of events."[100] The authors concluded that DD's new accounting was a mixture or contamination of both memory and fantasy, which was even evident before the hypnosis was started. It appears that hypnosis reinforced his belief in the events and increased his confidence in the new beliefs.

Based on such investigations, the overwhelming conclusion is that hypnosis does not necessarily produce or lead to enhanced memory or to veridical memories; rather, it enhances suggestibility and prompts pseudomemories.[101] There is no evidence to support the notion that memories emerging under hypnosis are more accurate than those in the waking state.[102] Thus, taking a person under hypnosis to a particular place or time does not necessarily enable a patient to produce accurate historical details. There appears to be a blend of some true details intermixed with confabulation in an attempt to give the hypnotherapist material that accords with the demand characteristics of the situation. That is, patients tell the therapist what they believe the therapist would like to hear.

Another line of research examined whether the diagnostic symptoms of DID could be induced in the experimental laboratory, so to speak. Spanos et al. predicate their studies on two points: most patients do not generally receive a diagnosis of DID before they enter therapy or display the symptoms beforehand.[103] Second, the diagnosis of DID usually involves hypnosis or similar suggestive procedures. Thus, patients are directly asked for the "alter" to come out and communicate with the therapist.

In one study, subjects were hypnotized and asked whether instructions for amnesia could be overcome.[104] The subjects were asked to use a hidden self in order to retain what was supposed to be forgotten. The subjects were able to do so. Spanos concluded that the findings are "consistent with the hypothesis that the identity enactments and recall performance of DID alters ... can be understood in terms of contextually generated role enactments."[105] When role-playing DID, subjects could relate a made-up negative childhood and offer descriptions of alters.[106]

Spanos further opines that DID memories of satanic ritual abuse are most likely therapy-induced fantasies. The development of "alters" is shaped to conform with the expectations of the treating therapist, but the alters can also come from TV, movies and other cultural sources.[107]

Since hypnosis involves the psychological interaction between two persons, use of a drug might be expected to be a more effective and direct way to access the unconscious. Over the years, sodium amytal has been used in an attempt to unclog the buried arteries of the patient's past. It was presumed that what emerges will be truth. For that reason, sodium amytal has been called a truth serum. In the famous Ramona case, the patient was given sodium amytal in order to confirm what seemed to be emerging in therapy, namely, that her father had molested her. The sodium amytal interview elicited apparent confirmation of the molestation. With this data in hand, her father was confronted with the details of the accusation.[108]

Clinical and experimental research on the use of sodium amytal directly contradicts the notion of a "truth serum."[109] If anything, when subjects respond after being administered sodium amytal, there is no way to discern truth from fabrication. When subjects are asked to lie or make up symptoms, they can do so under sodium amytal. Sodium amytal is an extremely unreliable method for retrieving memories in that there is no way to determine the truth or falsity without corroboration. Moreover, the demand characteristics of the setting may exert pressure to conform to the wishes and expectations of the therapist. Thus, why would a therapist have a patient undergo an unusual procedure involving IV administration of drugs unless there was something to it? The therapist's cues in these instances are similar to those in the Orne and Scheibe[110] hallucination-generating sensory deprivation study discussed in Chapter 1. If the patient has begun to believe she was molested, the therapist administers the sodium amytal with the notion that it will assist in unblocking the unconscious in order to offer confirmation for what the patient already suspects. The patients are not told, "This is an experimental procedure that has not been validated. There is no basis for determining whether what you say is true or false."

On the contrary, the patient undergoing many recovery therapy techniques is assured that what emerges will be a bona fide memory. Thus, when the subject gets drowsy and begins to talk, the patient may be telling the therapist (experimenter) what the patient thinks will please the therapist and satisfy the therapist-experimenter's expectation. As Piper concluded, sodium amytal interviews that are "intended to uncover memories of childhood sexual abuse are worse than useless, because they may encourage patient's beliefs in mythical events."[111]

Perhaps, then, it might be argued that at least journal-writing is a fairly good technique since the therapist may not be present when the writing is done. Furthermore, how could the written word be affected by outside sources? Unfortunately, there is a rather dramatic example in facilitated communication that demonstrates how a therapist could unwittingly determine what a person writes. Facilitated communication is used with nonverbal people who usually have a diagnosis of autism. The facilitator attempts to train the subject to type out his or her thoughts by way of typewriter, thereby obviating the deficient verbal skills. The facilitator guides the subject's hands but presumably does not direct the subject to a particular key. There are examples of autistic children miraculously typing out meaningful language. At times the statements refer to sexual abuse.[112]

In order to determine the validity of this procedure, experiments have been conducted to see if the subject can type without the facilitator knowing the target word. The results have indicated that there is an abysmal failure when the facilitator is "blind" as to the target word. For example, when the facilitator can see a word, then the subject can type correctly, but when the facilitator cannot see the word, the subject generally cannot type in the correct target word. Rather, in most instances, when the subject is shown one word and the facilitator is shown another word, it is the facilitator's word that is identified and typed by the autistic person.[113] Clearly, then, the communication was likely influenced and directed by the facilitator. Equally fascinating, the facilitators were not aware that they were influencing the subjects. Wheeler et al.[114] conclude that such communications cannot be accepted as valid and authentic.

In the case of Jane and other journal writers, a hidden hand may be influencing what is written. Topics and statements that emerge in this type of uncensored writing may be subtly or not so subtly reinforced when the therapist offers feedback. Furthermore, the interaction of the various techniques is bound to be synergistic with respect to influencing the patient in a certain direction.[115] Self-authenticating by means of journal-writing is fraught with peril in terms of documenting or confirming events of the past.

CRITIQUE AND ANALYSIS

Building on Freud's Flawed Edifice

To rest on Freud's theory of the etiological significance of repressed memories is akin to walking in quicksand. As demonstrated in Chapter 2, there is virtually no empirical support for the major tenets of Freud's theory.[116] To follow or build on this flawed theory only multiplies the erroneous assumptions of psychoanalysis. This is precisely what the recovered memory therapists and theorists have done.

Lynn's case of the numb hand being associated to touching her father's penis is the equivalent of Freud knowing that Dora felt Herr H's erect member (see Chapter 2). These assertions have a psychic and speculative quality. The therapists in Lynn's case could no more know she felt her father's penis than Freud knew Dora was subjected to an erect penis. Thus, Herman's statement may serve as a basis for an apt epitaph for Recovered Memory Therapy: Therapy clients who retrieve memories of childhood sexual abuse in many instances may be distorting what is recalled, and therapists may be inducing or reinforcing the distortions.[117]

Now that more than ten years have gone by since the beginning of Recovered Memory Therapy, the question is where are the individuals who attest to the improvement in their clinical conditions or their lives? Recovered Memory Therapy may be another in a long line of placebo engendering procedures somewhat akin to *est*, Neurolinguistic Programming or Primal Therapy. These therapies and techniques have not stood the test of time (Chapters 3 and 7). There was great initial enthusiasm, but as time passed, it appears the so-called effective results have diminished or disappeared. The initial excitement of finding the cause of psychopathology by extracting forgotten memories needs to be viewed with caution. The memories may or may not be true. The therapists may or may not have found the source of psychopathology. As the next decade may prove, much of the work of these therapists borders on the search for fictional causes.

THE DIAGNOSIS AND TREATMENT OF DID

Amazingly, the DSM-IV fails to delineate the most critical ingredient of a so-called dissociation. That is, what is the exact definition of "dissociation"? In actual clinical practice, typically there are no reports of persons who purportedly have DID who present at work dressing and talking differently and/or have several childhood years unaccounted for. But even if there are gaps in one's memory, what type or duration of memory deficit constitutes a sign of dissociation?

At work here may be role-play or enactment.[118] The patients have a conscious recall of all the so-called alters and often do not display these alters outside of the office or hospital setting. In the writer's experience, with clients who still believed they suffered from DID during lengthy and stressful litigation, there has been no switching or discernible difference in the patient/plaintiff's personality. Simply asking alters to emerge and dealing with the alters is not the same thing as blocking out portions of time, assuming a new identity and not having recall of the other parts of one's conscious existence.

In many of these instances, when the patient is asked to display what's inside, the alters will emerge. Based on the notion of positive reinforcement, if the therapist is giving more attention and praise to the client, it tends to reinforce these prompted behaviors. To base a diagnosis on simply asking alters to come out is not much different from asking a patient to pretend to be depressed and then giving a diagnosis of depression. The diagnostic criteria remain vague[119] and subject to the discretion of the clinician. Simply calling out and identifying alters and presuming memory gaps does not establish the diagnosis of DID.

The diagnosis may have more to do with social psychology than a clinical or mental disorder. It says more about the influence of the authoritarian therapist who is able to control and manipulate a patient into believing that the subpersonalities are real. After a patient recants or retracts the notion that he or she was abused, he or she also tends to find the notion of being DID illusory. In the case of Lynn, there appears to be a fictional history of sexual abuse and a fictional diagnosis of DID.

VALIDITY OF THE SYMPTOM CHECKLISTS

No evidence has been presented to date that causally relates childhood sexual abuse to adult symptoms. One of the major fictions in this arena is that the checklists offered by Fredrickson or Bass and Davis have validity. The symptoms can mean something or not mean something. It's like Freud's word play, in which a word can mean one thing or the opposite, but especially whatever fits the theory in an after-the-fact rationalization.

Thus, fear of pickles, avoidance of mayonnaise, eating too much food or too little, wearing long hair or short hair, fear of the dark, poor relationships and so on have not been reliably used alone to determine whether an adult was previously sexually abused. Use of any checklist to assess for SRA appears to be the mere figment of the therapists' imagination. There are no published studies showing that aversion to the color red, for example, indicates cult involvement.

SRA—THE ACHILLES HEEL OF RECOVERED MEMORY THERAPY

When certain therapies are examined critically, severe deficits are found in the underlying theory or assumptions. For example, NLP has little or nothing to do with eye gaze (see Chapter 7). Primal Therapy offers no proof of a prenatal memory or effect on later behavior. In Recovered Memory Therapy, the assertion that persons have killed, mutilated and eaten their own or other children has not been subjected to empirical verification. No empirical demonstration has been made that adults can be programmed by clicks or tones. Cult ties to the CIA or aliens have not been demonstrated. Dissociative identity disorder has not been shown to be a reliable diagnosis, nor is there any verification that there is a cause/effect relationship between repressed childhood trauma, especially childhood sexual trauma, and DID.

Thus, as Ofshe notes,[120] most reasonable people would question the validity of the claims made regarding satanic ritual abuse. To accept or not accept these claims puts recovered memory therapists on the horns of a dilemma. To declare satanic ritual abuse nonsense puts at risk the other claims of recovered memory therapists. To believe the notions related to satanic ritual abuse, the therapist must accept bizarre and conspiratorial ideas, including cult-created alters.

THE COPY-CAT THERAPIST

As indicated in the case of Barbara, it appears that a new technique is easily and quickly assimilated into the therapists' repertoire. Hearing about *Michelle Remembers* may have had a profound influence on Feldman, as noted by the similarities of the two cases.[121] Almost as an afterthought, Feldman seamlessly incorporates Past-Lives Therapy into her Recovered Memory Therapy. There is no indication that Feldman properly investigated the Recovered Memory Therapy and past-lives tools, let alone offered the patient a reasonable informed consent regarding the controversial nature of these techniques. Patients should at the very least be apprised of the controversy in the field.[122]

It appears that if a few prominent therapists contend that there is a special technique to treat DID, then hundreds, if not thousands of therapists simply copy the untested and at times absurd notions. For example, no research has been published demonstrating that persons can be programmed in childhood to respond as adults via operant or classical conditioning and modeling paradigms to whistles, touches or sounds on the phone line as suggested by Neswald.[123] Yet in this arena of Recovered Memory Therapy and treatment of DID, therapists will simply imitate what sounds exciting or innovative without assessing the scientific value of the procedure. At times there appears to be little awareness or concern with the professional literature.[124] At a conference sponsored by a group dealing with ritual and cult abuse, there was an aversion to and a quick dismissal of major studies, including Ceci. Although analogue studies may have problems with generalizability, it is troubling that an entire panel had never heard of his well-known research.[125]

In part due to the copycat behavior, some therapists uncritically follow the new gurus who have evolved from Freud. Little or no attempt is made to conduct a scientific analysis of the techniques used. With respect to cult programming, to this writer's knowledge, there has never been a documented instance of adult mind control programming that can produce Manchurian Candidate–like behavior. More probably, some therapists are exerting extreme influence on the vulnerable patients which induces these bizarre beliefs and behaviors. As Spanos shows, it is at least possible to convince a random group of subjects to display the signs and symptoms of DID.[126] This does not prove that any cases of alleged DID are role-playing, but it does suggest that the therapist's demand characteristics and influence may be unwittingly shaping some clients to conform to the therapists' symptomatic and behavioral parameters.[127]

It is more probable that the therapist shapes the patient's beliefs when affirmative recovery techniques such as hypnosis or visual imagery are employed. The Recovered Memory Therapy approach is somewhat reminiscent of psychoanalysis in general. When a new procedure is advocated, it may gain general acceptance without much concern for clinical efficacy. To date, no experimental or scientific proof has been offered that Recovered Memory Therapy has produced any significant improvement in the mental health of the treated patients that is more effective than a placebo or any alternative type of therapy. From Freud's original seduction theory to present-day Recovered Memory Therapy, no demonstrable evidence shows that the underlying treatment is responsible for any clinical improvement. Therefore, in many instances, a fictional history is treated with a fictional psychotherapy. How can a person abreact to an event that never happened? As with psychoanalysis, the latter-day legacy of Recovered Memory Therapy leads to erroneous trails on the way to uncovering the cause of emotional functioning.

NOTES

1. Bass, E. & Davis, L. (1988). *The courage to heal: A guide for women survivors of child sexual abuse.* New York: Harper & Row.

2. Spanos, N. P. (1996). *Multiple identities and false memories: A socio-cognitive perspective* (p. 234). Washington, D.C.: American Psychological Association.

3. Masson, J. M. (1984). *The assault on truth: Freud's suppression of the seduction theory.* New York: HarperPerennial.

4. Masson, *The assault on truth* (p. 190).

5. Herman, J. L. (1992). *Trauma and recovery.* New York: Basic Books.

6. Herman, *Trauma and recovery* (p. 13).

7. Bass & Davis, *The courage to heal* (p. 22).

8. Bradshaw, J. (1988). *Healing the shame that binds you.* Deerfield Beach, Fla.: Health Communications.

9. Goldstein, E. & Farmer, K. (1993). *True stories of false memories* (p. 194). Boca Raton, Fla.: SIRS.

10. Pendergrast, Mark. (1995). *Victims of memory: Incest accusations and shattered lives* (p. 473). Hinesburg, Vt.: Upper Access, Inc.

11. Bradshaw, *Healing the shame that binds you.*

12. Fredrickson, R. (1992). *Repressed memories: A journey to recovery from sexual abuse.* New York: Fireside/Parkside.

13. Putnam, F. W. (1989). *Diagnosis and treatment of multiple personality disorder.* London: Guilford Press; Ross, C. A. (1989). *Multiple personality disorder: Diagnosis, clinical features and treatment.* New York: Wiley.

14. Neswald, D. W. & Gould, C. (1992). Basic treatment and program neutralization strategies for adult MPD survivors of satanic ritual abuse. *Treating Abuse Today, 2* (pp. 5–10).

15. Neswald & Gould, Basic treatment for adult MPD survivors (pp. 5–10).

16. Whitfield, C. L. (1995). *Memory and abuse: Remembering and healing the effects of trauma.* Deerfield Beach, Fla.: Health Communications.

17. Whitfield, *Memory and abuse* (p. 11).

18. Terr, Lenore (1994). *Unchained memories: True stories of traumatic memories lost and found.* New York: Basic Books.

19. Feldman, G. C. (1993). *Lessons in evil, lessons from the light—A true story of satanic abuse and spiritual healing.* New York: Crown Publishers.

20. Goldstein & Farmer, *True stories of false memories*.

21. Pendergrast, *Victims of memory*.

22. Loftus, E. & Ketcham, K. (1994). *The myth of repressed memories: False memories and allegations of sexual abuse*. New York: St. Martin's Press.

23. Yapko, N. D. (1994). *Suggestions of abuse: True and false memories of childhood sexual trauma*. New York: Simon & Schuster.

24. Ofshe, R. & Watters, E. (1994). *Making monsters: False memories, psychotherapy and sexual hysteria*. New York: Charles Scribner's Sons.

25. Crews, F. (1995). *The memory wars: Freud's legacy in dispute* (p. 298). New York: New York Review.

26. Webster, R. (1995). *Why Freud was wrong: Sin, science and psychoanalysis*. New York: Basic Books.

27. Pope, K. S. & Brown, L. S. (1996). *Recovered memories of abuse: Assessment, therapy, forensics*. Washington, D.C.: American Psychological Association.

28. Pope & Brown, *Recovered memories of abuse* (p. 20).

29. Whitfield, *Memory and abuse* (p. 151).

30. Bass & Davis, *The courage to heal* (pp. 35–39).

31. Fredrickson, *Repressed memories* (p. 47).

32. Whitfield, *Memory and abuse* (p. 199); *Los Angeles Times* (May 14, 1994). Father Wins Suit in "False Memory" Case (pp. A8, A27).

33. *Diagnostic and Statistical Manual of Mental Disorders* (4th ed., 1996) (p. 486). Washington, D.C.: American Psychiatric Association.

34. Gould, C. (1995). Denying ritual abuse of children. *Journal of Psychohistory, 22* (pp. 329–339).

35. Gould, C. (1992). Diagnosis and treatment of ritually abused children. In Sackheim, D. K. & Devine, S. E. (Eds.), *Out of darkness: Exploring satanism and ritual abuse* (pp. 207–248). New York: Lexington Books.

36. Gould, Diagnosis and treatment of ritually abused children (pp. 207–248).

37. Gould, Denying ritual abuse (pp. 329–339).

38. Gould, C. & Cozolino, L. (1992). Ritual abuse, multiplicity, and mind-control. *Journal of Psychology and Theology, 20* (pp. 195–196).

39. Gould & Cozolino. Ritual abuse (pp. 195–196).

40. Fredrickson, *Repressed memories* (p. 150).

41. Fredrickson, *Repressed memories* (p. 45).

42. Fredrickson, *Repressed memories* (p. 45).

43. Fredrickson, *Repressed memories* (p. 126).

44. Fredrickson, *Repressed memories* (p. 127).

45. Fredrickson, *Repressed memories* (p. 146).

46. Pendergrast, *Victims of memory* (p. 223).

47. Fredrickson, *Repressed memories* (p. 141).

48. Fredrickson, *Repressed memories* (p. 150).

49. Bradshaw, *Healing the shame that binds you*.

50. Whitfield, *Memory and abuse* (p. 314).

51. Feldman, *Lessons in evil* (p. 8).

52. Feldman, *Lessons in evil* (p. 43).

53. Feldman, *Lessons in evil* (p. 46).

54. Feldman, *Lessons in evil* (p. 48).

55. Feldman, *Lessons in evil* (p. 96).

56. Feldman, *Lessons in evil* (p. 173).
57. Feldman, *Lessons in evil* (p. 186).
58. Feldman, *Lessons in evil* (p. 189).
59. Feldman, *Lessons in evil* (p. 197).
60. Feldman, *Lessons in evil* (p. 243).
61. Feldman, *Lessons in evil* (p. 243).
62. Feldman, *Lessons in evil* (p. 282).
63. Goldstein & Farmer, *True stories of false memories* (p. 368).
64. Goldstein & Farmer, *True stories of false memories* (p. 368).
65. Goldstein & Farmer, *True stories of false memories* (p. 369).
66. Goldstein & Farmer, *True stories of false memories* (p. 373).
67. Goldstein & Farmer, *True stories of false memories* (p. 375).
68. Goldstein & Farmer, *True stories of false memories* (p. 377).
69. Goldstein & Farmer, *True stories of false memories* (p. 384).
70. Whitfield, *Memory and abuse* (p. 70).
71. Herman, J. L. & Schatzow, E. (1987). Recovery and verification of memories of childhood sexual trauma. *Psychoanalytic Psychology, 4* (pp. 1–14).
72. Herman & Schatzow, Recovery and verification (pp. 1–14).
73. Herman & Schatzow, Recovery and verification (pp. 1–14).
74. Rosenthal, R. (1966). *Experimenter effects in behavioral research*. New York: Appleton-Century-Crofts.
75. Kazdin, A. E. (1980). *Research design in clinical psychology* (p. 294). New York: Harper & Row.
76. Kazdin, *Research design in clinical psychology* (p. 295).
77. Orne, M. T. & Scheibe, K. E. (1964). The contribution of nondeprivation factors in the production of sensory deprivation effects: The psychology of the "panic button." *Journal of Abnormal and Social Psychology, 68* (pp. 3–12).
78. Pendergrast, *Victims of memory* (p. 96).
79. Williams, L. M. (1994). Recall of childhood trauma: A prospective study of women's memories of child sexual abuse. *Journal of Consulting & Clinical Psychology, 62* (pp. 1167–1176).
80. McCahill, T., Meyer, L. C. & Fischman, A. (1979). *The aftermath of rape*. Lexington, Mass.: Lexington Books.
81. Williams, L. M. (1994). Recall of childhood trauma. *Journal of Consulting & Clinical Psychology, 62* (pp. 1167–1176).
82. Williams, L. M., Recall of childhood trauma, (pp. 1167–1176); Williams, L. M. (1995). Recovered memories of abuse. *Journal of Traumatic Stress, 8* (pp. 649–671).
83. Loftus, E. F., Gerry, M. & Feldman, J. (1994). Forgetting sexual trauma: What does it mean when 38% forget? *Journal of Consulting Clinical Psychology, 62* (pp. 1177–1181).
84. Pendergrast, *Victims of memory* (p. 98).
85. Williams, Recovered memories of abuse.
86. Williams, Recovered memories of abuse.
87. Williams, Recovered memories of abuse.
88. Ofshe & Watters, *Making monsters*.
89. Ceci, S. J., Huffman, M. J. C., Smith, E. & Loftus, E. F. (1994). Repeatedly

thinking about a non-event: Source misattributions among preschoolers. *Consciousness and Cognition, 3* (pp. 388–407).

90. Ceci et al., Source misattributions among preschoolers (pp. 388–407).

91. Ceci et al., Source misattributions among preschoolers.

92. Garry, M. & Loftus, E. (1994). Pseudo-memories without hypnosis. *International Journal of Clinical and Experimental Hypnosis, 42* (pp. 363–378).

93. Garry & Loftus, Pseudo-memories (pp. 363–378).

94. Ofshe & Watters, *Making monsters* (p. 165).

95. Ofshe & Watters, *Making monsters* (p. 172).

96. Spanos, N. P., Burgess, M. F., Samuel, C., Blois, W. O. & Burgess, C. A. (1994). *False memory reports in hypnotic and nonhypnotic subjects.* Unpublished manuscript, Carleton University, Ottawa, Ontario, Canada. Cited in Spanos, *Multiple identities* (p. 107).

97. Spanos, *Multiple identities* (p. 107).

98. Spanos, *Multiple identities* (p. 107).

99. McConkey, K. M. & Sheehan, P. W. (1995). *Hypnosis, memory, and behavior in criminal investigation* (p. 109). New York: Guilford Press.

100. McConkey & Sheehan, *Hypnosis, memory, and behavior* (p. 123).

101. Pope, K. S. & Brown, L. S. (1996). *Recovered memories of abuse* (p. 59). Washington, D.C.: American Psychological Association Press.

102. McConkey & Sheehan, *Hypnosis, memory, and behavior* (p. 210).

103. Spanos, N. P. et al. (1994). Past-life identities. *International Journal of Clinical and Experimental Hypnosis, 42* (pp. 433–446).

104. Spanos, N. P., Radtke, H. L. & Bertrand, L. D. (1984). Hypnotic amnesia as a strategic enactment: Breaching amnesia in highly hypnotizible subjects. *Journal of Personality and Social Psychology, 47* (pp. 1155–1169).

105. Spanos, *Multiple identities* (pp. 134–135).

106. Spanos, *Multiple identities* (p. 240).

107. Spanos, *Multiple identities* (pp. 284–285).

108. Whitfield, *Memory and abuse* (p. 194).

109. Piper, A., Jr. "Truth serum" and "recovered memories" of sexual abuse: A review of the evidence. *The Journal of Psychiatry and Law* (pp. 447–471).

110. Orne & Scheibe, The psychology of the "panic button" (pp. 3–12).

111. Piper, "Truth serum" and "recovered memories" (pp. 447–471).

112. Pendergrast, *Victims of memory* (p. 310).

113. Wheeler, D. L., Jacobson, J. W., Paglieri, R. A. & Schwartz, A. A. (1993). An experimental assessment of facilitated communication. *Mental Retardation, 31* (pp. 49–60).

114. Wheeler et al., An experimental assessment (pp. 49–60).

115. Loftus & Ketcham, *The myth of repressed memories* (p. 161).

116. Crews, F. (1995). *The memory wars: Freud's legacy in dispute* (p. 298). New York: New York Review.

117. Herman & Schatzow, Recovery and verification (pp. 1–14).

118. Spanos, *Multiple identities*.

119. Piper, A., Jr. (1994). Treatment for multiple personality disorder at what cost? *American Journal of Psychiatry, 48* (pp. 392–400).

120. Ofshe & Watters, *Making monsters* (p. 194).

121. Smith, M. & Pazder, L. (1980). *Michelle remembers.* New York: Simon & Schuster.

122. Harris. G. C. (1997). Claims of forgotten trauma. *Journal of Psychiatry & the Law, 24* (pp. 401–419).

123. Neswald, D. (1991). "Common" programs observed in survivors of satanic ritual abuse. *California Therapist, 3* (pp. 47–50).

124. Harrington, E. (1996, September–October). Conspiracy theories and paranoia: Notes from a mind-control conference. *Skeptical Inquirer* (pp. 35–42).

125. Harrington, Conspiracy theories and paranoia (pp. 35–42).

126. Spanos, N. P. (1994). Multiple identity enactments and multiple personality disorder: A sociocognitive perspective. *Psychological Bulletin, 116* (pp. 143–165).

127. Gleaves, D. H. (1996). The sociocognitive model of dissociative identity disorder: A re-examination of the evidence. *Psychological Bulletin, 120* (pp. 42–59).

Chapter 5

Humanistic Psychotherapy

Emerging in the 1950s were two major competitors to the dominance of psychoanalysis. The Behavior Therapy approach dealt with observable or overt behavior and was unconcerned with the unconscious dynamics. The third force was humanistic psychotherapy. Unlike the other approaches, humanistic psychotherapy saw people as individuals with unlimited potential. A patient was prevented from maximizing his or her potential not by dark lurking forces, but rather by not knowing oneself, the true self. There was little if any concern, for example, with analyzing the transference relationship. The therapist did not necessarily dwell on major traumas or attempt a catharsis.

In the Person-Centered Therapy of Carl Rogers, it is the *client* who directs and controls the treatment issues. In Gestalt Therapy (see below, "Gestalt Therapy of Fritz Perls"), personal growth is achieved through enhancing personal awareness and breaking down defenses. In the Experiential Therapy of Alvin Mahrer, the therapist attempts to enter the phenomenological field or world of the patient and share in the experience of therapy.

PERSON-CENTERED THERAPY

The major proponent of humanistic psychology was Carl Rogers, who developed what was first called client-centered, but later became known as person-centered, psychotherapy.[1] For the past 50 years, person-centered psychotherapy has been extremely popular and influential, particularly in the United States and on college campuses. In the last several decades, the influence has permeated into other arenas, including governmental agencies and businesses. Rogers' therapeutic approach became crystallized in the academic setting during the 1940s and 1950s, resulting in two important books: *Counseling and Psychotherapy*[2] and *Client-Centered Therapy*.[3]

Theoretical Rationale and Background

According to Rogers, there is an inherent *actualizing tendency*, which is observed in a person moving toward more order and complexity. Self-actualization refers to the realization of a human's full potential.[4] Psychopathology and maladjustment are defined as the consistency or lack thereof between the patient's experiencing of the world and his or her self-concept.[5] Negative or weak self-concept leads to the "symbolization of failure experiences."[6] The individual may have a distorted self-concept and not accurately perceive who he or she is. Significant developmental influences exerted by caretakers and parents serve to shape the child's self-concept.

Although allowing for defense mechanisms, no attempt is made to plumb the hidden unconscious to deal with dreams. Similarly, little interest is shown in analyzing the transference relationship. Unlike Cognitive and Behaviorist Therapy (see Chapter 6), Person-Centered Therapy does not focus on the client's deficiencies but rather accepts the client's point of view. There is no reassurance, criticism or interpretation. Taking the patient as is, therapy starts immediately with no history-taking, psychodiagnosis or even a determination of whether the patient is treatable.[7]

The Necessary and Sufficient Conditions of Psychotherapy

Rogers' landmark contribution was his formulation and assessment of the alleged critical ingredients of effective psychotherapy. The basic factors in effective therapy are *congruence, unconditional positive regard* and *empathy*.[8] Congruence means that the thoughts and behaviors of the therapist and client correspond. The therapist does not put up a false front or facade. For example, if the therapist is tired, he should express the fatigue to the patient. Person-Centered Therapy does not, however, advocate inappropriate or extensive self-disclosure. By not covering up a true feeling, Rogers contends that the therapeutic relationship is strengthened.

Unconditional positive regard refers to accepting, caring and even prizing the client.[9] Thus, the therapist is non-judgmental toward whatever the client is doing at the moment. The therapist does not challenge or confront the client even if therapy issues are being avoided. This stance on the part of the therapist is thought to lead to an increase in the client's own self-regard, and it allows forward movement in therapy.

A therapist who is empathic displays a genuine interest in the client's world and makes a concerted effort to "get within and live the attitudes expressed" by the patient.[10] When the therapist understands the patient, he can reflect or clarify meanings both at and just below the level of aware-ness.[11] "When empathy is at its best, the two individuals are participating in a process comparable to that of a couple dancing, with the client leading and the therapist following."[12]

Case Reports

Portions of a transcript from a previously unpublished article by Rogers concern a woman who has difficulty dealing with her dependence on her daughter and her inability to let go.[13] The half-hour session is initiated by the therapist offering her the opportunity to express what's on her mind and informing her that he hopes both can "get to know each other as deeply as possible."[14] In the interview, the patient displays guilt and anger, and also experiences a "lot of empty places" when the daughter is not around.

The therapist reflects the client's feelings: Her feelings of empty places are paraphrased as "the old vacuum" when the daughter is not nearby. The therapist states that part of her feeling is that, "Damn it, I want you." The other part is, "Oh my God, what a monster I am to not let you go." As the session proceeds, the patient comes to realize that there is an inner child part of herself that she can prize and hold onto. Finally, the therapist asks why she is smiling. When the client responds: "It's your eyes are twinkling," both laugh, as the therapist concludes "Yours twinkle too."

This one session demonstrates how Rogers accepts the client's problem as presented but allows the issue to move from something external to a more internal focus, i.e., how she feels about herself. The therapist makes no mental status evaluation or attempt to obtain any particular history. The therapist attempts to see the world from the client's perspective (empathy) and to show that she has feelings too (congruence). It is immediately ob-vious that this approach is drastically different from psychodynamic and cognitive-based therapies in that the client is not offered specific interpretations, on the one hand, or given directions on the other.

By providing the core conditions for change, this client was helped to shift responsibility from others onto herself, experience various emotions during the session, accept aspects of the "self" that were formerly denied to awareness and increase the level of self-regard. The client was able in this one session to experience "anger, pain, loneliness, tearfulness, nurturance, disgust, tenderness and compassion."[15]

A famous psychotherapy film, *Three Approaches to Psychotherapy*, including Rogers, Fritz Perls and Albert Ellis, has probably been seen by tens of thousands of psychology students.[16] Each therapist saw "Gloria" for one session and provided Person-Centered Therapy, Gestalt Therapy and Ra-tional Emotive Therapy (now called Rational Emotive Behavior Therapy). As noted in the next section, controversy still swirls around this landmark presentation of Person-Centered Therapy.

Gloria is a 30-year-old divorcee who agreed to be interviewed on film by three well-known therapists. The issue presented by Gloria is how or whether to tell her 9-year-old daughter about her sexual relationships. She has not been honest with her daughter and, as a result, is having conflicts about having lied. Gloria wonders whether her daughter or even she would accept the negative side of her personality. She specifically asks Rogers on several occasions for a direct answer. Based on the tenets of his therapy, Rogers demurs and tells Gloria, "This is the kind of private thing that I couldn't possibly answer for you."

After hearing Rogers' reflection of her conflict and that, if she feels secure about her feelings, there will be little concern, Gloria seems to conclude that the focus of attention is on self-acceptance. Thus, Gloria has now moved from needing an opinion from an authoritative source to understanding that the answer to her dilemma is in herself.[17] She seems emboldened and willing to take more risks. When Gloria says she feels backing from Rogers, she is referring to his empathic support.

As Gloria continues to experience her inner conflicts and reveal her inner feelings, she becomes tearful. In the middle of her crying, she tells Rogers that it is nice that she can talk to him and that he approves of her, and she respects him. Finally, she says she would like Rogers for her father. Rogers tells Gloria that "You look to me like a pretty nice daughter."

As Gloria moves from a distance of feelings to an immediate awareness and expression of her feelings, Rogers' theoretical and therapeutic predictions are supported. The therapy interaction is characterized like a piece of music "that begins on a thin persistent note and gradually adds dimensions and levels until the whole orchestra is playing."[18] The therapeutic enterprise is viewed as creative and intuitive.[19]

The controversy revolving around Gloria, in part, devolves from Weinrach apparently locating an additional 249 words from the filmed therapy session with Rogers.[20] Was Rogers displaying countertransference when he told Gloria that she looks like a pretty nice daughter? In the missing portion, Gloria says she would like to find someone who "loves me like a father." The session does not delve into transference issues but rather focuses on her choice of a mate.

The answer might remain unclear except for what happened after the session and during the next fifteen years. As a result of continued interest in this case, Rogers provided a postscript.[21] For the first ten years after the interview, Gloria wrote to Rogers about once or twice a year. The last letter was written before her death, fifteen years after the filmed interview. About one year after the interview, Gloria attended a weekend retreat during which she requested that Rogers and his wife Helene allow her to view them as her spiritual parents, that is, the ones she would have liked to have had. Rogers replied that he and his wife would be pleased and honored to have that status in her life. From a psychoanalytic standpoint, it appears that an important issue was overlooked, but from the person-centered point of view, Rogers was simply displaying a caring attitude and interconnectedness between himself and this stranger.[22]

Research on Person-Centered Psychotherapy

A hallmark of Person-Centered Therapy is that attempts have been made to validate the major aspects of the theory. Such research has sometimes been enhanced by the use of verbatim transcripts. The first area of research concerns the necessary and sufficient conditions of effective therapy: congruence, unconditional positive regard and empathy. The second is whether any research has demonstrated the superiority of Person-Centered Therapy over that of a placebo.

Based on an overall review, and even "reviews of reviews," there appears to be little empirical support for Rogers' three basic ingredients.[23] Thus, the clinical research on "empathy, genuineness, and prizing . . . has demonstrated that these facilitative interpersonal conditions are valuable contributors to outcome but are neither necessary nor sufficient."[24]

At least two major difficulties are encountered in assessing the relationship between the core conditions and outcomes of psychotherapy. First, how is it possible to determine what is meant by genuineness, unconditional positive regard and empathy? To use independent judges would seem to violate Rogers' position that it is the client who is to be the judge of the facilitative conditions.[25] But if trained psychologists and clients are not in agreement over who is facilitative, then the question is raised as to what the client is responding to. Is it simply liking the therapist and feeling you are improved, or is it some other factor? These ingredients of the therapeutic relationship are difficult for a client to evaluate objectively.

The second and perhaps more technical problem is that an experimental test has not been conducted.[26] None of the prior studies has properly tested whether a causal connection exists between the core conditions and therapeutic improvement. For example, if a therapist with higher levels of empathy, congruence and unconditional positive regard produces more therapeutic improvement than a therapist with lower levels, it may be concluded that there is a direct causal link between these conditions and therapeutic change. In order to reach this conclusion, the level of the facilitative conditions needs to be manipulated. One way to do so is to randomly assign therapists into groups providing different levels of the core conditions. But by whom and how are the levels going to be validated and assessed? To get a grasp on all three ingredients with objective measures may be an insurmountable task. As noted below, these concepts are not easily subjected to objective definitions and assessments.

A research project on seriously disturbed patients compared eight schizophrenics who received either a high level of the core conditions or lower levels of the core conditions.[27] The measure of therapeutic effectiveness was the amount of time patients spent outside the hospital during the subsequent nine years after entry into the research project. College students with no training or background in psychotherapy made an evaluation of the level of therapy characteristics of empathy, genuineness and unconditional positive regard. The three aspects of therapy effectiveness were grouped together into a single measure. The prediction was that people who received a higher level of the necessary and sufficient therapy conditions would spend fewer days in the hospital subsequent to discharge. It appears that the hypothesis was not supported, but with a sophisticated statistical analysis, there were indications that the group receiving therapy high in empathy, nonpossessive warmth and genuineness was more likely to get out and stay out of the hospital compared to patients in the group receiving less of the three core characteristics. Indeed, the authors point out that, despite selecting therapists thought to possess the necessary ingredients for effective therapy, some proved to be unhelpful or harmful.[28]

In the comparative reviews by Smith and Glass, there seemed to be very little difference between placebo treatment and Person-Centered Therapy.[29] In this so-called meta-analysis of studies, Person-Centered Therapy was on a par with insight-oriented therapy but perhaps slightly less effective than behaviorally oriented therapies.

Critique and Analysis of Person-Centered Therapy

Without doubt Person-Centered Therapy presents a dramatic departure from the psychoanalytic perspective. In almost direct opposition to psychoanalysis, Rogers views the positive side of the human organism, one that inexorably moves toward growth and fulfillment. The therapist simply nourishes the patients and allows this growth to flourish. The ingredients sprinkled into therapy are the three core ingredients: congruence, empathy and unconditional positive regard.

It would be critical to the successful outcome of psychotherapy if it were confirmed that congruence, empathy and unconditional positive regard lead to emotional change. At least five methodological errors preclude any conclusions at present.[30] (1) Some control subjects were not proper candidates for therapy. (2) There was a lack of untreated control groups for comparison purposes. (3) Controls for placebo effects were lacking. (4) Too much reliance was placed on self-reports, which may in part be an attempt to please the experimenter. (But, as noted above, it appears that the core conditions must be evaluated by the clients themselves.) (5)"Neglect [of] the actual behavior and functioning of clients in favor of their subjective experiences."[31]

Can the case of Gloria be an exemplary, yet anecdotal, indicator of the efficacy of Person-Centered Therapy? Rogers clearly believes so. He was awed by the fact that his 15-year association with Gloria grew out of a 30-minute contact when they truly met as persons. He seems to suggest that even one brief meeting can make a difference.

First, this relationship may not be a typical "case" in that the client volunteered to present herself on film to three therapists. For Rogers to conclude that her self-concept became more complex, that she was less rigid after his brief encounter, is quite a stretch.[32] He totally discounts the effect, if any, of the other two therapists and concludes that the changes he apparently observes are due to his therapeutic techniques.

Even therapists within the person-centered camp cannot agree to what extent Rogers employs reflection or interpretation in the Gloria case. Weinrach, who asserted that Rogers displays countertransference in his reaction to Gloria, contends that Rogers used interpretation 38 percent of the time.[33] Bohart, on the other hand, who "informally scored the transcript" found only 14 percent interpretation.[34]

The conclusions reached on the schizophrenia research suggest overreaching on the part of Rogers.[35] There were only eight subjects in each group in the Truax study.[36] Apparently, the article does not present the difference between the two groups. The outcome measure related to length of time out of the hospital, which may or may not be a good measure of clinical improvement. Most noteworthy, however, is that, first, other therapists cannot informally determine who has the critical characteristics that can produce change. Second and most astounding, if these results are to be accepted, there are a significant number of therapists who provide inadequate and harmful therapy because they don't possess these characteristics. The decrease in the hospital stay in the control group and the high-conditions group, however, and the converse increase in the low-condition therapy group could be due to a host of unknown variables.

Without empirical demonstration, how can therapy changes be documented? There is a great lack of specificity in determining a change in someone's self-concept or the complexity thereof. There are at least fourteen other theoretical formulations of the "self," so at the very least it would be necessary to pin down the definitions with precision so as to provide objective measures of such alterations in self-concept.[37] The concept of empathy raises thorny measurement issues. Does empathy mean directly contacting another person and experiencing their feelings, or is the therapist relating to his own set of feelings based on his cognitive reconstruction of the clients' feelings and attitudes?[38]

Thus, to date, there has been no confirmation that the major ingredients postulated by Rogers for effective psychotherapy are necessary and sufficient. Therefore, there is no scientific basis for asserting that the essential fundamentals that produce therapeutic change have been uncovered and verified. The metaphysical nature of self-concept, empathy and congruence has led at best to uncertain results.

On a more global level, Rogers' therapy is not necessarily person-directed. As is true of virtually all therapies, the clinicians bring their theoretical bias into the clinic or office. The therapist may give more attention and respond more favorably when the patient begins to talk about areas that are germane to the therapist's psychotherapeutic approach. Thus, in psychoanalysis, it seems that the patient is more likely to mention dreams and make comments and perceptions about the therapist. In Person-Centered Therapy, feelings and how one feels about oneself seem to be the main topic for discussion. Thus, subtly or overtly, the person-centered therapist is construing and constricting the range of acceptable grist for the therapy mill.

An early study by Truax suggests that changes in clients' behavior may be explained within a behavioral framework of reinforcement.[39] The question was whether Rogers offered empathy and acceptance independent of what the client said. The results indicate that Rogers was more likely to offer empathy and unconditional positive regard when the client made insightful statements, focused on the problem, or expressed him- or herself in a way similar to that of Rogers. What this study demonstrates is that Person-Centered Therapy is "very directive in reinforcing certain kinds of client behavior."[40]

More specifically, Rogers' therapeutic philosophy may be too restrictive and optimistic. Other views of human nature suggest that people do not inherently move toward fulfillment or self-actualization.[41] If the client does not have the innate ability to move forward in his or her growth and development, then simply to reflect and clarify for a patient may be wasteful. Thus, under the proper circumstances, shouldn't a patient be confronted with some harsh realities? For Quinn, some patients need contradiction and learning the hard truths in order to move toward fuller functioning.[42]

Last, is the therapeutic arena envisioned by Rogers artificial and hypocritical? Can a therapist really like all his patients? Undoubtedly, there will be clients for whom one might have natural revulsion, e.g., a child molester. The therapist must then pretend to accept the patient for who he is. In such a circumstance, the therapist is playacting. Such behavior is the opposite of the essential congruence ingredient.[43]

Apparently, Masson correctly observed that this therapeutic interaction is artificial.[44] One does not meet people in real life who are so accepting and nonjudgmental. It is purposefully foisted onto the patient in order to produce cognitive, behavioral and attitudinal change. The major difficulty is that, once the patient leaves the therapy room, he or she does not experience this kind of behavior among others. The gains in therapy, if any, meet up with harsh realities when these patients encounter people who don't like them and are judgmental or less than empathic, for example. The pretense of unconditional acceptance may be a disservice to clients since the real world is filled with conditions. Thus, such pretense and artificiality can lead to the client believing that "only a therapist could love them."[45]

The range of clients who are amenable to Person-Centered Therapy may be limited to higher functioning people. Conflict resolution, between individuals or countries, may be a proper forum for this non-confrontational approach. Unfortunately, however, no recent studies have been done with schizophrenics or borderline personalty disorders, for example. Since Person-Centered Therapy emanated from the university setting, it appealed mainly to college students. As Prochaska and Norcross further note, the theory and the therapy seem suitable to the ambitious person "whose typically American drive to achieve is mistaken for some tendency to actualize."[46]

Thus, do schizophrenics operate with the same innate actualizing tendency such that providing Person-Centered Therapy will lead to personal growth and a more productive life? What about a chemical imbalance and psychopharmacological treatment? As may be true with other forms of humanistic therapy, there may be a limitation on who may profit. For those who are able to attend a seminar or are in the work environment but display no major debilitating mental illness, it may be helpful to listen to a caring, professional adult. Whether a professional can be trained to be a good listener is debatable.

THE GESTALT THERAPY OF FRITZ PERLS

In a drastic divergence from Freud, Gestalt Therapy viewed psychopathology as originating in the interaction of the person with the environment. In the middle of the twentieth century, a major sector of psychotherapeutic attention shifted from archeological explorations to a formulation of personal growth. The humanistic/existential approach developed as a major alternative to psychoanalysis. One of the major players was Fritz Perls, who developed Gestalt Therapy. Interestingly, as noted earlier, Fritz Perls was analyzed by Wilhelm Reich, who had been trained in psychoanalysis. The focus was on here-and-now awareness. The patient examines what is going on at the moment. For the most part, the patient does not dwell on the past or try to seek etiological explanations from childhood to explain current behavior.

The therapist does not perform a psychodiagnostic history, administer psychological tests, or engage in long-term therapy. (Some gestalt therapists, however, may see the patient on an extended basis.) Rather, the situation is immediately sized up, and treatment is offered on the spot, which in workshop situations may last five or ten minutes. In the here-and-now gestalt approaches, the patient may participate in a group setting over the course of just one weekend in a hotel conference room or at a scenic location. In both gestalt and the newer experiential approaches of Mahrer, the therapist relies on the material that is brought to the session, such as a dream or a feeling.[47]

Gestalt Therapy seeks to "promote the growth process and develop the human potential."[48] Fritz Perls, the originator of Gestalt Therapy, viewed his approach as within the framework of humanistic and existential psychology.[49] There is a major difference between Carl Rogers' Person-Centered Therapy and Gestalt Therapy in that the former places a premium on empathy with and acceptance of the patient. Perls was more active and verbally confrontive. The aim of the gestalt approach is to have the patient get in touch with his or her immediate perceptual and phenomenological field.[50]

"Gestalt" is a German word that refers to a pattern or configuration. The individual parts of the organization make up the whole.[51] These organizational principles were developed in the area of perception, i.e., figure versus ground. For example, in viewing people in a crowded room, a person does not see a blur of colors and shapes but rather organizes the scene into a meaningful array so that people may be in the foreground as distinct figures, while other perceptual stimuli recede into the background.[52] The gestalt view sees individuals as interacting among themselves and the environment.[53]

The integrity of the person is maintained in a "continual process of bringing completeness to our needs," which is the process of forming *wholes* or gestalts.[54]

In Perls' humanistic approach, little remains of the psychoanalytic explanation of psychopathology. The energizing force of our actions is emotion.[55] Psychopathology is described in terms of neurosis. A neurosis arises "when the individual somehow interrupts the ongoing process of life and saddles himself with so many unfinished situations that he cannot satisfactorily get on with the process of living."[56] For Perls, a neurosis is a defensive strategy that serves to protect the individual against the threat of an overwhelming and encroaching world.[57]

Perls described four types of defensive strategies: introjection, projection, confluence and retroflection. With introjection, there is a problem in self/other differentiation or discrimination wherein the individual has problems with boundaries and allows others' ideas and attitudes to overly intrude and become incorporated as his own. For example, the comment "I think" really means "they think."[58]

Projection is the opposite of introjection in that the person tends to make the environment responsible for what is really originating within the self. A prime example is an overly cautious person who wants to have friends but contends he can't trust anyone because others are selfish.[59]

A person who feels no boundaries between himself and others displays confluence. For example, newborn infants cannot distinguish between what is outside and inside or between the self and other. The generic "we" at times can represent the defense of confluence.[60]

The fourth defensive mechanism, retroflection, is a turning back against the self. Thus, the retroflector does to himself what he actually would like to do to another person. A linguistic example of retroflection is found in the phrase "I am ashamed of myself," but this really refers to being ashamed of someone else.

The Gestalt Psychotherapeutic Technique

Since Gestalt Therapy is experiential, no preliminary history-taking, problem identification or psychodiagnosis is required. In the group format volunteers become the identified "patient." The patient is asked to re-experience problems or traumas in the here and now.[61] The patient is asked to become aware not only of overt language, but also breathing, emotions, sound of the voice and gestures.

To facilitate the focus on the present, several exercises or games have been developed. When there is an entrenched focus on the past, the empty-chair technique may be used. Here the patient imagines that a parent is in the empty chair, and the patient now can say in the present what he or she never was able to say beforehand.

The resentment game involves couples who say first negative and then positive things to each other.[62] The patients state in the present tense what they resent about the partner, followed by what is appreciated. During exercises, it is the therapist who keeps the individual on target by interjecting comments but not directly interpreting. As the verbatim transcript makes clear, the therapist can become enmeshed in the scenarios, but Perls, at least, seems to extricate himself and puts the spotlight back on the participants.

A number of other exercises are used, such as dialogue games in which different aspects of a personality confront each other,[63] and "Top Dog/Underdog": The Top Dog can be described as "righteous, bullying, punishing, authoritarian, and primitive" and demanding.[64] Perls viewed the Top Dog as Freud's superego.[65] The Underdog is "apologetic, wheedling" and plays the cry-baby.[66] Underdog acquiesces to Top Dog, at least on the surface. Underdog, however, has developed skill in evading the demands of Top Dog and may respond with "I'll do better next time."

Here is a brief snippet of a Top Dog/Underdog dialogue:

A divorcee at a workshop had disclosed an interest in remarriage but seemed to be engaging in behavior that defeated her purpose.[67]

Underdog: I'm so lonely, I wish I had someone to come home to at the end of the day.

Top Dog: You have the children; that should certainly be enough for you.

Underdog: I'm all right during the day as long as I'm busy at night, I'm all right if I'm tired enough but. . . .

Top Dog: Don't be such a baby; you should certainly be more self-sufficient than that.

Under Dog: But I don't want to be self-sufficient! I want a man to take care of me, and make decisions for me, and. . . .

At the gestalt workshops, the participants are asked to bring in dreams. For Perls, different parts of the dreams are fragments of the personality.[68] In order to become a unified whole individual, the patient, needs to "re-own these projected fragmented parts of our personality."[69] In so doing, the person can reclaim the hidden potential that is depicted in the dream.

In Linda's dream, she is watching a lake dry up in which there is a small island in the middle.[70] At the bottom, there is an old license plate. Perls asked her to play the license plate:

Linda: I am an old license plate, thrown in the bottom of the lake, I have no use because I'm of no value.

Linda is asked how she feels about this.

Linda: I don't like it, I don't like being a license plate—useless.

Linda is then asked to play the lake.

Linda: I'm a lake. I'm drying up.

Although she is drying up, Linda exclaims that "new life can grow from me" and cries. Perls asks if Linda gets the existential message.

Linda replies: "Yes. I can paint. I can no longer reproduce, I water the earth and give life."

Perls then states, "You see the contrast: On the surface, you find something, some artifact—the license plate, the artificial you—but then when you go deeper, you find the apparent death of the lake is actually fertility."

This self-confrontation highlights the unfinished business, patching up the holes in the personality, bringing enhanced awareness, allowing the completion of the gestalt, making the person whole. What Perls attempts to do is have the patient re-experience her problems and trauma. In order to close the book on her unfinished business, the patient must confront and deal with the problem in the present.[71] The disowned parts of the personality are to be re-owned. The games or exercises bring out in broad daylight the major conflicts and present to the patient the key to unlocking the different parts of the personality, thus helping to close the incomplete gestalt.[72]

Research on Gestalt Therapy

Prior to 1980, 18 studies were analyzed in a large survey on the effect-iveness of various psychotherapies.[73] The results of the survey suggested that Gestalt Therapy was not significantly better than a placebo and appeared to be less effective than behavioral and cognitive approaches.[74]

Much of the research as well as the clinical activities have involved highly functioning adults who are interested in seeking a growth experience. When psychiatric in-patients are examined, the results are disappointing and suggest there may be more deterioration in experiential and gestalt approaches compared to behavioral or process-oriented groups.[75]

In a study by Beutler, the patients were diagnosed with substance abuse, schizophrenia, bipolar affective disorder, personality disorder, adjustment re-action, anxiety disorder, major depressive disorder and dysthymic disorder. All the therapists were in training with the exception of one staff nurse. The behavior task group included relaxation training, anxiety management and exercise. The expressive-experiential group asked patients to "exaggerate negative feelings." Role-playing was used, as were a two-chair dialogue and imagined conversations with significant people. The interactive group em-phasized interpersonal roles, which focused on the group interaction. There was no group therapy control group.

The clear-cut results demonstrated that patients in the expressive-experiential group showed no improvement and may have experienced some deterioration. The authors suggested that in acute psychiatric inpatient treat-ment, "emotional display, exaggeration of anger, and increased sensitivity may not be warranted."[76] With this population in this setting, it seems con-traindicated to try to break down defenses rapidly or exaggerate negative feelings. Improvement, on the other hand, was found for patients in the interactive group. Due to attrition of the sample, there were no reliable long-term follow-up results after discharge from the hospital.

A study on mildly disturbed adults was performed by Paivio and Green-berg.[77] The rationale underlying the empty-chair technique is to allow the patient to engage in an imaginary dialogue with important people in his or her life such that hitherto restricted feelings can be accessed and dealt with in the security of the therapist's office.[78] This technique may allow resolution of unfinished business, which includes a shift in the patient's self-perception from weak and victimized to one of self-empowerment.

Patients were recruited through newspaper and radio notices. The subjects were selected on the basis of a rating checklist for symptoms and features of "unfinished business" rather than formal DSM-III-R criteria.[79] Sixteen people were placed in either an empty-chair group or a psychoeducation group which was construed as an attention-placebo minimal treatment con-dition. The participants in the placebo control met in a group setting that offered emotional support and information in a lecture/discussion format.

The empty-chair participants experienced more decrease in symptoms compared to the control group. Even after one year, there was measurable improvement in the empty-chair people on various self-reports and therapist ratings. The authors report an increase in self-acceptance, which supports the notion of "greater understanding of the other and self-empowerment."

Although this study is intriguing, the authors point out three methodological problems.

1. The mild symptoms in this recruited sample may not be generalized to other samples.

2. Since the main experimenter participated or supervised both the empty-chair and the placebo group, there could be the intrusion of experimenter bias.

3. The control group may not have been interesting enough to provide a valid comparison with the experimental group. Meeting in a non-clinical group setting may raise different expectancy levels than the intense individual treatment.

Two other methodological issues not addressed by the authors are as follows:

4. The empty-chair technique was combined with an empathic client-centered approach. Since these approaches are somewhat contradictory, it is not clear how the therapist is to integrate the two. That is, at times the gestalt-oriented therapist must be directive, whereas the person-centered therapist allows the client to set the agenda, with the therapist reflecting the clients' comments. Parenthetically, it is interesting to note that the empty-chair technique is just one of the gestalt exercises that was employed. Thus, it is not known whether a panoply of procedures would lead to substantial change in reducing unfinished business.

5. Finally, the main contention regarding resolution of unfinished business by self-acceptance and empowerment was not actually measured. It is not necessarily the case that decrease in hostility or increase in affiliation is related to more self-acceptance or coming to terms with negative feelings about someone else.

Critique and Analysis of Gestalt Therapy

The first issue is whether Gestalt Therapy is appropriate for most mental disorders. One of the major myths of Gestalt Therapy is that it is applicable to a broad array of clientele. In the workshops at Esalen and in many of the research projects, highly functioning college students or professionals participated. With respect to psychiatric in-patients, Gestalt Therapy appears contraindicated. As noted by Beutler et al., patients with severe mental disorders may deteriorate when subjected to experiential techniques.[80] People who have intractable defenses may be immune to the short-term workshop attempts to produce insight and growth. Gestalt Therapy may be helpful with emotionally intact people as a learning or psychoeducational approach to demonstrate how we interact with others.

There appears to be no attempt to verify the nature of the defense mechanisms or to show that a person has actually achieved closure by getting in touch with the repressions of the unconscious.[81] Does establishing a novel interpersonal contact at seminars or having a person get into the hot seat allow the person to get beyond the superficial? The group participants and the leaders may be able to see the defensive maneuvers, but the patient can remain blissfully unaware. A case in point may be Judy.[82] A somewhat reluctant volunteer, she doesn't comply with Perls' directive to make statements but rather suggests that it is up to Perls to make something happen. Judy may present a classic example of resistance, avoidance and projection in this brief encounter. As Perls pretends to sleep, Judy says, "You're breathing too deeply for one asleep"; then he says, "don't make me kick you." This draws a burst of laughter from the audience. Perls may get to the nub of the issue and has the audience laughing at Judy, but, alas, Judy doesn't seem to understand the laughter or the connections the audience is making. In all fairness, it should be pointed out that this episode took only several minutes. The issue remains, however: would ongoing therapy games penetrate the thicket of defenses?

By avoiding the generally acceptable procedures of psychological testing and assessment, treatment plan, problem identification and follow-up, the traditional gestaltist has no way of knowing who he is helping and, perhaps as significantly, whether he is helping anyone. No scientific data have yet been presented showing that Gestalt Therapy has produced measurable improvement in any appreciable fashion. As noted, the study by Paivio, which suggests that a certain type of patient might be helped, is too flawed to change the conclusion that Gestalt Therapy by itself has little or no utility.[83] Thus, there is no scientific basis for concluding that Gestalt Therapy is effective.

A major problem in Gestalt Therapy is that the underlying theory is not translatable from its presumed origin in gestalt psychology to the psychotherapy arena. In a scathing review, Henle disputes the connection and kinship between gestalt psychology and Gestalt Therapy.[84] Gestalt psychology originated around the turn of the twentieth century and was focused primarily on the area of perception. The issues of figure/ground and perceptual closure were typical areas of research. The problem for Gestalt Therapy is that there is no easy way to traverse from one segmented arena of human ability to a larger one, i.e., personality and psychopathology. Looking back at Perls, we see that he was apparently analogizing from the perceptual domain, i.e., lack of closure in personality was unfinished business. It never became clear how gestalt psychology or "field psychology" has relevance for psychotherapy. What does figure/ground perception, for example, have to do with holes in the personality or making a person whole? Little if any research has apparently been done on this depiction of the above-mentioned quartet of defense mechanisms or how they are related to the gestalt position.

The stature and time of the innovator may preclude generalizations across generations. What happens if the therapy seems relevant to a certain historical time and is largely dependent on the fame of the originator? In the turbulent 1960s, the here-and-now focus of gestalt may have very well meshed with the zeitgeist, especially for highly functioning growth-oriented adults. As Masson muses, the gestalt prayer in which you do your thing and I do my thing may be a bit outdated.[85] The focus on the "I" versus the group may portray the cultural bias of the American scene circa 1960–1970.[86]

Perls became larger than life as a therapist and was at the peak of his fame in the late 1960s. To what extent are his personality and the charisma of the therapist responsible for the reported therapeutic effects and growth experiences? To date no new data have been presented suggesting that other gestalt therapists produce significant clinical changes. There do not appear to be any surveys that record any former gestalt patients who can now claim they have been helped. Perhaps at that time in the late 1960s and 1970s, some patients had the perception of personal growth. Thus, the alleged improvement in emotional functioning that occurred in the 1960s and 1970s may have had more to do with the charisma of the leader and the cultural time zone than any actual change in personal growth.

EXPERIENTIAL THERAPY

One humanistic alterative to Gestalt Therapy has been termed Experiential Therapy.[87] The essence of Experiential Therapy is to *experience* during the therapeutic session. Experiential Therapy has similarities to a number of other psychotherapies, including Gestalt, elements of Primal (see Chapter 3) and Behavioral Therapy (Chapter 6). There are, however, no group therapy sessions or workshops, but rather intense individual sessions, with each session apparently standing on its own. Thus, Mahrer advocates an open-ended, go-with-the-flow type of therapy, with each session an entity unto itself.[88] The same four-step process is repeated in each treatment session. Both the client and therapist recline on different chairs but facing in the same direction and with eyes closed.

There is no concern with transference, insight, therapeutic support or empathy or overt behavior change. There is no psychological assessment or psychodiagnosis. What occurs is a set four-step procedure that is repeated every session, allowing the patient to delve into scenes that reflect strong feelings. The therapist goes along for the ride and attempts to direct the patient to fully explore his or her emotions and feelings. There is no intake or psychological testing prior to any of the sessions.

In the first step of each session, the patient "attains a level of strong feeling."[89] In the moment of strong feeling, the patient accesses his or her inner "deeper potential way of being-behaving."[90] Both the patient and the therapist are to live and be in the moment of strong feeling.[91] A case example of what appears to be claustrophobia is presented.[92] At the beginning of the session, the patient describes his frustration when in enclosed places, followed by crying, trembling and screaming while experiencing his feelings. Thus, the patient returns to a real or imagined emotionally charged event wherein it can be fully sensorily explored.

The second step focuses on reconstructing the experience in a positive fashion. The person senses, feels, welcomes and accepts the accessed explosive energy emanating from step one. The second step takes ten to twenty minutes.[93] In step two, attention is geared to bodily sensations such as warmth of the hands, electrical impulses on the skin and heart palpitations. The patient may be asked what he or she is feeling inside the body, and the therapist can describe what he or she is feeling.[94] The strong emotional state abates, so that what was once unpleasant may now seem pleasant and positive. Mahrer reports that the patient was able to appreciate his inner experiencing.[95]

The third step gives the patient an opportunity to disengage from his ordinary personality by using the explosive energy in a new and creative way.[96] The patient re-experiences a negative scene from childhood—being taunted and ridiculed, for example. The new inner experience allows the phobic patient to laugh at his tormentors in the childhood scene. A whole new person emerges during the third step. When reaching the deeper potential during this phase, there are feelings of actualization such as "bodily excitement, aliveness, vitality, vibrancy" and the bodily tingling that accompanies actualization.[97] This step appears to be similar to age regression, with the implementation of reframing and recasting past events in a more favorable light and the patient presenting him- or herself as a wonderful, worthy person.

Last, the patient imagines prospective scenes wherein he is the qualitatively new person. Thus, the patient imagines how he would feel or react outside the therapy session. What was gained in step three by visualizing or inner experiencing past scenes moves to the future in step four. The therapist may envision fame and fortune for the patient: "Yes, I think I got it! Your sculpture is everywhere—galleries across the country."[98] Mahrer reports that at the end of the 1½- to 2-hour session, the phobic patient left as a new person, not scared of enclosed places.

Critique and Analysis

Mahrer's latest book does not carry a single comment regarding scientific verification[99] and cites no peer-reviewed articles. His approach is virtually untested. No attempt is made to illuminate how experiencing in the therapy sessions leads to improvement in reducing a phobia, for example. Mahrer provides no documentation that accessing earlier scenes via imagination leads to changes in emotional function (step 3) or how imagining your new self (step 4) leads to altered behavior. He does not cite any related literature in the cognitive behavioral arena or hypnosis that might support his theory and practice. The similarities to implosion, systematic desensitization (Chapter 6) or visualization seem to be ignored. He provides no yardstick for change other than what the patient reports. What he offers are a series of anecdotal reports.

The alleged improvement in reported changes in behavior should not be viewed as anything more than a placebo. It appears that the patient and therapist embark on an unscripted journey without a real beginning, middle or end. His approach does not seem distinguishable from entering into a virtual reality game. No data are presented that jumping into the narrative history world provided any help whatsoever. Mahrer's experiential psychotherapy is radical, extreme, untested and unscientific, but not any more than psychoanalysis.

NOTES

1. Raskin, N. J. & Rogers, C. R. (1994). Person-centered therapy. In Corsini, R. J. & Wedding, D. (Eds.), *Current psychotherapies* (5th ed.) (pp. 128–161). Itasca, Ill.: Peacock Publishers.

2. Rogers, C. R. (1942). *Counseling and psychotherapy.* Boston: Houghton Mifflin.

3. Rogers, C. R. (1951). *Client-Centered Therapy.* Boston: Houghton Mifflin.

4. Raskin & Rogers, Person-centered therapy (p. 128).

5. Raskin & Rogers, Person-centered therapy (p. 140).

6. Raskin & Rogers, Person-centered therapy (p. 140).

7. Raskin & Rogers, Person-centered therapy (p. 144).

8. Raskin & Rogers, Person-centered therapy (pp. 142, 143).

9. Raskin & Rogers, Person-centered therapy (p. 143).

10. Raskin & Rogers, Person-centered therapy (p. 142).

11. Raskin & Rogers, Person-centered therapy (p. 143).

12. Raskin & Rogers, Person-centered therapy (p. 130).

13. Raskin & Rogers, Person-centered therapy (p. 144).

14. Raskin & Rogers, Person-centered therapy (p. 144).

15. Raskin & Rogers, Person-centered therapy (p. 149).

16. Shostrom, E. L. (Producer) (1965). *Three approaches to psychotherapy.* [Film]. Orange, Calif.: Psychological Films.

17. Raskin & Rogers, Person-centered therapy (p. 155).

18. Raskin & Rogers, Person-centered therapy (p. 157).

19. Raskin & Rogers, Person-centered therapy (p. 157).

20. Weinrach, S. G. (1990). Rogers and Gloria: The controversial film and the enduring relationship. *Psychotherapy, 27* (pp. 282–290).

21. Rogers, C. R. (1984). A historical note—Gloria. In Levant, R. F. & Shlien, J. M. (Eds.), *Client-Centered Therapy and the Person-Centered Approach* (pp. 423–425). New York: Praeger. (Cited in Raskin & Rogers, Person-centered therapy.)

22. Bohart, A. C. (1991). The missing 249 words: In search of objectivity. *Psychotherapy, 28* (pp. 497–503).

23. Prochaska, J. O. & Norcross, J. C. (1994). *Systems of psychotherapy: A transtheoretical analysis* (3rd ed.) (p. 146). Pacific Grove, Calif.: Brooks/Cole.

24. Prochaska & Norcross, *Systems of psychotherapy* (p. 146).

25. Cramer, D. (1990). Towards assessing the therapeutic value of Rogers' core conditions. *Counselling Psychology Quarterly, 3* (pp. 57–66).

26. Cramer, Towards assessing the therapeutic value of Rogers' core conditions (pp. 57–66).

27. Truax, C. B. (1970). Effects of client-centered psychotherapy with schizophrenic patients: Nine years pre-therapy and nine years post-therapy hospitalization. *Journal of Consulting & Clinical Psychology, 35* (pp. 417–422).

28. Truax, Effects of client-centered psychotherapy (pp. 417–422).

29. Smith, M. L. & Glass, G. V. (1977). Meta-analysis of psychotherapy outcome studies. *American Psychologist, 32* (pp. 752–760).

30. Prochaska & Norcross, *Systems of psychotherapy* (p. 150).

31. Prochaska & Norcross, *Systems of psychotherapy* (p. 150).

32. Raskin & Rogers, Person-centered therapy (p. 157).

33. Weinrach, Rogers and Gloria (pp. 282–290).

34. Bohart, The missing 249 words (pp. 497–503).

35. Raskin & Rogers, Person-centered therapy (p. 135).

36. Truax, Effects of client-centered psychotherapy (pp. 417–422).

37. Hall, C. S. & Lindzey, G. (1970). *Theories of personality* (2nd ed.) (pp. 517–523). New York: John Wiley.

38. Hanna, F. J. & Shank, G. (1995). The specter of metaphysics in counselling research and practice: The qualitative challenge. *Journal of Counseling and Development, 74* (pp. 53–59).

39. Truax, C. B. (1966). Reinforcement and nonreinforcement in Rogerian psychotherapy. *Journal of Abnormal Psychology, 71* (pp. 1–9).

40. Kazdin, A. E. (1980). *Research design in clinical psychology* (p. 96). New York: Harper & Row.

41. Quinn, R. (1993). Confronting Carl Rogers: A developmental interactional approach to person-centered therapy. *Journal of Humanistic Psychology, 33* (pp. 6–23).

42. Quinn, R. (1993). Confronting Carl Rogers. *Journal of Humanistic Psychology, 33* (pp. 6–23).

43. Masson, J. M. (1994). *Against therapy* (p. 232). Monroe, Maine: Common Courage Press.

44. Masson, *Against therapy* (p. 232).

45. Prochaska & Norcross, *Systems of psychotherapy* (p. 151).

46. Prochaska & Norcross, *Systems of psychotherapy* (p. 150).

47. Mahrer, A. R. (1906). *The complete guide to experiential psychotherapy.* New York: John Wiley & Sons.

48. Perls, F. (1969). *Gestalt therapy verbatim* (p. 2). New York: Bantam Books.

49. Perls, *Gestalt therapy verbatim* (pp. 1, 16).

50. Brown, M. (1973). The new body psychotherapies. *Psychotherapy: Theory of research and practice, 10* (pp. 98–116).

51. Perls, F. (1973). *The Gestalt approach and eye witness to history* (p. 3). Toronto: Science and Behavior Books.

52. Perls, *The Gestalt approach* (p. 3).

53. Perls, *The Gestalt approach* (p. 25).

54. Prochaska & Norcross, *Systems of psychotherapy* (p. 159).

55. Perls, *The Gestalt approach* (p. 23).

56. Perls, *The Gestalt approach* (p. 23).

57. Perls, *The Gestalt approach* (p. 31).

58. Perls, *The Gestalt approach* (p. 35).

59. Perls, *The Gestalt approach* (p. 38).

60. Perls, *The Gestalt approach* (p. 40).

61. Perls, *The Gestalt approach* (p. 63).

62. Perls, *The Gestalt approach* (p. 158).

63. Prochaska & Norcross, *Systems of psychotherapy* (p. 167).

64. Stephenson, S. F. (Ed.) (1978). *Gestalt therapy primer* (p. 77). New York: Jason Aronson.

65. Perls, *Gestalt therapy verbatim* (p. 18).

66. Perls, *Gestalt therapy verbatim* (p. 19).

67. Fantz, R. (1978). Polarities: Differentiation and integration. In Stephenson, F. D. (Ed.), *Gestalt therapy primer* (pp. 87–96). New York: Jason Aronson.

68. Perls, *Gestalt therapy verbatim* (p. 71).

69. Perls, *Gestalt therapy verbatim* (p. 72).

70. Perls, *Gestalt therapy verbatim* (p. 84).

71. Perls, *The gestalt approach* (p. 63).

72. Perls, *Gestalt therapy verbatim* (p. 41).

73. Smith, M. L., Glass, G. V. & Miller, G. I. (1980). *The benefits of psychotherapy.* Baltimore: Johns Hopkins University Press.

74. Prochaska & Norcross, *Systems of psychotherapy* (p. 185).

75. Beutler, L. E., Frank, M., Scheiber, S. C., Calvert, S. & Gaines, J. (1984). Comparative effects of group psychotherapies in a short-term inpatient setting: An experience with deterioration effects. *Psychiatry, 47* (pp. 66–76).

76. Beutler et al., Comparative effects (pp. 66–76).

77. Paivio, S. C. & Greenberg, L. S. (1995). Resolving "unfinished business": Efficacy of experiential therapy using empty-chair dialogue. *Journal of Consulting and Clinical Psychology, 63* (pp. 419–425).

78. Paivio & Greenberg, Resolving "unfinished business."

79. Derogatis, L. R. (1983). *SCL-90-R administration scoring and procedures manual.* Towson, Md.: Clinical Psychiatric Research.

80. Beutler et al., Comparative effects (pp. 66–76).

81. Brown, M. (1973). The new body psychotherapies. *Psychotherapy, 10* (pp. 98–116).

82. Perls, *Gestalt therapy verbatim* (p. 137).

83. Paivio & Greenberg, Resolving "unfinished business."

84. Henle, M. (1978). Gestalt psychology and gestalt therapy. *Journal of the History of the Behavioral Sciences, 14* (pp. 23–32).

85. Masson, *Against therapy* (p. 254).

86. Saner, R. (1989). Culture bias of gestalt therapy made-in-the-USA. *The Gestalt Journal,* 12 (pp. 57–71).

87. Mahrer, A. R. (1996). *The complete guide to experiential psychotherapy.* New York: John Wiley.

88. Mahrer, *The complete guide* (p. 299).

89. Mahrer, A. R. (1991). Experiential psychotherapy, simple phobias and a recasting of prescriptive treatment. *Psychotherapy, 28* (pp. 448–451).

90. Mahrer, A. R. & Fairweather, D. R. (1993). What is "experiencing"? *The Humanistic Psychologist, 21* (pp. 2–25).

91. Mahrer, *The complete guide* (p. 215).

92. Mahrer, Experiential psychotherapy (pp. 448–451).

93. Mahrer, *The complete guide* (p. 299).

94. Mahrer, *The complete guide* (p. 270).

95. Mahrer, Experiential psychotherapy.

96. Mahrer, Experiential psychotherapy.

97. Mahrer, *The complete guide* (p. 300).

98. Mahrer, *The complete guide* (p. 344).

99. Mahrer, *The complete guide.*

Chapter 6

Behavioral and Cognitive Therapy

Behavior Therapy can be traced to the clinical observations of animals during the early part of the twentieth century. The behaviorists were interested in overt behavior, not the hidden and subjective terrain of the mind. One of the major figures was Pavlov, who classically conditioned dogs to salivate to the sound of a bell. First, a bell was paired with food, so that a connection was made between the food and the bell. After a number of such pairings, the bell alone was produced. In the absence of food, the dog would still salivate as if the food were present.

In the middle of the twentieth century, several therapists attempted to apply behavioristic principles to a wide array of emotional problems. Behavior Therapy and Humanistic Therapy were the first major psychotherapy alternatives to psychoanalysis. Behavior Therapy in particular was scorned by the psychoanalysts, who claimed that even if symptoms were eliminated, new ones would crop up and be substituted to fill the patient's mental vacuum.

One of the first important figures in Behavior Therapy is Joseph Wolpe, who devised *systematic desensitization*. As Behavior Therapy evolved, several variations of Wolpe's paradigm emerged: Implosion Therapy, visualizing the actual trauma in Exposure Therapy scenarios, and, most recently, Eye Movement Desensitization-Reprocessing (EMDR).

Cognitive Therapy is covered in the second part of this chapter. Whereas Behavior Therapy focuses on overt behavior and specifically altering readily identifiable responses, Cognitive Therapy is concerned with mental thought processes and beliefs. There is no bright line distinction between Behavior Therapy and Cognitive Therapy. In the 1970s and up to the present, many therapists are described as performing Cognitive-Behavior Therapy. Some of the behavioral techniques may be readily incorporated into the cognitive therapist's arsenal.

The most extensive version of Cognitive Therapy is exemplified in the "broad-band" Multimodal Therapy of Lazarus.[1] Although Multimodal Therapy could be credited for its flexibility and innovation, the indeterminacy of its methods seems to preclude adequate experimental testing. In addition, behavioral and psychoanalytic combination approaches are also subject to severe problems in terms of experimental validation. With the proliferation of behavioral, cognitive and psychodynamic approaches, attempts have been made to integrate the various approaches.[2] Because of the almost insurmountable difficulties in providing standardization of a blended therapy, it is almost impossible to conduct credible research on these somewhat amorphous, contourless therapies. To put it another way, the criticisms of the behavioral, cognitive and psychodynamic therapy are in essence multiplied exponentially when attempting a mode of therapy combining behavioral, cognitive and psychodynamic approaches.

SYSTEMATIC DESENSITIZATION

Based on animal research, Wolpe developed an approach to deal with anxiety.[3] Not only is anxiety one of the causative factors in psychopathology, but also such responses are learned. The idea in therapy is to "unlearn" or counter-condition fear responses. Such learning may take place as Pavlov first described, i.e., classical conditioning. In humans, a neutral stimulus, which hitherto never aroused fear, can become associated with (conditioned to) fear if it is contemporaneously paired with a fear-inducing stimulus. What is happening is conditioned avoidance to anxiety-inducing stimuli. For example, being trapped in an elevator for a number of hours may produce future fear of riding in an elevator. The focus is on overt observable events rather than hidden subterranean inferred mental events.

The first step is to teach the client a response that is incompatible with anxiety. Not too surprisingly, the patient is taught how to relax. Specifically, the patient is asked to tense and relax various muscular groups. Second, an anxiety hierarchy is constructed, which asks the client to rank anxiety-provoking stimuli from the most anxiety-inducing to the least anxiety-inducing. The scenes are based on real situations. The client is asked to imagine the least anxiety-provoking scene, followed by the second least anxiety-producing scene in the hierarchy. If there is no appreciable increase in anxiety, the client moves up the hierarchy to the last item, which is the target. The visualizations occur while the patient is in a relatively relaxed state due to the above-mentioned relaxation exercises.

After the completion of in-office systematic desensitization, the client tests the new behavior in the outside world. As a result of the disconnection between the stimulus and the fear, the patient may be able to confront the once-feared situation. The therapy includes no specific focus on the patient's childhood, no discussion of dreams, and no reference to transference or its implications.

Clinical Research

In a major study on systematic desensitization conducted over 30 years ago, Paul compared individual and group administration of this behaviorial approach against an active placebo control.[4] The special control was used in an attempt to rule out expectancy effects and allow for identification of the active ingredients of systematic desensitization.

Paul compared the effect of systematic desensitization with insight-oriented therapy in college students who experienced anxiety related to public speaking. The subjects were 50 college students enrolled in a public speaking course, divided into five groups of ten students each. Each group was given one of the following modalities: (1) individual systematic desensitization, (2) insight-oriented psychotherapy, (3) attention-placebo, (4) group desensitization (the group that was originally the wait-list control group), and (5) an untreated control group. The individual treatments were one hour in duration over a six-week period.

The focus of the insight-oriented group was an examination of the historical basis for speaking anxiety. Other problems or issues were not dealt with. The therapists administering this treatment indicated "a high level of confidence in effecting therapeutic change," even with the time constraints.[5] Systematic desensitization was based on the Wolpe approach. The main features included training in deep muscle relaxation, constructing an anxiety hierarchy list and imagining items for the list while in a state of relaxation (counter-conditioning).

In an attempt to control for placebo effects and demand characteristics, the attention-placebo group was utilized to control for changes owing to nonspecific effects. The subjects were told that they would be learning how to function better while under stress after taking a "tranquilizer." Unbeknownst to the subjects, the so-called tranquilizer was actually sodium bicarbonate. The subjects were given a task to perform for 45 minutes and had no verbal interaction with the therapist. The subjects' pulse and pupillary responses were taken.

The nine sessions of group desensitization consisted of discussions, relaxation training and construction of anxiety hierarchies. The group interactions focused on building self-confidence, as well as becoming aware of the interpersonal aspects and effects of interpersonal relationships.

The results indicated that group methods could be successfully applied to systematic desensitization of public speaking performance anxiety. In fact, the students in the group generally demonstrated more anxiety reduction compared to the individual desensitization, insight therapy and the attention-placebo. A two-year follow-up also reflected the improvements in the desensitization groups, although on some measures, the placebo-attention group was somewhat improved. Two years later there was no evidence of symptom substitution or relapse.[6]

IMPLOSION AND EXPOSURE THERAPY

Both systematic desensitization and implosion have been developed from analogical research on animals. Thus, an animal who learns to fear an electric shock when it is paired with a buzzer may continue to respond to the buzzer, even though the animal is not shocked again. The animal never learns that it will not receive a shock because it manages to either avoid or escape from the area where it was given the shock. Implosion, however, seems to be the flip side of desensitization. Namely, rather than reduce anxiety incrementally with incompatible responses, Implosion Therapy presents stimuli that increase and enhance fear. The patient is made to confront the most imaginable or unimaginable fear. Although attempts have been made to combine implosion with psychodynamics, the context of this discussion is restricted to the behavioral approach.

The first advocate of Implosion Therapy was Stampl.[7] The client not only is immersed in imagining fearful situations but is asked to enhance or exaggerate the fears. For example, a patient who could not swim and was afraid of water was asked to imagine taking a bath without a life preserver and to see herself going under the water. What generally happens is that, when the patient "learns" that nothing bad occurs after intense increases in anxiety, the anxiety decreases. The patient must learn to confront the fear in order to experience the lack of aversive consequences. Thus, the patient or animal is no longer rewarded with anxiety reduction when avoiding the feared stimulus. In Implosion Therapy, unlike Systematic Desensitization, the patient is therefore not restricted to visualizing just the feared event or image.

Clinical Research

Many of the clinical studies involved treatment of traumatized individuals. In a study by Cooper and Crum, 26 Vietnam War veterans served as subjects.[8] At least ten participants dropped out of the study, and two more were not included in the data analysis. Thus, only 14 of the original 26 completed the study. All had diagnoses of post-traumatic stress disorder (PTSD) with symptoms of nightmares, flashbacks, re-experiencing of trauma, and/or intrusive thoughts. Half of the group received what was described as standard treatment, while the experimental group received imaginal flooding, which is essentially similar to implosion. Four subjects in each half were receiving psychotropic medication.

Subjects in the flooding group received from six to fourteen 90-minute sessions. A number of scenes were presented starting with the least distressing. If the anxiety proved overwhelming, however, the patient was switched to positive scenes and provided with relaxation in order to reduce agitation before the end of the session. A description was not given for what constitutes the standard therapy. Both the experimental group and the standard group also received an educational aspect, which consisted of lectures and discussions focused on their social isolation upon returning from the war.

As a result of the flooding experience, patients showed more improvement in several areas, including decreases in re-experiencing symptoms and sleep disturbance. Psychological assessment procedures such as the Beck Depression Inventory indicated that levels of depression and current levels of anxiety symptoms were not significantly changed. In addition, the flooding procedure failed to reduce heart rate during a presentation of sights and sounds of the Vietnam War. Because of mixed results, the small number of subjects and the dropout rate, this study offers very limited support for the effectiveness of imaginal flooding.

Implosion or Flooding Therapy was provided to a group of 24 Vietnam veterans.[9] Each of the eleven patients in the flooding group was given two or three initial sessions in relaxation training. The flooding lasted 45 minutes, preceded and followed by relaxation training. In order to enhance the fear arousal, each patient was asked to visualize the entire traumatic event with a special attention to bodily injury, abandonment, rejection and loss of control. The wait-list control group consisted of thirteen subjects who received no psychotherapy treatment; however, ten of these subjects were taking psychotropic medication. A variety of measures administered included the Beck Depression Inventory, the Zung Depression Scale and the MMPI.

The people in the implosion group showed less depression and short-term anxiety after the treatment compared to the control group. The results were seen as confirming the avoidance model, i.e., anxiety-reduction occurred by exposure to and confronting the traumatic episodes. By experiencing the traumatic memories, the fear attached to the memory became extinguished. An additional theoretical explanation was offered, which included aspects of information processing and extended to aspects of Cognitive Therapy, i.e., challenging irrational belief and disabling attitudes.

DIRECT EXPOSURE THERAPY

The necessary ingredients for effective treatment of anxiety or PTSD were twofold: (1) The memories of the trauma must be activated or engaged. (2) New information must be introduced that is incompatible with the trauma. One of the unique features in this study was that facial expression of fear was used as the indication of fear activation. The researchers rated physical or anatomical facial displays that comport with signs of fear.[10]

A total of 12 subjects were included in the study, all of whom had been either physically or sexually assaulted. There was no placebo or control group. The therapeutic treatment involved twice weekly 90-minute sessions over a nine-week period. The subjects were asked to re-experience the emotions related to the assaults, including all the attendant events. Each subject closed his eyes and related the incident in the present tense. During the session, the subject's level of anxiety was monitored by Subjective Units of Distress (SUD). The subject continued to recount the trauma until the SUD diminished somewhat.

After the exposure treatment, all twelve clients showed some reduction in symptoms. Thus, repeated reliving of physical assault in one's mind's eye decreases post-trauma symptoms. Greater pretreatment trauma was positively correlated with more intense facial fear expression. This finding implicates the need for fear activation as a necessary ingredient in reducing the symptoms related to experienced trauma.

EYE MOVEMENT DESENSITIZATION-REPROCESSING (EMDR)

A newly developed method of dealing with the aftermath of trauma was discovered in 1987 by Francine Shapiro.[11] While walking in the park one day, she noticed that some disturbing thoughts had suddenly disappeared. And when the disturbing thoughts were brought back to the mind's eye, they were not as upsetting. She next noticed that when the disturbing thoughts were brought up, there was spontaneous eye movement. As the thoughts disappeared, the negative affect also diminished. The next step was to intentionally make the eye movements. The final step was to use her hand or finger to guide the eye movements to duplicate the spontaneous eye movements. Eye Movement Desensitization-Reprocessing is a technique in which the therapist moves his fingers in front of the patient with the intention of defusing the negative affect associated with traumatic memories.

A tentative theoretical basis for EMDR has been proposed to explain the rapidity of the achieved results. The theoretical model is called Accelerated Information Processing. Psychopathology is seen as developing from prior life experiences. The pathological memories are "represented by dysfunctional information," which is not only physiologically stored in some fashion, but is able to be accessed and transformed by means of the EMDR procedures. Blockage of innate information processing is the reason that the mental trauma remains.[12] EMDR is the key that unlocks the door to the negative affect, behavior and cognition related to the mental trauma and memories. Shapiro states that her theory converges with the major approaches in psychotherapy: namely, the psychodynamic, humanistic, behavioral and cognitive.[13] Despite making reference to constructs as "neuro networks,"[14] Shapiro indicates that the efficacy of EMDR is based on the validity of the physiological model she is presenting.[15] Shapiro notes that "the successful clinical results achieved with EMDR by the approximately 10,000 clinicians trained to date indicate the wide range of applicability" of EMDR.[16]

Case Reports

The excitement generated by EMDR has led to several clinical trials using the technique in single subjects. The founder of Systematic Desensitization even tried his hand, so to speak, at EMDR.[17] A second report was on a Vietnam War veteran.[18]

The Case of Failed Psychoanalysis

The patient was a 43-year-old corporate executive who was first treated by Abrams in 1989.[19] Her presenting problem included difficulties in getting along with co-workers and fears of being alone. Her fears apparently stemmed from a rape in 1980. For the first 15 sessions, Abrams used psychodynamically oriented therapy. Because of the client's dissatisfaction with treatment progress, she began to miss appointments. At this point, Wolpe was called into the case, and after his examination, the patient received a formal diagnosis of PTSD.

The first behavioral technique was to give the patient training in muscle relaxation. Some improvement took place, but it was not noteworthy. As a result, Abrams and Wolpe decided to try EMDR. A hierarchy of anxiety-producing scenes was developed, which reflected subjective units of anxiety. The various scenes were visualized while the EMDR procedure was employed. This included four sets of 25 finger movements in front of the patient's eyes. As a result of the sessions, her ability to travel outside the home improved markedly, she was getting along better at work, and she was not afraid of losing control. In many ways, this person was greatly improved in that she could enjoy walking alone on the beach, reduced her drinking almost completely, became more sociable and was generally less phobic.

The Case of the Vietnam Veteran

A 46-year-old man was suffering from severe guilt and intrusive images of a helicopter explosion. He also experienced "numbing, isolation, irritability alternating with panic attacks, flashbacks and dissociative symptoms."[20] These post-traumatic stress disorder symptoms were described as incapacitating. Over the course of the 24 years he suffered from PTSD, he was hospitalized eight times and received traditional supportive therapy and desensitization. No treatment, including antidepressants, had been successful.

An initial session of EMDR focused on the traumatic memory related to the death of his friend during the Vietnam War. After 30 minutes, there was significant improvement. Based on the patient's self-report, he felt a "sense of calm" about the traumatic episode. Because of this success, a second memory was dealt with. After one hour, the patient no longer felt distressed when recalling the previously traumatic incidents. He continued to feel better the following day, and he was able to sleep well for the first time in 20 years. The dramatic improvement was seen in a nine-month follow-up.

Clinical Research

There has been a plethora of studies on EMDR that contain at least one experimental and one control group. A few examples are explored here. Because of the large number of studies that have emerged, the three selected here are not necessarily representative but serve to illustrate several methodological points.

A relatively large sample was included in an experiment by Wilson, Becker and Tinker.[21] Eighty participants were assigned to either an immediate EMDR treatment or a delayed EMDR treatment group. The traumas experienced by these individuals included physical or mental abuse, deaths of significant others, rape and molestations. All of the participants met at least one symptom criterion for PTSD. Outcome measures (dependent variables) included SUDs, Impact of Event Scale, State-Trait Anxiety Inventory and the Symptom Check List (SCL-90-R).

Both groups showed improvement after three sessions of EMDR treatment. The positive effects of treatment were maintained at the 90-day follow-up. Thus, the authors concluded that "EMDR was effective in decreasing symptoms and anxiety associated with traumatic memory."[22] The authors also note that nonspecific treatment effects may have played an unknown role in this study. There was not a so-called placebo control but rather a type of wait-list control.

In Sanderson and Carpenter (1992), EMDR was contrasted with an *image confrontation* group.[23] The subjects had complaints of phobias: e.g., spiders, insects, flying, vomiting. Both groups were given seven sets of EMDR for 20 seconds. Before and after each set, the SUD scale was given in response to the feared image. In order to simplify the study, the Validity of Cognition Scale was omitted. The participants were asked to focus on the most disturbing image while the "experimenter's" finger was held at eye level about twelve to fourteen inches from their faces. The EMDR subjects tracked the finger as it moved back and forth horizontally. The image confrontation subjects kept their eyes closed and motionless. These subjects were asked to image with their eyes shut.

The results indicated significant improvement in both groups in terms of reduction of a feared object or a feared image. Based on this study, it appears that eye movements do not play a role in the clinical improvement. The implication is that repeated visual imagery of the trauma may be the effective tool that leads to reduction in phobias and possibly post-traumatic stress disorder.

A more sophisticated experiment compared three procedures: Image Habituation Training (IHT), Applied Muscle Relaxation (AMR) and EMDR.[24] People in the IHT group listened to continuous taped descriptions of their traumas for 60 minutes per day; people in the AMR group practiced relaxation techniques for two 20-minute periods per day; and the EMDR group followed the protocol described by Shapiro.[25] There was also a wait-list control group. Approximately 80 percent of subjects were diagnosed as PTSD, and all reported a traumatic experience and at least one re-experiencing or intrusion of symptoms as well as hyper-arousal.

All three groups showed clinical improvement. There were reductions in their PTSD symptoms, and at a three-month follow-up, only 30 percent were given this diagnosis. A general conclusion is that no one particular treatment was superior to the others.

Critique and Analysis of Behavioral Approaches to the Treatment of Anxiety

Generalization of Results

One of the most sophisticated designs in the history of psychotherapy research is the above-mentioned study by Paul.[26] The contention that systematic desensitization is superior to other forms of therapy needs to be tempered by one significant fact—namely, the issue in Paul's study was whether speech anxiety could be reduced in a sample of college students. In this extensive attempt to provide for experimental controls of unwanted artifacts, it appears that the study has limited generalizability. Thus, the particular complaint in his study probably would not warrant major scrutiny by the mental health profession, nor would a unitary symptom of speech anxiety necessarily be a sign of a mental disorder. Lastly, the fear related to public speaking does not rise to the level of the trauma addressed by the other research covered in this chapter.

The bulk of research to date has focused on anxiety reduction and management of post-traumatic stress disorder. Thus, if the DSM-IV is to be any guide, behavior-oriented techniques do not deal with the overwhelming number of mental disorders.

Implosion Therapy Appears to Have Imploded

The more recent attempts at Implosion Therapy (i.e., Cooper & Crum[27]) seem quite tame by comparison to Stampl's original approach.[28] At times, there appears to be little difference between implosion (or flooding) and Direct Exposure Therapy. Since Direct Exposure Therapy is less drastic and asks the patient to imagine the actual trauma, it may be a more effective way to battle anxiety-related symptoms. Comparative studies that include exposure-type groups suggest that people with traumatic stressors could be treated with less drastic methods (e.g., Sanderson and Carpenter).[29]

EMDR May Be a Technique Without an Adequate Explanation

EMDR is accessible to clinical research, and Shapiro and other investigators have conducted numerous studies on it.[30] In the few examples cited, there is no clear superiority of EMDR over other methods of trauma-related anxiety reduction. What appears abundantly clear is that EMDR does not require eye movements in order to be effective. If so, the name of this procedure alone seems somewhat nonsensical. As noted in just the few studies in the above section, there can be apparent clinical improvement with one's eyes closed.

Whether there is a theory that can explain the results is also not clear. If eye movements are not necessary to this procedure, then the underlying neurobiological explanation needs to be altered. Furthermore, as noted, exposure techniques appear to be as effective as EMDR. Without further research, it is too early to tell whether EMDR is truly a major breakthrough or just another crazy therapy.[31]

Brevity of Treatment

Like the cognitive therapies (see below), the behavioral approaches are usually conducted over a period of several months to perhaps one year. To the extent that there is clinical improvement, it tends to belie the need for dealing with issues of transference, for example. The patient appears to play a large role in the treatments, particularly when assessing the level of anxiety by way of the SUD.

Direct exposure to a trauma appears to have some promise, but as yet there is no clear-cut explanatory concept. The possibility remains that the variants of exposure (flooding, Direct Exposure, EMDR and systematic desensitization) may all rest on the patient's expectancies and hopes. With further research certain types of trauma or fears may be reliably reduced by a presentation of the fear-inducing or traumatic stimuli. At present, however, it is odd that theoretical models advocating either anxiety-reduction, on the one hand, or anxiety increase, on the other hand, seem at times to produce an apparent change in behavior.

COGNITIVE THERAPY

Two major cognitive therapies have developed over the last 30 to 40 years: the cognitive approach of Aaron Beck[32] and the Rational Emotive

Behavior Therapy of Albert Ellis.[33] These two approaches have also been called cognitive-behavioral in that there is a basic cognitive approach, which can easily incorporate various behavioral techniques. More recently, an Interpersonal Therapy has been presented as an alternative to psychodynamic therapy.[34] Interpersonal Therapy is presented in this chapter since it appears to be more closely aligned to Cognitive Therapy than to its reputed psychoanalytic predecessors.

THE RATIONAL EMOTIVE BEHAVIOR THERAPY (REBT) OF ALBERT ELLIS

At the forefront of the anti-psychoanalytic approach has been Albert Ellis, a prolific author, psychotherapist and lecturer. As of 1994, he had already written over 500 articles and 60 books.[35] Originally, the therapy he developed was termed Rational-Emotive; despite the name change, the therapy appears to be clearly in the cognitive sphere.

Background

The origins of Rational Emotive Behavior Therapy (REBT) are multifaceted. Ellis gives credit to ancient Asian and Greek philosophers as well as twentieth-century psychotherapists, including Alfred Adler.[36] Ellis was originally a psychoanalyst but ultimately rejected the psychodynamic approach. In the newly developed REBT, he did not attempt to analyze a patient's transference or dwell on the past. The motto of REBT is: So as a person thinks, that is how he or she feels. A person's cognitive interpretation of events will determine his or her attitude and emotions.

Although REBT has had several precursors such as Adlerian psychotherapy and some of Jung's ideas, it diverges sharply from all other non-cognitive approaches. REBT does not concern itself with the warmth of the therapist or unconditional positive regard, does not look to dreams for material and is generally not concerned with the unconscious.[37] Similar to the experiential and humanistic methods, the REBT therapist may jump right into the issues and not take a preliminary or a comprehensive intake history. Most important, REBT deals with the philosophical basis of neurosis—namely, a person's belief in certain "shoulds" or "musts."

Rational Emotive Behavior Therapy is fairly straightforward in terms of assessing the problem and how to effect change. The therapist deals with (1) activating events, such as the person's inability to get good grades, and (2) beliefs about the activating events. An example of an irrational belief is: it's awful that I can't get good grades. The third aspect is (3) the emotional consequences.

REBT views emotional upsets as stemming largely from irrational beliefs. Thus, a person believes that something "ought" to be, and if it isn't, then it's a catastrophe. The last step for the therapist is to actively intervene and

(4) dispute the irrational beliefs. The therapist might inform the patient that it is unfortunate not to be a good student and get good grades, but it is not a horrible circumstance or a catastrophe. Thus, what is initially perceived as negative, impacting on the person's view of himself (e.g., I'm also a bad person) and perhaps generating feelings of worthlessness is put into a new light and perspective by the active confrontation of the therapist.

The REBT therapist may employ a number of external behavior methods in order to help the patient disprove the irrational belief. The techniques might include assertiveness training, role-playing and risk-taking assignments, such as where a person might ask someone for a date, throwing oneself in a possibly humiliating experience. Ellis has suggested going to a large department store at 12 noon and yelling out "it's 12 o'clock," or asking a obvious question about directions.

Case Report

A 25-year-old woman entered therapy and received six individual sessions, 24 weeks of group REBT and one weekend encounter.[38] Ellis notes that she was fairly attractive but was ashamed of her body and did little dating. Her focus was on her work. Her current problems included overdrinking and overeating. Aware of her constant drinking, the president of her company requested that she see a therapist.

Ellis provides a verbatim transcript of the first session.[39] The cognitive aspect of therapy dealt with her belief that she had to be perfect and immune from criticism. She was given emotional support during the marathon and group sessions to freely vent her real feelings. In the behavioral arena, she was given an assignment that included speaking to men in public places with the goal of overcoming her fears of being rejected.[40]

The therapy has a didactic-educational, Socratic quality (italics in original).

Client Statement 27: I can't imagine existing, or that there would be any reason for existing without a purpose.

Therapist Statement 29: No, No, No. . . . You see, you said a sane sentence and an *insane* sentence. . . . What you really mean is "It *would be better* if I had a purpose."

Therapist Statement 30: But then you magically jump to "Therefore, I *should*."

Therapist Statement 35: Whatever you *believe* you feel. . . . Practically every time you're disturbed, you're changing *it would be better to a must*. That's all neurosis is.

According to Ellis, after the brief intervention, the client showed remarkable improvement: She stopped drinking, lost 25 pounds, was less condemning of herself, began to make close friends, had satisfactory sexual relations, and only rarely made herself feel guilty or depressed. A two-and-a-half-year follow-up revealed that she had married one of her boyfriends, and all was going well in her marriage, job and social life.

Research

Several so-called meta-analyses have been performed on REBT. A number of methodological problems have been highlighted in previous studies that attempt to demonstrate the effectiveness of what was then termed Rational Emotive Therapy.[41] Most significantly, the independent variable was not clearly delineated. Thus, it was not clear what, if anything, was being varied or manipulated in order to produce the particular outcome. A particular result could be due to any number of factors, which may or may not be related to the specific elements of Rational Emotive Therapy.

The alleged mediator, the irrational beliefs, are also ambiguous. Prior to 1990, Dryden et al. concluded that "there are numerous indications that definition and measurement of RET for research purposes has been inadequate."[42] Ellis defends his approach by claiming that some of the unimpressive results are due to experimenters not really doing RET.[43] Apparently, both a real kind of RET and a bootleg copy exist. Needless to say, if the psychotherapy approach cannot be replicated, then the results are due to a host of uncontrolled idiosyncratic factors.

What Dryden et al. attempted to do first was to assess adherence or integrity to the RET methods. By examining 41 outcome studies, it was not possible to determine with any great degree of assurance the "purity of interventions." For example, in at least 22 of the studies, there was no information as to whether manuals were used to guide the therapist/experimenters. When manuals were used, often little published information was provided.

Lyons and Woods conducted another meta-analysis on 70 studies.[44] To be included, RET needed to be compared with a baseline, a control group or another psychotherapy. Some studies were rejected because of uninterpretable statistics or inadequate information regarding critical elements of any study—the actual treatment and experimental procedures.

After subjecting the studies to a number of complex statistical analyses, the authors concluded that the data show RET to be an effective form of psychotherapy. The next sentence in the article states that there were no differences between RET, Cognitive Therapy and Behavior Therapy.[45] Despite the sweeping conclusion, in the context of discussing therapist experience and effectiveness, it is admitted that "there is no guarantee that the therapy being used was actually RET as practiced and taught by the Institute of Rational-Emotive Therapy.[46] Finally, it is pointed out that over 80 percent of the studies did not report follow-up data. Thus, there is little information on the long-term effectiveness of Rational Emotive Behavior Therapy.

Critique of REBT

The only rational conclusion, therefore, is that the effectiveness of Rational Emotive Therapy has not been demonstrated. Some people may improve, but as shown in the *Consumer Reports* article discussed in Chapter 1, merely showing improvement does not demonstrate that psychotherapy is responsible for the alleged gains in mental status or a person's feelings or change in attitudes.

Imagine that the effectiveness of Prozac is being evaluated, but the experimenter informs the scientific community that it is not known if the pills being given are actually *Prozac*! Imagine further that the clinician has no way of determining that the actual ingredients in Prozac are responsible for any alleged behavioral or physiological change. If this state of affairs is unacceptable in the drug research area, why should psychotherapy research be more lax?

Several limitations apply to how emotional problems are dealt with and the type of patients seen in therapy. The question is whether Ellis trivializes severe emotional trauma. Can it be that horrendous events such as a rape can be viewed within the context of unfortunate events but not as a catastrophe? Is getting a poor grade in a class on the same level as getting fired from a job? For people who do not suffer from moderate or extreme trauma, the clash between therapist and patient may be helpful in producing a new perspective. But in the instance of real and severe trauma, it appears that REBT trivializes the underlying events.[47]

Moreover, REBT may be useful only for fairly verbal, higher functioning patients who are capable of entering into a philosophical debate with their instructor. In this view then, REBT would fit into the Department of Philosophy or Education and would not be in the purview of psychology or psychotherapy.

BECK'S COGNITIVE BEHAVIOR THERAPY

Developing along similar lines as REBT is Beck's Cognitive Behavior Therapy (BCBT). How a person thinks is a major determinant of how one feels and behaves.[48] Beck's approach is short-term, here and now, and it avoids looking into a person's alleged unconscious causes of psychopathology. One of the major innovations and hallmarks of Beck's Cognitive Behavior Therapy is its brevity. This highly structured form of Cognitive-Behavior Therapy is short-term and lasts twelve to sixteen weeks.[49]

At least three major distinctions can be made between BCBT and REBT. First, BCBT does not view a person's distorted cognition as irrational as does Ellis. The perspective is that a person may have dysfunctional thoughts.

At the root of psychopathology are core beliefs.[50] A core belief is the most central idea about the self that develops in childhood.

Second, BCBT, unlike REBT, maintains that various mental disorders have their own typical cognitive contents. Thus, REBT maintains that virtually all emotional disorders stem from the same or similar sets of underlying irrational beliefs. Beck's Cognitive Therapy, on the other hand, asserts that "each disorder has its own typical cognitive content."[51] Thus, the cognitive elements are different in panic disorder, depression or anxiety, for example. The cognitive error in depression is a negative view of self, experience and the future, whereas in anxiety disorder, the distortion is viewed as a "sense of physical or psychological danger."[52] REBT, on the other hand, assumes that a similar set of irrational beliefs is at the basis of all of these mental disorders.

Last, there is less argumentation and debate in BCBT and more of a collaborative effort with the patient. Ellis has a "direct confrontational style, while Beck's approach is essentially Socratic."[53] It is a matter of more tact versus less tact. As shown in the example above, Ellis directly attacks the alleged irrational or distorted cognition. Beck, on the other hand, helps the client discover the distorted cognition.

Numerous behavioral techniques may be used: progressive relaxation, guided imagery, activity scheduling, behavioral rehearsal, exposure therapy, role-playing and homework assignments.

Case Report

A 21-year-old male college student had complaints of insomnia, speech difficulties and symptoms of anxiety.[54] His speech problems were heightened prior to exams or athletic events.

The early session included history-taking and forming a diagnosis. The therapist's task is to show how the patient's cognition contributed to his distress.

Therapist: What thoughts go through your mind, let's say, when you don't do so well at swimming?
Patient: I think people think much less of me if I'm not on top.

Thus, the patient was able to acknowledge that his mood depended on what others thought of him.

Visual imagery was used so that the patient could imagine being less anxious when well prepared. Homework assignments included recording automatic thoughts and recognizing cognitive distortions. For example, if the patient ruminated about the exam, he offered a retort, "Thinking about the exam is not going to make a difference at this point. I did study."

In the later sessions, the focus turned to social interaction. The patient practiced initiating conversations as well as being more tactful. At the conclusion of therapy, the patient was able to pursue interests that were not related to achievement.

Clinical Research

Beck has proposed that a major component of his Cognitive Therapy for depression is changing negative underlying thoughts.[55] A recent study attempted to ascertain whether there might be a more parsimonious explanation of the efficacy of Beck's Cognitive Behavior Therapy.[56] Three treatments for depression were compared. The first treatment included only behavioral activation (BA). A second treatment included BA plus modifying automatic thoughts (AT). The third group included the full complement of Cognitive Therapy, i.e., BA plus AT, and identifying and modifying core negative thoughts.

The sample consisted of 152 patients who met the DSM-III-R criteria for major depression and scored at least 20 on the Beck Depression Inventory and 14 or more on the Hamilton Rating Scale for Depression. The patients were randomly assigned to one of the three groups. There was an equivalence in each group on the following: number of previous episodes of depression, presence or absence of dysthymic severity of depression, gender and marital status.

The therapy was delivered by four experienced cognitive therapists. Each treatment group had its own manual. Protocol adherence was calibrated by listening to 20 percent of the audiotaped sessions.

The BA Condition

The focus was on activating patients in their natural environment. This intervention included monitoring daily activities, assessing pleasure or mastery when accomplishing various tasks, cognitive rehearsal wherein the patient imagines engaging in the activities but finds obstacles to achieving the desired result, assertiveness training to improve social skill deficits and discussion of various problems related to depression such as insomnia. The entire 20 sessions used only BA.

BA Plus AT Condition

The focus was on identifying and modifying cognitive distortions that manifested in dysfunctional automatic thoughts. Cognitive Therapy conceptualizes that negative perception of events precipitates depression. The techniques used to alter dysfunctional thinking are: recording of these thoughts by way of a diary, attempting to ascertain what thought preceded a mood shift and assessing the validity of the dysfunctional thoughts.

CT Condition

The focus was on identifying and modifying the basic underlying cognitive distortions that allegedly cause depression. Thus, a person may hold the core belief that he or she is incompetent. Interventions to modify a core belief include: identification of alternative assumptions and homework assignments both to ascertain if the patient is using the core beliefs in his or her daily life and to try out other assumptions.

The major conclusion was that the full Cognitive Therapy (CT) was no more effective in reducing depression than either of the two components, BA or AT. Thus, people who received BA alone showed decreases in depression at the same level as those who were also taught coping skills (AT) to counter depression. Finally, both groups (BA and BA plus AT) improved as much as the subjects who received the so-called full complement of Cognitive Therapy. These results imply that dealing with core beliefs as a necessary precursor to behavioral or attitudinal change does not appear warranted.

Critique of Beck's Cognitive Behavior Therapy

Can the special ingredients that are essential to Cognitive Behavior Therapy be identified? If not, then improvement as a result of Beck's Cognitive Behavior Therapy may be due to placebo or general verbal interactive factors between therapist and patient. This argument is also pertinent to the comparisons to Beck's Cognitive Behavior Therapy and Interpersonal Therapy (see below). A meta-analysis of 43 studies on depression revealed no difference between drug treatment, Cognitive Behavior Therapy and other types of therapy as assessed by the Beck Depression Inventory. Thus, these studies "taken as a whole . . . do not provide strong evidence for specific action in cognitive therapy for depression."[57] It has not been determined what, if any, element is necessary for effecting the change observed in the cognitive treatment of depression.

Although Beck has provided a coherent and testable theory regarding the etiology of mental disorders and how to bring about change, little support exists for the major tenet of his theory. As demonstrated by Jacobson et al., there was a failure to find evidence that the basic change mechanisms were needed.[58] A simplified version of behavioral-type therapy was able to produce a decrease in depression. As noted by the Jacobson study, both the theory and therapy are in need of revision. The implication is that self-administered or peer support groups may be more cost-effective and as helpful as formal psychotherapy.[59]

INTERPERSONAL THERAPY (IPT)

A new psychotherapy that burst into the mainstream is called Interpersonal Psychotherapy (IPT).[60] The precursors to IPT are psychoanalytic, including the work of Harry Stack Sullivan and Adolph Meyer. Sullivan focuses on interpersonal relations[61] whereas Meyer viewed psychopathology within the context of an individual attempting to adapt to the environment.[62] Although there is psychoanalytic heritage, it appears that the focus on current environmental and social stressors is more closely aligned to the cognitive-behavioral approach.[63] Interpersonal Therapy does not attempt to resurrect the past but rather focuses on current issues. IPT is short term, usually twelve to sixteen sessions, with specific goals for each section of the therapeutic relationship. It features no discussion or analysis of transference or attempt to ferret unconscious dynamics. Whereas Beck's Cognitive Behavior Therapy and REBT attempt to challenge negative self-images, IPT views dysfunctional self-perceptions as part of the symptoms package, which are alleviated as the interpersonal problems are resolved.[64]

The initial sessions of Interpersonal Therapy in the treatment of depression focus on (1) establishing the specific diagnosis, e.g., dysthymia; (2) taking a comprehensive medical history and an interpersonal inventory; (3) explaining the nature of the depressive disorder and the person's role in it; (4) establishing the interpersonal treatment areas and relating them to the diagnosis; and (5) forming a treatment alliance, which includes a psychoeducational approach as well as offering hope.

The diagnosis of depression and other mental disorders begins with a psychiatric and mental status evaluation, psychological testing and a psychosocial history. In contrast to a number of other therapeutic approaches, IPT attempts to have a firm grasp on both diagnosis and some of the current factors related to the depression. Special attention is given to the patient's important past and present relationships.[65]

Once the diagnosis is assured, the therapist explains that the various somatic, cognitive and emotional symptoms are a treatable condition. The patient may be shown the DSM-III as a way to demonstrate that the patient has a particular disorder. The psycho-educational aspect involves explaining the nature and course of the mental disorder. One significant aspect in IPT is the imparting of hope. Thus, the therapist must convey that the patient has a good chance of improving. The patient is informed that dysthymia, for example, is a treatable mental illness and IPT is an effective treatment.[66]

The second phase of treatment encompasses the fourth through twelfth sessions. The goal in these sessions is to alleviate the depression and to help the patient explore and reconceptualize her identified interpersonal problems. The main area of difficulty could involve grief, interpersonal disputes, role transitions or interpersonal deficits.

In the IPT framework, grief refers to the death of a close relative or friend.

Generally, an acute grief reaction is not the focus of concern in IPT. Chronic grief, however, requires professional attention.

Interpersonal disputes may arise owing to feelings of inadequacy on the part of the dysthymic patient who may remain in an unsatisfying relationship, and be afraid to speak up and perhaps rock the boat.

Role transition refers to "difficulties in coping with life changes that require an alteration in one's social or occupational status or self view."[67] Interpersonal deficits may involve social isolation, a sense of inadequacy, a lack of self-assertion and a guilty inability to express anger.

The last four sessions (thirteen to sixteen) focus on termination. The patient gives up any reliance on the therapist and learns that she must deal with her situation on an independent basis. The interpersonal issues are reviewed, and the improvements made are consolidated.

Case Report: "Changing Long-Standing Behaviors That Are Contributing to Dysthymia"

A single, 29-year-old Hispanic woman entered treatment for depression that she felt was out of control.[68] She feared that her boyfriend would desert her. Role dispute was selected as the initial problem area. The patient needed to be able to re-negotiate the lack of reciprocity in the relationship with her boyfriend. This patient deferred to her parents in an attempt to avoid disapproval. The therapist conceptualized her interpersonal problem as follows: The patient needed to depend on someone else for sustenance and, in so doing, would compromise her own feelings. As a result, she felt less than competent and adequate.

Her maladaptive interpersonal style was clarified. The patient was then helped to relinquish her life-long dependency on others in order to obtain emotional stability. At termination, the patient's depression had significantly decreased, even though her boyfriend left her at the time of her seventh session. At the end of twelve sessions, the patient was able to enter a Ph.D. program and obtain a professional-level job.

Clinical Research

In a major investigation of depression, Beck's Cognitive Behavior Therapy and IPT were chosen as the gold standards.[69] The research was sponsored by the National Institute of Mental Health (NIMH) and was a multi-site study designed to assess the value of collaborative work and to evaluate the effectiveness of Beck's version of Cognitive Behavior Therapy and Klerman's Interpersonal Therapy. The patients in this study were non-bipolar, nonpsychotic depressed outpatients. To help determine the efficacy of the psychotherapy approaches, a standard psychopharmacological treatment of proven effectiveness was used as comparison. A tricylic antidepressant, Imipramine, was given in a double-blind portion of this study along with clinical management. The latter was described as a type of mini-supportive therapy.

To be included in the study, the patients had to satisfy rigorous criteria. All patients were interviewed and given the Hamilton Rating Scale for Depression. The participants needed to have the required symptoms for a major depression. Patients with various other mental disorders were excluded. A total of 250 patients passed the various screening measures and were included in the study.

There were four manualized treatment conditions: (1) Cognitive Behavior Therapy (CBT) as described by Beck, (2) Interpersonal Therapy (IPT) as described by Klerman, (3) Imipramine-Clinical Management (ICM) in which medication was given along with clinical management, and (4) Placebo-Clinical Management (Pla-CM) in which a placebo pill was given along with clinical management, which included information regarding the use and side effects of the medication, encouragement and support, and direct advice if required.

The patients were assessed before, during and after treatment. Four scales were used in the assessment of change in the level of depression: the Hamilton Rating Scale for Depression, the Global Assessment of Functioning, the Beck Depression Inventory and the Hopkins Symptoms Checklist-90 Total Score (HSCL-90T).

Data analyses were conducted on patients who completed at least twelve sessions and fifteen weeks of treatment. It appears that data for only 155 patients were included in the statistical computations.[70] The analysis did not take into effect differential attrition rates across the groups.

The results indicate significant pre- to post-treatment scores in all groups including the Pla-CM. For example, in the Beck Depression Inventory, the CBT patients had an initial score of 26.8 and a termination score of 10.2. The Pla-CM had an initial score of 28.1 and a termination score of 11.0. Similarly, on the Global Assessment of Functioning, all groups improved, including the Pla-CM.

The effects of exercise on depression were compared with the interpersonal and cognitive approaches as well as a meditation/relaxation group.[71] The subjects were given a number of assessment batteries, including the Symptom Checklist (SCL)-Revised; a Structural Analysis of Social Behavior, which measures self-image; a Social Adjustment Self-Report Questionnaire, which measures functioning in different role domains such as work, school and family patterns; the Cornell Medical Index, which covers somatic and physical health; and a role rating questionnaire, which looked at the cognitive aspects of depression including negative self-views. The measures were repeated at termination after twelve weeks and at a nine-month follow-up.

In the exercise group, the subjects met with mental health professionals who had experience in personal exercise. There were two 45-minute sessions each week, which consisted of a warmup, breathing and stretching, and aerobic walking/running. If subjects brought up psychological problems, the therapist focused only on the physical exercise.

The meditation/relaxation group involved weekly two-hour group sessions in which subjects were taught to relax in order to reduce stress. There were readings from meditation texts, meditation in silence, and Yoga stretching exercises.

Group therapy included elements of interpersonal and Cognitive Therapy. The sessions were held for twelve two-hour sessions. The focus was on helping the members to recognize and change problem communication patterns such as submissiveness and withdrawal. There were psycho-educational lectures that focused on the cognitive errors that may induce depression.

The results indicated that subjects in each group showed a decrease in depressive symptoms at the end of twelve weeks. Thus, there were improvements in global functioning, as well as interpersonal and somatic problems, anxiety and tension. Perhaps even more significant, depression was reduced at the end of the nine-month follow-up. The overall results did not show any differences between the three treatment groups in terms of effectiveness.

Critique and Analysis of Interpersonal Therapy

On the positive side, research on IPT as well as Beck's Cognitive Behavior Therapy in the NIMH study was a serious attempt to compare at least two types of therapies. There were manuals and training so that there could be some degree of assurance that the clinicians were adhering to the specific mode of treatment. There were extensive pre- and post-test assessments. The results implied that clinical improvement could be obtained in a four-month period. This is a far cry from what is allegedly required in some instances of psychoanalysis, for example.

Unfortunately, despite the incredible amount of effort that went into this research, there are at least four major criticisms. Paradoxically, the better controlled the study, the less likely it can be generalized to private practice in the field. Thus, very few clinicians will record their patient's diagnosis in as great detail or do such extensive follow-up. Furthermore, even in the presence of manuals, clinicians tend to do their own thing, so it cannot be verified that what happens in an antiseptic and monitored research project will carry over to a typical clinical practice.

The second problem is that Beck's therapy and IPT may really be alternative versions of Cognitive Therapy. On the one hand, there is emphasis on a person's thinking, and on the other hand, there is focus on a person's perspective in social interactions. So what emerges are two examples of the alleged effectiveness of Cognitive Therapy. Thus, this study really did not address what active or critical elements may underlie change in one's mental status.

A major problem in any study is the dropout rate. It appears that out of

250 patients only 150 completed the study. This represented a 40 percent attrition rate. In a short period of time, this meant a significant loss of research participants.

Finally, the placebo control group (with clinical management) showed noteworthy changes, virtually on a par with the so-called active treatment groups. Without additional studies across a wider spectrum of therapies and control groups, the NIMH research does not support the stated equivalent effectiveness of two types of psychotherapy over a clinical management group.

There appears to be little, if any, clinical significance between the active treatment and the so-called placebo group.[72] Furthermore, exercise seems to be as effective in decreasing many depressive symptoms as is Interpersonal Therapy or Cognitive Therapy.[73] The implication is that expectancy and demand characteristics intruded into the elaborately designed NIMH study.[74]

NOTES

1. Lazarus, A. A. (1989). *The practice of multimodal therapy.* Baltimore: Johns Hopkins University Press.

2. Prochaska, J. O. & Norcross, J. C. (1994). *Systems of psychotherapy: A transtheoretical analysis* (3rd ed.) (p. 30). Belmont, Calif.: Brooks/Cole.

3. Wolpe, J. (1990). *The practice of behavior therapy* (4th ed.). Elmsford, N.Y.: Pergamon.

4. Paul, G. L. & Shannon, D. T. (1966). Treatment of anxiety through systematic desensitization in therapy groups. *Journal of Abnormal Psychology, 71* (pp. 124–135).

Paul, G. L. (1967). Insight versus desensitization in psychotherapy two years after termination. *Journal of Consulting Psychology, 31* (pp. 333–348).

5. Paul & Shannon, Treatment of anxiety (pp. 124–135).

6. Paul, Insight versus desensitization (pp. 333–348).

7. Stampl, T. & Levis, D. (1973). The essentials of implosive therapy: A learning theory based on psychodynamic behavioral therapy. *Journal of Abnormal Psychology, 72* (pp. 496–503).

8. Cooper, N. A. & Crum, G. A. (1989). Imaginal flooding as a supplementary treatment for PTSD in combat veterans: A controlled study. *Behavior Therapy, 20* (pp. 381–391).

9. Keane, T. M., Fairbank, J. A., Caddell, J. M. & Zimmering, R. T. (1989). Implosive (flooding) therapy reduces symptoms of PTSD in Vietnam combat veterans. *Behavior Therapy, 20* (pp. 245–260).

10. Foa, E. B., Riggs, D. S., Massie, E. D. & Yarczower, M. (1995). The impact of fear activation and anger on the efficacy of exposure treatment for post-traumatic stress disorder. *Behavior Therapy, 26* (pp. 487–499).

11. Shapiro, F. (1995). *Eye-movement desensitization and reprocessing.* New York: Guilford Press.

12. Shapiro, *Eye-movement desensitization and reprocessing* (p. 15).

13. Shapiro, *Eye-movement desensitization and reprocessing* (p. 17).
14. Shapiro, *Eye-movement desensitization and reprocessing* (p. 29).
15. Shapiro, *Eye-movement desensitization and reprocessing* (p. 13).
16. Shapiro, *Eye-movement desensitization and reprocessing* (p. 10).
17. Wolpe, J. & Abrams, J. (1991). Post-traumatic stress disorder overcome by eye-movement desensitization: A case report. *Journal of Behavior Therapy & Experimental Psychiatry, 22* (pp. 39–43).
18. Young, W. C. (1995). Eye-movement desensitization/reprocessing: Its use in resolving the trauma caused by the loss of a war buddy. *American Journal of Psychotherapy, 49* (pp. 282–291).
19. Wolpe & Abrams, PTSD overcome (pp. 39–43).
20. Young, Eye-movement desensitization (pp. 282–291).
21. Wilson, S. A., Becker, L. A. & Tinker, R. H. (1995). Eye-movement desensitization and reprocessing (EMDR) treatment for psychologically traumatized individuals. *Journal of Consulting and Clinical Psychology, 63* (pp. 928–937).
22. Wilson, Becker & Tinker, EMDR treatment (pp. 928–937).
23. Sanderson, A. A. & Carpenter, R. (1992). Eye-movement desensitization versus image confrontation: A single-session crossover study of 58 phobic subjects. *Journal of Behavior Therapy and Experimental Psychiatry, 23* (pp. 269–275).
24. Vaughan, K., Armstrong, M. F., Gold, R., O'Connor, N., Jenneke, W. & Tarrier, N. (1994). A trial of eye-movement desensitization compared to image habituation training and applied muscle relaxation in post-traumatic stress disorder. *Journal of Behavior Therapy and Experimental Psychiatry, 25* (pp. 283–291).
25. Shapiro, F. (1989). Eye-movement desensitization: A new treatment for Post-Traumatic Stress Disorder. *Journal of Behavior Therapy and Experimental Psychiatry, 20* (pp. 211–217).
26. Paul & Shannon, Treatment of anxiety (pp. 124–135).
27. Cooper & Crum, Imaginal flooding (pp. 381–391).
28. Stampl & Levis, Essentials of implosive therapy (pp. 496–503).
29. Sanderson & Carpenter, Eye-movement desensitization versus image confrontation (pp. 269–275).
30. Shapiro, *Eye-movement desensitization and reprocessing.*
31. Singer, M. T. & Lalich, J. (1996). *Crazy therapies: What are they? Do they work?* San Francisco: Jossey-Bass.
32. Beck, A. T. & Weishaar, M. (1994). Cognitive therapy. In Corsini, R. J. & Wedding, D. (Eds.), *Current psychotherapies* (5th ed.) (pp. 229–261). Itasca, Ill.: Peacock Publishers.
33. Ellis, A. (1994). Rational emotive behavior therapy. In Corsini & Wedding (Eds.), *Current psychotherapies* (pp. 162–196).
34. Klerman, G. L. & Weissman, M. W. (1993). *New applications of interpersonal therapy.* Washington, D.C.: American Psychiatric Press.
35. Prochaska & Norcross, *Systems of psychotherapy* (p. 315).
36. Ellis, Rational emotive behavior therapy.
37. Ellis, Rational emotive behavior therapy.
38. Ellis, Rational emotive behavior therapy.
39. Ellis, Rational emotive behavior therapy.
40. Ellis, Rational emotive behavior therapy.
41. Haaga, D. F., Dryden, W. & Dancy, C. P. (1991). Measurement of rational-

emotive therapy in outcome studies. *Journal of Rational Emotive and Cognitive-Behavior Therapy, 9,* (pp. 73–93).

42. Haaga et al., Measurement of rational-emotive therapy (pp. 73–93).

43. Ellis, Rational emotive behavior therapy.

44. Lyons, L. C. & Woods, P. J. (1991). The efficacy of rational-emotive therapy: A quantitative review of the outcome research. *Clinical Psychology Review, 11* (pp. 357–369).

45. Lyons & Woods, The efficacy of rational-emotive therapy.

46. Lyons & Woods, The efficacy of rational-emotive therapy.

47. Prochaska & Norcross, *Systems of psychotherapy* (pp. 340–341).

48. Beck & Weishaar, Cognitive therapy.

49. Beck & Weishaar, Cognitive therapy.

50. Beck, J. S. (1995). *Cognitive therapy basics and beyond* (p. 166). New York: Guilford Press.

51. Beck & Weishaar, Cognitive therapy.

52. Beck & Weishaar, Cognitive therapy.

53. Prochaska & Norcross, *Systems of psychotherapy* (p. 332).

54. Beck & Weishaar, Cognitive therapy.

55. Beck & Weishaar, Cognitive therapy.

56. Jacobson, N. S. et al. (1996). A component analysis of cognitive-behavioral treatment for depression. *Journal of Consulting Clinical Psychology, 64* (pp. 295–304).

57. Oei, T.P.S. & Shuttlewood, G. J. (1996). Specific and nonspecific factors in psychotherapy: A case of cognitive therapy for depression. *Clinical Psychology Review, 16* (pp. 83–103).

58. Jacobson et al., A component analysis.

59. Jacobson et al., A component analysis.

60. Klerman & Weissman, *New applications of interpersonal therapy.*

61. Sullivan, H. S. (1953). *The interpersonal theory of psychiatry.* New York: Norton.

62. Meyer, A. (1957). *Psychobiology: A science of man.* Springfield, Ill.: Charles C. Thomas.

63. Prochaska & Norcross, *Systems of psychotherapy* (p. 213).

64. Klerman & Weissman, *New applications of interpersonal therapy* (p. 15).

65. Klerman & Weissman, *New applications of interpersonal therapy* (p. 234).

66. Klerman & Weissman, *New applications of interpersonal therapy* (p. 238).

67. Klerman & Weissman, *New applications of interpersonal therapy* (p. 242).

68. Klerman & Weissman, *New applications of interpersonal therapy* (p. 249).

69. Elkind, I. et al. (1989). National Institute of Mental Health Treatment of Depression Collaborative Research Program. *Archives of General Psychiatry, 46* (pp. 971–982).

70. Elkind et al., National Institute of Mental Health Treatment of Depression Collaborative Research Program.

71. Klein, M. H. et al. (1985). A comparative outcome study of group psychotherapy vs. exercise treatment for depression. *International Journal of Mental Health, 13* (pp. 148–177).

72. Ogles, B. M., Lambert, M. J. & Sawyer, J. D. (1995). Clinical significance of the National Institute of Mental Health Treatment of Depression Collaborative Re-

search Program data. *Journal of Consulting and Clinical Psychology, 63* (pp. 321–326).

73. Klein, M. H. et al. (1985). Group psychotherapy vs. exercise. *International Journal of Mental Health, 13* (pp. 148–177).

74. Elkind et al., National Institute of Mental Health Treatment of Depression Collaborative Research Program.

Chapter 7

Strategic Family Systems Therapy and Neurolinguistic Programming

THE STRATEGIC THERAPY OF JAY HALEY

In Strategic Family Systems Therapy, little or no reliance is placed on the patient's early developmental history. Excavating repressed memories and thoughts is not recommended and is actively avoided.[1] Thus, a person in crisis is not questioned about possible ancient origins of psychopathology. For Haley, it may be impossible to know the actual or truthful cause of a symptom or an emotional disorder. Similarly, what was fundamental in psychoanalysis, i.e., the transference relationship, is virtually ignored.

With respect to the humanistic orientation, there is perhaps a more superficial similarity to the gestalt technique versus Person-Centered Therapy in that the systems approach does not let the client direct the therapy. (See Chapter 5 on Humanistic Psychotherapy.) In Strategic Therapy no attempt is made to be empathic or be in tune with the patient. Furthermore, no interest is shown in producing personal growth or helping someone to become "self-actualized."

Haley parts company with the behavioral and cognitive approaches to the extent that he pays attention to past learning or experiences.[2] "Cognitive theory, . . . includes most of the hypotheses of psychodynamic therapy but struggles to be more rational with irrational problems."[3] The strategic therapist does not collaborate with the patient regarding treatment goals but rather imposes the solution on the patient. The patient doesn't need to know what is happening; rather, it's the therapist-determined results that matter.

The Origin of Psychopathology Within a Communication Systems Theory

Strategic Therapy focuses on the dynamics of the family. The family is held to be a self-correcting system, and the behaviors of the individual members are thought to maintain that system.[4] Thus, "the motivation of a person's behavior, and the cause of a problem, was not in the past but in the current sequence in which the person was enmeshed."[5] In the systems approach, the major psychoanalytic tenet that the past causes behavior problems is abandoned and instead the present comes under scrutiny. In this view, a change in the social setting is required to produce change in the individual. Family therapy is considered the proper format to produce such changes.[6]

In therapy, generally three persons should be the focus of attention: the patient, the therapist and at least one other significant individual. In the case of a woman who is afraid to leave her home, Haley suggests that the patient is in a triangle with her mother and husband. In this instance, all three do not necessarily need to be in the therapy room, but attention must be given to elements outside the therapeutic arena. A child in school might be enmeshed in a triangle between his parents or between a parent and teacher.[7] The therapist focuses essentially on the presenting problem or symptom without gathering historical information. Thus, the system has to change in order for the individual to change.[8]

The origin of Strategic Therapy was premised on the notion that people respond to others in a sequential manner and symptoms of an emotional disorder cannot change unless someone else in the system changes.[9] One of Haley's early observations involved parents who were in therapy with their young boy. Haley observed the interaction from behind a mirror. As the boy began to touch the microphone, the father told him not to fool with it. His mother interjected and asked the father not to pick on the boy. As these events evolved, Haley was not concerned with measuring the perceptions of the family, but rather with assessing the sequential communications.

Strategic Therapy even views schizophrenia within the social and family context. Haley ruminates that these serious mental disorders might more appropriately be considered psychological and social problems rather than medical ones. Hence, the interest in physiological treatments via medication may be misplaced.[10] The implication for treatment is that instead of using "brain-damaging chemicals," the family- or systems-oriented therapist can return to more benign procedures such as hot tubs or cold packs.[11]

Techniques of Strategic Therapy

Although Strategic Therapy does not specifically use hypnosis, many of the ideas have been borrowed from the work of Milton Erickson.[12] What strategic family systems therapy has in common with Erickson's approach is that the therapist devises the treatment but does not necessarily inform the patient as to the actual rationale and why. This view contrasts with other approaches that spell out the treatment and do not mislead or misinform a patient as sometimes occurs in Strategic Therapy.

The essence of behavioral change is based on the interpersonal impact of the therapist that is outside of the patient's awareness.[13] Unlike Person-Centered Therapy and psychoanalysis, the strategic therapist initiates what happens during therapy, custom designs an approach for each person[14] and directly influences the patient.

One of the major ways to produce change within the Strategic Therapy arena is to deal in analogies or metaphor.[15] Particularly when a patient is resistant, an indirect approach may be useful. The therapist or hypnotist talks about a related topic, so as not to produce defensiveness in the patient. By so doing, the patient may "spontaneously" (as Haley describes it) connect the two topics and thereby respond appropriately.[16] A nonverbal metaphor is found in the hypnotic induction: when suggesting that the subject's hand get lighter and lighter and lift up toward the face, the hypnotist may lift his own head and raise his voice.

Haley[17] provides the following example of the use of metaphor: a married couple having difficulty talking directly about their sexual conflicts. Rather than confront the issue directly, Erickson analogizes a dinner scenario. He discusses appetizers with the wife and mention how the husband prefers to dive into the meat and potatoes. If the couple connects the sexual context to what Erickson is saying, he will move quickly to another topic. At the end of the session, he might give a directive for the couple to actually have a pleasant dinner that is mutually satisfying.

The Use of Directives

Strategic Therapy employs the use of directives, that is, telling a patient what to do. Haley advocates that the trainee therapist talk about issues from within a psychodynamic approach.[18] When directives are given, however, there is a specific topic that can be discussed. Therapist and client don't need to talk about the past, dreams or fantasies but rather about the directive and what is happening at the present.[19]

In one example, a woman complained that when vacuuming her home on Saturday mornings, her husband continually followed her from room to room.[20] The issue was how to stop the husband from engaging in this behavior. Haley asked Erickson for assistance. Erickson's advice was quite direct: the woman should continue to vacuum the room as usual, allowing her husband to follow her as before. After cleaning, however, the patient was to dump the vacuum bags into piles of dirt and leave the bags until the following Saturday. When this task was carried out, the husband stopped his following behavior. According to Erickson, this plan worked because the husband could not tolerate the absurd situation and voluntarily left the field, so to speak.

Erickson and Haley use paradoxical directives quite frequently. A therapeutic double bind is created by requesting that the patient continue or even increase the behavior that is the targeted symptom. The patient can either follow the therapist's paradoxical request and persist in the symptomatic acts or resist the therapist and eliminate the problem behavior. For example, an overprotective mother is not told to do this but rather to do more. If the therapist suggests that part of the problem is that she is overprotective, she is likely to resist. Thus, the mother is given the paradoxical directive to spend the next week hovering over the child. The actual rationale is not given to the mother, but rather a plausible reason may be cited so that the mother might engage in what seems to be a counter-intuitive action. The therapist may inform the mother that the reason for the assignment is that "she can find out how she really feels in this situation or so that she can observe herself and the child."[21]

The patient is asked to show more extreme behavior than she had been presenting. What happens in some cases is that the mother rebels against the directive and thus diminishes her overprotectiveness. Or in the case of a patient with a bed wetting problem, the patient is asked to indulge in this behavior. In this instance, when the patient does not follow the idiosyncratic advice, change for the better is produced. Obviously, no insight is gained, there is no analysis of transference, nor is there collaboration with the patient in terms of designing the treatment plan.

A nine-year-old boy presented with compulsive public masturbation. The problem had persisted for four years. Apparently, there had been some psychodynamic as well as Behavioral Therapy. When seeing the boy alone, the therapist gave a paradoxical request for an increase in masturbation. By the fifth interview, the young patient began to rebel and decreased his masturbation activity. After several more weeks, the problem diminished and disappeared. The paradoxical directives were within the family context; first the young patient was treated, then the focus was on the mother, so that she did not overreact to his improvement.[22]

When a supervisee was not profiting from coaching and a straightforward directive, the indirect approach was used.[23] The therapist in training was described as nervous and afraid of making mistakes when treating a family in therapy. The nervousness was apparent not only to her supervisor but to the family. The following family directives were given: The supervising therapist directed the acting therapist to make three special mistakes.[24] The first mistake is one that both the acting therapist and the supervisor know is a mistake. The second mistake should only be known to the therapist. Finally, the therapist is to make a mistake that she doesn't know is a mistake. Needless to say, the therapist conducted a better interview and was less nervous. Even if the paradox is transparent to a patient, it still may work. Thus, if the patient says, "You are using reverse psychology on me," the therapist can inform the patient that it is one of the things that is being done.[25]

Paradoxes may be offered either as a means of inducing or enhancing the hypnotic trance: "Would you like to experience a light, medium or deep trance?" "Would you like to enter a trance now or in a few minutes?" "Will you be ready to get over that habit this week or the next?" or "You don't need to listen to me. Your unconscious mind can listen without your knowledge."[26] Therapeutic double-bind in hypnosis is used to face important issues and to produce reorientation.[27] Classic examples include asking the patient why she must have a headache on weekends. Thus, if the patient is told to have a headache during the week, the double-bind is formed. In the case of acrophobia, the following double-bind is suggested: Have the patient be on the lookout for a special building that can actually increase her fear.[28]

Case Reports

In *Uncommon Therapy: The Psychiatric Techniques of Milton H. Erickson, M.D.*, Haley covers a multitude of cases from both a family and strategic perspective.[29] The cases are mainly from Erickson's articles and were edited for presentation in *Uncommon Therapy*.[30] As Haley states, the book is essentially comprised of anecdotes with no critical analysis.[31]

The Case of the Falling-Down Patient

A young man displayed numerous phobias and avoidant behavior. When he had to cross certain streets or go into certain buildings, he would faint.[32] There was even one particular restaurant he was unable to enter. By getting over the problem of entering restaurants, Erickson hoped also to have the patient overcome his fears of women.

Erickson arranged for the patient to arrive at Erickson's home at 7 o'clock. The patient was to take the Ericksons and a divorcee to the restaurant. When they arrived at the location, Erickson pointed out that the parking lot was graveled and suggested the patient look for a better spot to faint. The patient was able to enter and sit at a table without any appreciable problem. When the waitress came to the table, Erickson purposely picked a fight with her. He also had a verbal fight with the manager and demanded to see the kitchen. The intent was to embarrass and ignore the patient while at the restaurant.

Apparently, when Erickson entered the kitchen, he informed the waitress and the manager that he was kidding his friend.[33] After dinner, the patient and the divorcee went dancing. It was not clear what the divorcee knew about the case or how Erickson knew her. It also was not clear how or if the patient was identified to any of the participants. The results were startling: The patient was able to go to the restaurant and enter buildings without incident.

The Case of the Non-Patient

Haley states that sometimes Erickson does not directly attack fears but is protective and subtle in his attempt to change the person and gracefully eases the patient into treatment.[34] Although this is an early case, it is contained in the 1986 (and 1993 paper edition) of Haley's book.

The patient who was to be the focus of attention was a 23-year-old woman who showed signs of social withdrawal and decrease in work performance.[35] She was tearful and expressed a wish to die. Because of the patient's aversion to psychiatrists at this point in time, he approached the woman's roommate and asked her to tell the patient that the roommate was receiving psychotherapy from Erickson. The roommate asked the patient to be present at one of her hypnosis sessions. As both subjects sat in adjacent chairs, Erickson provided a long and laborious hypnotic induction. The roommate achieved an excellent trance and thereby set "an effective example for the intended patient."[36]

Erickson was able to induce suggestions to the patient as she sat listening and watching her roommate. "Gradually, it became possible *while looking directly at the patient*, thus creating in the patient an impulse to respond" (emphasis in original). After an hour and a half, the patient fell into a deep hypnotic trance. The patient was age-regressed to the ten-to-thirteen age range, since it coincided with her mother's death and was thought to be the onset of menstruation. In the next hypnotic session, the patient informed Erickson what her mother taught her about sexual activity. During the third session, in the waking state, Erickson provided instruction on the development of primary and secondary sex characteristics, including the growth of her nipples and wearing of a bra. Just after the third session, the patient became engaged and "had a new understanding of things," which made it possible for her to enjoy the company of others and to fall in love.[37]

The patient was married about a year later and was the happy mother of a baby girl. According to Haley, the patient was offered permission to engage in adult behavior that was formerly forbidden. This case demonstrates Erickson's indirect approach to providing suggestions and how he can provide new ideas that are not actively resisted and in fact are accepted.

The Case of the Pleasingly Plump Patient

The patient was an overweight 35-year-old woman who was referred by a mutual friend of Erickson and the patient. The patient's main complaint was her inability to get a date. Her personal grooming and hygiene were quite poor: unkempt hair, dirty ears and neck, and obnoxiously dirty fingernails. She had accepted a job in another city and had limited funds to pay for therapy. Thus, Erickson determined that something drastic had to be done.

Erickson gained her consent to provide "drastic therapy" and informed her that there would be a therapeutic assault. Over the course of three hours, Erickson painstakingly covered her grooming and hygiene. He commented critically on her uncombed hair and her poorly fitting and unmatching clothes. Next, the patient was instructed to wash one side of her face and notice the contrast with the unwashed side.

At the next appointment two days later, the patient's grooming was significantly improved. At the end of the session, Erickson imparted the following: "You are never going to be able to forget again that you have a pretty patch of fur between your legs." She was also to take note in front of a mirror the three badges of womanhood.[38] At the next appointment, she was told to go to a beauty consultant at a department store and obtain grooming and clothing tips. Finally, she was to take dance lessons and then go to the company dance. This she did.

Three months after taking the new position in another town, she became acquainted with a college professor. A year later they were married and subsequently had four children. Haley reports that Erickson's approach involves the "use of sensible, ordinary procedures, such as learning to groom oneself or to dance." Erickson also makes use of community resources such as beauty consultants.[39]

The Case of the Unfair Therapist

Haley presents another recent supervised case of marital therapy. The question is whether a therapist can make an unfair statement in the interest of producing change.[40] This was a case presented as an exemplar of supervision; thus, the supervisor asked the therapist in training if it was possible to be unfair. The issue was whether the therapist could select one spouse and inform them that "one was entirely wrong and the other was entirely right."[41] The supervisor engages in a series of steps in order to persuade the reluctant therapist that he should be unfair to one of the patients. Thus, the supervisor told the therapist to side with one spouse. In order to help the therapist, the supervisor said that others were able to be unfair.

The therapist informed the husband that he was entirely wrong in the relationship and that the wife was not "doing anything to create the problem."[42] The wife was told she was not doing anything to create the problem and should insist that the husband do the work to save the marriage. The husband, as part of his work, was to court his wife again. The husband was told by the therapist that the marital problem was his fault, he was making a mess of things, doing things to turn his wife off and did not seek her out or court her.

At the next interview, the couple appeared more cheerful. The husband had made an attempt to court or be more involved with his wife. During this session, it was apparent that both had decided to take steps to make the marriage work. No follow-up or outcome was reported.

Clinical Research

There appears to be a severe shortage of any systematic clinical research regarding the efficacy or effectiveness of Strategic Therapy. Not a single citation or reference to such research appears in Haley's latest book (1996).[43] Reportedly, three studies are classified as Strategic Therapy. Because of the multitude of approaches, it was not always clear to these investigators how to classify the theoretical orientation or approach.[44] This paltry amount of research is not too surprising given Haley's attitude toward psychologists and the scientific method: "Psychologists can develop a handicap as therapists if the research attitude they learn permeates their therapy approach."[45] Thus, rather than an objective attempt to learn what makes for behavioral changes, Haley espouses a non-neutral attitude that affects the person. The main task in therapy is to influence and change the data, i.e., person.

Critique and Analysis

Ethical Issues in Strategic Therapy

A reasonable observation is that therapists may manipulate a patient so that some influence is exerted in order to change the patient.[46] The controversial questions regard forcing a patient to accept the directives of the therapist and actively deceiving the patient.

When a patient is placed into a double-bind, is the patient really free to choose one of the alternatives? The patient may be given the illusion of choice but must, in many instances, resist the therapist's commands or maintain the unwanted behavior. In situations where the patient is court-referred, for example, it would be difficult, if not impossible, to walk out. Patients who have made an investment of time and money for several months or so also may not find it easy to leave. In order to do so, one must have the audacity to tell the therapist that the treatment plan is ridiculous. Thus, no amount of semantic juggling can alter what is a forced choice into a free choice.[47] Just because the therapist construes the two alternatives as positive doesn't make the situation less intimidating to the patient. The patient may presume that the licensed professional has knowledge and expertise, and in reliance relinquishes common sense.

From the clinical standpoint, when the patient starts to take the bait, i.e., rebelling against the therapist, an unknown and possibly counterproductive resistance is created. Thus, the Haley/Erickson approach may produce the resistance that crops up regularly in many therapies. When a patient is told to purposely wet his bed or magnify a symptom, it is not too surprising that some patients might alter their behavior. But in so doing, this is the exact opposite of what many therapists would recommend. Prochaska and Norcross view the therapeutic arena as one of a power struggle wherein the therapists must win but perhaps with the ends justifying the means.[48] "How else can you justify such manipulative techniques as prescribing symptoms, placing patients in double-binds, and reducing their complaints to absurdities?"[49] Their position is that these techniques make for a good theater of the absurd but do not create a human system to assist troubled individuals.[50] It would be helpful to have some published data showing potential effects when patients are compelled to resist the therapist.

The issue of deceiving the patients deserves some comment. The double-binds and other prescribed techniques may be construed as overtly manipulative. At least the patient hears the actual game plan. But what about when the patient is purposely given deceptive information? Haley appears to believe it is ethical to deceive a patient if it is essential for the cure.[51] According to the unfair therapist, Haley blatantly condoned lying to the husband and wife. The husband, in the name of therapy, was deceived into thinking he was responsible for the failing marriage. This appears to be a gross ethical violation and a total lack of informed consent. Thus, the couple was never informed that, as part of therapy, the therapist would make up a bald-faced lie in order to help them. This story turned out positively, but if it had had negative consequences, would the therapist have taken responsibility or blamed it on something else?

Permeating several of the other cases presented are what currently would be considered ethical lapses and possibly boundary violations. For example, the phobic patient (the Falling-Down Patient) met with Erickson at his home, was introduced to a stranger by Erickson and was subjected to embarrassment in public. More bizarre is the entrapment of a patient into therapy by a roommate (the case of the Non-Patient). Erickson tricked the patient into therapy by using a third party. Even with the reported amazing results, there would be ethical land mines if this tactic were attempted now. Finally, patients should give informed consent if they are to be identified to outside consultants (Pleasingly Plump Patient) and are to be verbally assaulted.

The Haley/Erickson approach implies that the therapist may have inherent knowledge about the correct response for the patient. The treatment plan is implemented without the patient's collaboration and awareness. The supervisor engages in a series of steps in order to convince the reluctant therapist that he should be unfair to one of the patients. It is true that not everything can be told to the patient, since this would be disruptive of the ongoing therapy. Haley and Erickson seem to feel that it is proper to withhold vital information; however, in doing so, the patient cannot decide whether this type of therapy is suitable. Thus, the strategic therapist (and others) arrogate to themselves even after a few minutes what is the appropriate treatment plan. The patients, even children, are simply to sit back and let the therapist tell them what to do. Without input and consultation with the patient and some treatment disclosure, the patient is subject to the dictates of an authoritarian change agent.

Although creative, innovative and apparently producing amazing results, the strategic communication systems theory of Haley and Erickson suffers from a dearth of research. Haley presents a training model for new therapists, yet he never demonstrates how his approach leads to successful results.[52] Haley and Erickson's books essentially detail techniques and anecdotes and make no presentation of how the various techniques such as directives or altering the family system is essential to behavioral and attitudinal change. It would be helpful to know what effect if any there is on patients who are given double-binds. Do some patients feel that these kinds of therapists are tricky and manipulative?

If there is a family, social or even a communication systems basis of psychopathology, let alone schizophrenia, no current or recently published research supports this claim. Thus, Haley has de-emphasized what appears to be almost incontrovertible evidence supporting a genetic and biological basis to schizophrenia. There may also be a biological basis to some forms of depression and other mental disorders. If Haley espouses a social/communication approach to therapy, it is incumbent upon him to present some credible documentation to support his view. His one-paragraph critique of the side effects of medications is not on point. To ignore recent biobehavioral studies, using the PET scan, for example, suggests that the Haley communication and family systems may be immune to research.

Apparently, Haley and Erickson have not attempted to demonstrate the relationship between the theory and practice of Strategic Therapy. Thus, the same criticism launched against Gestalt Therapy is relevant here. As Prochaska and Norcross point out, how does a severely disturbed patient who lives alone fit into these schemes of family?[53] Haley and Erickson have not demonstrated that forgetting about prior development history or teaching a patient coping skills is useless. In the case of the Unfair Therapist, do we really know how the communication pattern was dysfunctional, let alone changed by the imposition of the therapist?

Thus, the most obvious shortcoming of Strategic Therapy is that no scientific confirmation exists. Haley apparently does not approve of the scientific method in that it interferes with the therapeutic task. It is not clear why therapists could not be enthusiastic about changing patients and still be involved in clinical research. The proper approach would be to compare the family systems methods with other therapies and wait-list controls. At the very least, it would be instructive to learn if placebo-type control groups showed as much improvement as is alleged in strategic family therapy.

The issue that crops up again and again is whether therapists other than the innovators can provide the same level of success. Part of Haley's and Erickson's success may be due to the mystique, talent and charisma of the innovator. Can students or followers duplicate what the master therapist does? In *Uncommon Therapy*, all of the presented cases were Erickson's. The question is whether the typical therapist can replicate the amazing stories in the book. If the results are due to Erickson's personal characteristics, then this approach has little generalizability or applicability to the wider range of therapists.

Since there is virtually no published research of any consequence, the active or necessary and sufficient ingredients in Strategic Therapy are based on speculation. Only successful case studies or anecdotes have been published. Little or nothing is known about unsuccessful cases or even the ratio of successful to unsuccessful cases. The clinician has mainly to rely on the word of Haley and Erickson. To do so ignores the placebo effects of the approach, not to mention the unmeasured impact of the master therapists whose positive reports are presented. What is the effect of an authoritarian therapist who controls and directs the goals of therapy and may mislead the patient as to what is really going on? Thus, at this point, Strategic Therapy is untested, unverified, and has no scientific viability.

NEUROLINGUISTIC PROGRAMMING (NLP)

Imagine that a phobia could be cured in less than an hour or that the limitations of learning disabilities could be overcome in an hour; or further that smoking, overeating and insomnia could be eliminated in a few sessions, and even physical and psychosomatic problems could be eliminated in a few sessions. These claims sound incredible, but in the foreword of *Frogs into Princes*, it is asserted that people experienced in NLP "can back them up with solid, visible results."[54] Thus, Bandler and Grinder have treated alcoholics and heroin addicts in one session and reported success after two-year follow-ups with these patients.[55]

Neurolinguistic Programming relies on ideas from Gestalt Therapy as well as Milton Erickson and a family therapist named Virginia Satir. The founders of NLP are Richard Bandler, who was a mathematician, and John Grinder, who was a linguist. Bandler edited the materials presented in Perls' posthumous work, *The Gestalt Approach* and *Eye Witness to Therapy*.[56] Bandler and Grinder have published material on Erickson's hypnotic techniques.[57] Originated in 1975, NLP had a meteoric rise in popularity in the next ten years. Commenting on the work of Bandler and Grinder, reviewers have claimed that NLP "has been clinically demonstrated as a powerful technology for engendering change.[58]

Neurolinguistic Programming has been described as a model of human behavior that is broken down into smaller pieces permitting earlier learning and behavior change. In addition, NLP helps the individual therapist to influence someone else's behavior.[59] An outgrowth of NLP is Design Human Engineering (DHE). Participants in DHE seminars learn to automate unconscious processes, and by building generalizations about human behavior, internal ecological changes can be created.[60]

Theory and Practice of NLP

In order to initiate change, it is important to gain rapport with the client. Similar to the Haley/Erickson approach, in the NLP approach there is little interest in exploring past developmental incidents. Nor is any attempt made to plumb the unconscious to attain insight. Rather, the therapist helps the client by matching his representational mode (visual, kinesthetic and auditory) to that of the patient. Mirroring and pacing can also establish rapport and alter behavior. Through a process called reframing, the therapist can swiftly re-cast a negative behavior or symptom in a more positive attribute. Both hypnosis and visual imagery may be used to facilitate reframing.[61]

Preferred Representational Systems

Corresponding to different ways of thinking are three main senses: vision, hearing and kinesthetic. Initially, people think in one of these representational systems. So, internally, an individual may be generating visual images, having bodily sensations or hearing sounds.[62] People characteristically move their eyes (pupils) in systematic directions, depending on the sensory mode being accessed. For example, when asked, "What color are your shoes?" the person's eyes move upward; when asked, "What was the last question I asked you?" the eyes remain level; and when asked, "What does it feel like to touch something hot?" the eyes move downward.[63] If attention is paid to the preferred representational system, the therapist can adjust his own behavior "to get the response you want."[64]

Mirroring and Pacing

At times, Erickson would match the breathing of the patient so as to enhance the hypnotic trance. Mirroring involves matching the patient's breathing, voice, facial expression, eye blinks and so on. In direct mirroring, the therapist breathes at exactly the same rate and depth as the patient. Examples of cross-over mirroring include moving the hand to the rise and fall of the patient's chest. A second example involves matching voice level to the rise and fall of the patient's chest.

Reframing

In reframing, one unwanted symptom is turned into another one.[65] This process involves six steps. In the first step of the trance version of this procedure, the unconscious is set up with yes/no signals. Thus, one finger might lift for "yes" and another finger would lift for "no." Reframing is effective because it is a channel to the unconscious.[66]

Second, the pattern of behavior to be changed is identified. While under hypnosis, the patient scans the unconscious and selects an important problem that needs to be changed. When this has been done, the unconscious mind is to signal with the "yes" response.

Third, the patient determines what is positive about the unwanted behavior. The idea is to find out what is of value when the patient indulges in the unwanted behavior or demonstrates the symptom. Fourth, the patient creates new alternatives to the target symptomatic behavior. The unconscious mind attempts a type of dreaming and brainstorming to create new choices. The fifth step is to evaluate the new alternatives, and last, the patient is to select one alternative. The unconscious part of the mind is asked "if it would be responsible for using the new choice instead of the old one for three weeks." If the first six steps are successful, then the patient is asked to have a fantasy of responding with the new alternative.[67]

In the case of an alcoholic, hypnosis might be used to get to the alcoholic aspects of one's personality. Thus, the patient might be asked to return to the time when he was drinking and try to experience the feel and smell of drinking.[68] Another way to get to the alcoholic state "is to pace and lead the client into a drunken state."[69] The therapist can mirror the client and may begin at act drunk as well. The patient is asked to increase the drunklike behaviors such as slurring the speech and walking in a tipsy fashion. This technique is so powerful that a given client might lapse into a psychotic state or have whole-body convulsions.[70]

Case Reports

Even in the case of catatonic schizophrenia, pacing may be helpful. Bandler and Grinder report that a catatonic patient had been sitting for several years in the day room of a state mental hospital.[71] The patient displayed no verbal communication. The therapist sat at about a 45-degree angle and matched the patient's body position. At first, the patient's breathing was mirrored, followed by slight deviations, which the patient then followed. It was apparent that at least some rapport was achieved. Next, the therapist shouted and asked for a cigarette. The patient jumped off the couch and verbalized a comment for the first time.

Reframing can be conducted while the patient is in a hypnotic trance or in the course of normal conversation. Reframing has been applied to dealing with alcoholism and family therapy as well as corporate business conflicts. For example, in the corporate arena, one party is interested in expanding the business, and the other wants stability rather than risk growth.[72] A strategy that reportedly will always work is to reframe the two responses so that both can agree on the outcome. The new frame is to have both parties agree that expansion is appropriate when the high level of service can be maintained. The conflicting parties are to draw up proposals that support their respective positions on expansion.

In a workshop, a woman described a freeway phobia. In reframing the phobia, the patient was asked to "go inside" and find what was scary about going near a freeway. The participant was asked further to see if her unconscious was willing to communicate with her. The inside part of her mind was construed as powerful and capable of doing something worthwhile. For example, the inside powerful part might be willing to have the client be comfortable, alert and feeling safe when entering a freeway ramp. The participant was asked to fantasize several freeway scenarios without increasing her level of anxiety. Afterward, she reportedly was able to drive on the freeway without difficulty.[73]

The Echoing Therapist

Patients who are suffering from serious emotional trauma may consult an NLP therapist in private practice for individual therapy. A patient named "Louise" was assaulted in her apartment during a nighttime robbery. She had one visit with an NLP therapist, who attempted to get her to picture things in her mind and continually repeated what she said.[74] Apparently, there was no formal intake, psychodiagnosis or focus on the major presenting problems.

Clinical Research

In order to determine the clinical utility of a particular psychotherapy approach, it is abundantly clear that some clinical research is required. Such research includes an experimental group that is compared with a control group or an alternative therapy. In addition, in the case of unique therapies such as NLP, it is helpful to assess the underlying theoretical tenets such as the effect and validity of focusing on the representational systems. Otherwise, stories and anecdotes must be relied on. In the case of NLP, there is no peer-reviewed research on the effectiveness of NLP. Although a flurry of doctoral dissertations appeared in the 1970s and 1980s, apparently none were presented for independent publication in a journal.

The effect of NLP on self-actualization and personal growth was examined in an Amsterdam study.[75] Self-actualization was assessed through the Personal Orientation Inventory, which measures, in part, whether a person is more present-oriented, inner-directed, flexible and self-aware.[76] The subjects—54 adults who participated in a 21-day NLP workshop—stated that they had good to excellent command of the English language. There was no control group, such as a wait-list of future participants.

All statistical comparisons were made on the basis of scores prior to and post-NLP. The results indicated a "strong movement toward self-actualization after completing the NLP workshop." Therefore it was concluded that significant changes occurred in the direction toward self-actualization as a result of the NLP workshop.[77]

A plethora of studies have been published examining the preferred representation systems described by Bandler and Grinder.[78] One study was premised on the notion that if the therapist can determine the preferred representational system, "enhanced communication, trust, and therapeutic progress will result."[79] The introductory psychology students were told that personality characteristics were being examined through the use of imagery.

A series of nine questions was asked, three from each of the main modalities: visual, auditory and kinesthetic. Special recording equipment was used to track eye movements. The results indicated that when comparing eye movement direction with modality, no relationship was found. The authors concluded that there is no support for the assertion that people respond based on the modality allegedly accessed by the therapist, and further that several modalities seem to operate simultaneously. Thus, eye movements, according to this study, are somewhat random and do not follow the predicted path of NLP. Finally, it was concluded that the concept of preferred representation system "is as slippery and elusive as a greased pig at a county fair."[80]

Despite broad claims and mass advertising, no studies have been published demonstrating the effectiveness of NLP.[81] The Sharpley article reviewed fifteen studies and found no consistent support for identifying the preferred sensory modality accessed by NLP. Proponents of NLP claim that the problem with the negative research in particular is due to deficiency in research design.[82] Although most of the research on the preferred representational systems has been negative, eye-scanning is considered to be an important, yet small, part of NLP. Thus, these flawed studies apparently have little relevance to the therapy and practice of NLP. No peer-reviewed studies are presented that support any aspect of clinical changes as a result of undergoing NLP.

Critique and Analysis of NLP

First, it should be noted that, although NLP has been utilized and advocated by people trained in the mental health field, there appears to be no restriction as to who can conduct NLP. This may lend ammunition to the promulgation of exaggerated claims and misleading statements. Various advertisements claim that NLP can help a person to stop addictive behaviors such as smoking, bring about weight loss, eliminate traumas, phobias and fears, produce abundance, motivate instantly, improve self-esteem, reduce stress and improve relationships.[83] It apparently is not illegal or unethical for a non-mental health professional to claim an instantaneous cure for a phobia.

Most striking of all, no apparent attempts have been made to provide confirmation of the effectiveness of NLP by means of clinical research. What is presented in workshops by Bandler and Grinder is little more than unverified stories. No verbatim transcripts appear in the literature so that an independent assessment can be made, and no reports have substantiated any of the miraculous cures. Does mirroring an alcoholic really work? The various advertisements and claims have no clinical support and are grossly misleading.

Second, there is the real question of whether the so-called tenets of the theory, such as eye-scanning and sensory mode, can really be accessed. At present the sophisticated studies that have been done suggest there is little or no scientific basis to the notion that a person's eyes move in a certain direction depending on her preferred sensory mode. It appears that this line of research as well as all others dropped off the radar map after Sharpley's second review.[84] Both Sharpley and Elich et al. conclude that NLP is akin to a cult and may be nothing more than a psychological fad.[85]

There is nothing new about NLP. It is a haphazard concoction of hypnosis and client empathy, with a little Gestalt and behavioral conditioning mixed in.[86] Singer and Lalich provide vignettes that resemble a *Saturday Night Live* parody of NLP:[87] In "The Echoing Therapist," the patient is subjected to the therapist repeating what is said and tempting her to expand on every statement. Furthermore, the therapist seems to be insisting that the patient access by way of the visual mode, requesting or suggesting that she picture something in her mind's eye. In "The Miming Therapist," a depressed patient was referred to a therapist using NLP. Every move the patient made, the therapist copied, so that when the patient crossed his leg, breathed or spoke in a certain tone, the therapist mimicked. Clearly, no evidence exists that the obvious or even subtle patient copying improves rapport.

Virtually no clinical support has been presented for the effectiveness of NLP. The studies without control groups are a typical example of extrapolating from misleading data.[88] Duncan's 21-day study in Amsterdam, in particular, was fatally flawed as a serious research project. Since there was no control group, how could the outcome studies be related to anything that happened in the 21-day workshop? It may be that the participants, all of whom paid a large sum of money and some of whom are from foreign countries, are more willing to endorse "uplifting" items on a psychological assessment tool. Obviously, all the participants and researchers knew that a study was under way. Based on the lack of empirical support for NLP, what remains are the guru and placebo effects. NLP appears to be a superficial and gimmicky approach to dealing with mental health problems. Unfortunately, NLP appears to be the first in a long line of mass marketing seminars that purport to virtually cure any mental disorder.

Originators and followers present a mystical, and magical, new theory that produces a climate for positive expectations. Amazing anecdotes are offered as confirmation of the theory and practice. Word-of-mouth reports tend to be unbelievable. As with psychoanalysis, Gestalt Therapy and Strategic Therapy, there is the impression that the practitioner of NLP somehow knows more than the patient. NLP seems to use the same kind of clinical divination that led Freud to know what was happening beneath the surface.

As a credible therapy technique, NLP seems to have gone under that radar screen in terms of providing clinical confirmation of the results of therapy. This way, there is no need to be concerned with proving any of the claims. Adherents of NLP simply declare that it works and move on. Costly three- and fourteen-day seminars are held to learn all the secrets of NLP. Any theory that relies on borrowed techniques needs to be careful that the methods have some validity. Since there is little support for the origins of NLP, it is not surprising that the concocted theoretical amalgam of NLP has failed to produce any credible substantial evidence of its effectiveness. At present, it appears that NLP has no empirical or scientific support as to the underlying tenets of its theory or clinical effectiveness. What remains is a mass-marketed serving of psychopablum.

NOTES

1. Haley, J. (1996). *Learning and teaching therapy*. New York: Guilford Press.
2. Haley, *Learning and teaching therapy* (pp. 81, 89).
3. Haley, *Learning and teaching therapy* (p. 89).
4. Haley, *Learning and teaching therapy* (p. 81).
5. Haley, J. (1997). Changes in therapy. In Zeig, J. (Ed.), *The evolution of psychotherapy: A third conference* (pp. 245–255). New York: Brunner/Mazel.
6. Haley, *Learning and teaching therapy* (p. 82).
7. Haley, *Learning and teaching therapy* (p. 91).
8. Haley, Changes in therapy.
9. Haley, Changes in therapy.
10. Haley, J. (1989). The effect of long-term outcome studies on the therapy of schizophrenia. *Journal of Marital and Family Therapy, 2* (pp. 127–132).
11. Haley, The effect of long-term outcome studies (pp. 127–132).
12. Haley, J. (1986). *Uncommon therapy: The psychiatric techniques of Milton H. Erickson, M.D.* New York: W. W. Norton.
13. Haley, *Uncommon therapy* (p. 39).
14. Haley, *Uncommon therapy* (p. 17).
15. Haley, *Uncommon therapy* (p. 26).
16. Haley, *Uncommon therapy* (p. 26).
17. Haley, *Uncommon therapy* (p. 27).
18. Haley, Changes in therapy (p. 253).
19. Haley, Changes in therapy (p. 253).
20. Haley, *Learning and teaching therapy* (p. 33).
21. Haley, J. (1987). *Problem-solving therapy* (2nd ed.) (p. 79). San Francisco: Jossey-Bass.
22. Haley, *Problem-solving therapy* (p. 84).

23. Haley, *Learning and teaching therapy* (p. 144).
24. Haley, *Learning and teaching therapy* (p. 165).
25. Haley, *Learning and teaching therapy* (p. 165).
26. Erickson, M. H., Rossi, E. L. & Rossi, S. I. (1976). *Hypnotic realities: The induction of clinical hypnosis and forms of indirect suggestion* (pp. 64, 65, 68). New York: John Wiley.
27. Rossi, E. L. & Ryan, M. O. (1992). Creative choice in hypnosis. In *The seminars, workshops and lectures of Milton H. Erickson*, Vol. 4 (p. 199). New York: Irvington Publishers.
28. Rossi & Ryan, Creative choice in hypnosis (p. 199).
29. Haley, *Uncommon therapy* (p. 39).
30. Haley, *Uncommon therapy* (p. 12).
31. Haley, *Uncommon therapy* (p. 13).
32. Haley, *Uncommon therapy* (p. 67).
33. Haley, *Uncommon therapy* (p. 69).
34. Haley, *Uncommon therapy* (pp. 75, 83).
35. Haley, *Uncommon therapy* (p. 75).
36. Haley, *Uncommon therapy* (p. 76).
37. Haley, *Uncommon therapy* (p. 82).
38. Haley, *Uncommon therapy* (p. 93).
39. Haley, *Uncommon therapy* (p. 94).
40. Haley, *Learning and teaching therapy* (p. 144).
41. Haley, *Learning and teaching therapy* (p. 145).
42. Haley, *Learning and teaching therapy* (p. 146).
43. Haley, *Learning and teaching therapy*.
44. Shadish, W. R., Montgomery, L. M., Wilson, P., Wilson, M. R., Bright, I. & Okwumabua, T. (1993). Effects of family and marital psychotherapies: A meta-analysis. *Journal of Consulting and Clinical Psychology, 61* (pp. 992–1002).
45. Haley, *Learning and teaching therapy* (p. 48).
46. Haley, *Problem-solving therapy* (p. 222).
47. Rossi & Ryan, Creative choice in hypnosis (p. xi).
48. Prochaska, J. O. & Norcross, J. C. (1994). *Systems of psychotherapy: A transtheoretical analysis* (3rd ed.) (p. 381). Pacific Grove, Calif.: Brooks/Cole.
49. Prochaska & Norcross, *Systems of psychotherapy* (p. 381).
50. Prochaska & Norcross, *Systems of psychotherapy* (p. 381).
51. Haley, *Problem-solving therapy* (p. 226).
52. Haley, *Learning and teaching therapy*.
53. Prochaska & Norcross, *Systems of psychotherapy* (p. 379).
54. Bandler, R. & Grinder, J. (1979). *Frogs into princes: Neurolinguistic programming* (p. ii). Moab, Utah: Real People Press.
55. Bandler, R. & Grinder, J. (1982). *Reframing: Neurolinguistic programming and the transformation of meaning.* (p. 185). Moab, Utah: Real People Press.
56. Perls, F. (1973). *The Gestalt approach and eye witness to history.* Toronto: Science and Behavior Books.
57. Bandler, R. & Grinder, J. (1975). *Patterns of the hypnotic techniques of Milton H. Erickson, M.D. 1.* Cupertino, Calif.: Meta Publications.
58. Einsbruch, E. R. & Forman, B. D. (1985). Observations concerning research

literature on neuro-linguistic programming. *Journal of Counseling Psychology, 32* (pp. 589–596).

59. DHEA Brochure. (1996). Brookfield, Wisconsin.

60. DHEA Brochure.

61. Bandler, R. & Grinder, J. (1981). *Trance-formations: Neuro-linguistic programming and the structure of hypnosis.* Moab, Utah: Real People Press.

62. Bandler & Grinder, *Frogs into princes* (pp. 14–15).

63. Bandler & Grinder, *Trance-formations* (p. 229).

64. Bandler & Grinder, *Frogs into princes* (p. 15).

65. Bandler & Grinder, *Trance-formations* (p. 142).

66. Bandler & Grinder, *Reframing neurolinguistic programming* (p. 179).

67. Bandler & Grinder, *Reframing neurolinguistic programming* (pp. 157–158).

68. Bandler & Grinder, *Frogs into princes* (p. 80).

69. Bandler & Grinder, *Reframing neurolinguistic programming* (p. 182).

70. Bandler & Grinder, *Reframing neurolinguistic programming* (p. 183).

71. Bandler & Grinder, *Frogs into princes* (p. 80).

72. Bandler & Grinder, *Frogs into princes* (p. 175).

73. Bandler & Grinder, *Frogs into princes* (pp. 154–155).

74. Singer, M. T. & Lalich, J. (1996). *Crazy therapies: What are they? Do they work?* (p. 173). San Francisco: Jossey-Bass.

75. Duncan, R. C. & Konefal, J. (1990). Effective neurolinguistic programming, training and self-actualization as measured by the personal orientation inventory. *Psychological Reports, 66* (pp. 1323–1330).

76. Shostrum, E. L. (1974). *Manual for the personal orientation inventory.* San Diego, Calif.: Educational and Industrial Testing Services.

77. Duncan & Konefal, Effective NLP (pp. 1323–1330).

78. Elich, M., Thompson, R. W. & Miller, L. (1985). Mental imagery as revealed by eye movements and spoken predicates: A test of neurolinguistic programming. *Journal of Counseling Psychology, 32* (pp. 622–625).

79. Elich et al., Mental imagery.

80. Elich et al., Mental imagery.

81. Sharpley, C. F. (1984). Predicate matching in NLP: A review of research on the preferred representational system. *Journal of Counseling Psychology, 31* (pp. 238–248).

82. Einsbruch & Forman, Observations on neuro-linguistic programming (pp. 589–596).

83. Singer & Lalich, *Crazy therapies* (p. 175).

84. Sharpley, C. F. (1987). Research findings on neurolinguistic programming: Nonsupportive data or an untestable theory? *Journal of Consulting Psychology, 34* (pp. 103–107).

85. Elich et al., Mental imagery.

86. Sharpley, Research findings on NLP.

87. Singer & Lalich, *Crazy therapies* (pp. 173–174).

88. Duncan & Konefal, Effective NLP.

Chapter 8

Spiritual Therapy

Spiritual Therapy encompasses a wide range of psychotherapeutic approaches that focus on extra corporeal influences on humans. In Past-Lives Therapy, a patient contacts his discarnate prior personality in a past life in an attempt to unlock and explain his current psychopathology. Christian Therapy spiritual warfare engages the alleged demons who are allied with Satan. There also may be hostile discarnate, deceased humans who invade other bodies and cause mischief as well as mental illness. Thus, entity depossession is a prescribed form of treatment when this occurs. On the other hand, benevolent entities, such as angels and spirit guides, can assist in improving a person's emotional health. Finally, A Course in Miracles is based on the words of Jesus Christ being channeled through a psychologist.

PAST-LIVES THERAPY

In Past-Lives Therapy, the regression is not just to the individual's own childhood but back before birth into another lifespan. There are some therapists who do Future Lives Therapy as well.[1] Past-Lives Therapy has origins in psychoanalysis and Eastern religions, as well as in Jungian Psychotherapy. The connection with psychoanalysis relates to the unlocking of repressed material, not available to conscious awareness. The Jungian notion of the collective unconscious is invoked by some past lives therapists to explain how the thoughts of previous generations can be embedded in the minds of current and future generations. Thus, all people have the ability "to dip into the vast collective memory bank of mankind."[2]

The aim of Past-Lives Therapy is to look for the cause of psychopathology not just in one's developmental history but in the decades and centuries prior to one's actual birth. Through hypnosis or guided imagery, the alleged source of mental disturbance may be uncovered. However, unlike traditional psychoanalysis, the source of the difficulty or mental block is not in this lifetime. A person's depression or phobia may be traced back to a prior lifetime.

It is contended that behind mental disorders and even personal complaints there are lurking "older, fuller stories with events often far more devastating and cataclysmic than the surface fear."[3] Under hypnosis, with the guidance of a psychotherapist, the patient retrieves memories from the prior lifetimes. When the patient is awakened, he can, as in psychoanalysis, integrate the new material and work through his current problems.

Past-Lives Therapy may be viewed in at least four ways. The first is a psychic approach.[4] From this perspective, a person who has psychic abilities is able to connect to traces of past-life memories and channel the thoughts to the present time. Tapping into the past life comports with the Jungian concept of the collective unconscious. That is, according to Jung, each person has a memory trace that contains eons of time. There are a number of noted channelers, including Edgar Cayce and Jane Roberts.[5]

The parapsychological approach is concerned with assessing in a critical and experimental way whether there is a scientific basis for reincarnation.[6] One avenue of attack on the validity of Past-Lives Therapy is to consider whether the patient is experiencing cryptoamnesia. Namely, the mind has unconsciously recorded virtually everything, including stories, films, TV, and so on, but has forgotten most of the material. These stories may become juxtaposed under hypnosis to reemerge as fresh and real past-life memories.[7] On this basis, the therapist would view past lives as a kind of free association technique.

The third view of past lives is the various religious approaches. Eastern religions in particular have focused on the concept of karma and reincarnation. Karma is a Sanskrit word that refers to the psychic inheritance from deeds and actions in this and previous lifetimes. Thus, one's destiny or karma is based not just on what happens in this lifetime, but on the accumulation of events in previous lifespans.[8] In Buddhism, there are karmic connections between lives, which are "similar in function to the DNA that makes up the chromosomes responsible for the inherited characteristics in the physical body."[9] In essence, the soul of the person returns by way of reincarnation.

The fourth view is termed the psychotherapeutic approach.[10] From this perspective, the therapist is somewhat akin to an agnostic. That is, a therapist neither believes nor disbelieves the reality of reincarnation, but rather, focuses on the meaning to the patient. In addition, the patient can be told that it doesn't matter if he believes in the validity of reincarnation for Past-Lives Therapy to work.[11]

Past-Lives Therapy may be conducted by anyone; there is no restriction on who can perform it. Furthermore, even when conducted by a licensed psychotherapist, all current problems are amenable to therapy. Thus, any mental disorder listed in the DSM-IV is considered appropriate for Past-Lives Therapy.

Case Reports

Elizabeth's Cats

The patient entered treatment due to anxiety over the thought of abandoning her cats when leaving the house. As a result, she found it difficult, if not impossible, to take vacations. On one occasion, when she left a cat with a friend, the cat got stuck in a closet and almost died.[12] As therapy progressed, two themes emerged: Elizabeth couldn't leave them alone because something would happen, and it was her fault for not caring enough for them.

In a past-life regression, the patient told a story with tears in her eyes. Elizabeth was an old woman in what might be northern Scotland. She was fighting with her husband who accused her of not caring for her children. The patient believed her husband might be right. The family was cast out into the storm, with the end result that they died. Elizabeth blamed herself for the tragedy.

This was "the appalling story that lay behind the fears of leaving her cats."[13] According to the past-lives therapist, the patient gained enormous relief and most significantly was able to take a two-week vacation and leave her cats with a friend.

Melinda's Sexual Abuse

Melinda had been consulting therapists about her inability to form close relationships and her sexual frigidity. In her history was "a clear memory of sexual molestation at 11 years."[14] Although she had discussed this matter in therapy and had attempted to ventilate her anger by hitting pillows and mattresses, some anger still remained. Initially, it appeared that the patient was re-experiencing the childhood traumas during her hypnosis sessions. Her words, however, indicated that she had slipped into another lifetime. Melinda found herself in Russia at the age of 11, where there was a group of soldiers who raped her. According to Woolger, the current life trauma served to "reawaken the latent past life level of the complex."[15]

Past-Lives Research

Perhaps the most carefully researched case was that of Bridey Murphy.[16] In 1956, a woman named Bridey Murphy was regressed to a past life by a neighbor. While under hypnosis, Bridey reported numerous details about her life in Ireland during the nineteenth century, including the date of her birth and a description of her marriage. It turns out, however, that the subject, under hypnosis, may have been recalling stories told to her by her nanny.[17] There were glaring historical inaccuracies that should give pause as to the veracity of her account.[18] Therefore, it can be reasonably concluded that people who are hypnotically age-regressed to a previous life may appear different in terms of developmental levels or speech or mannerisms due to an overlay of the current life perspective when responding.

Although thousands of patients have been subject to Past-Lives Therapy, virtually no clinical research demonstrates the validity of the reincarnation experiences. There is no basis in fact for the statement that "clinical research suggests that significant problems in this lifetime may be the direct result of previous past-life situations."[19] One of the major reasons that therapists persist in the face of no evidentiary support is that Woolger's "psychotherapeutic" view is adopted. Thus, it is not important whether the memories are true or false, but rather what importance they have to the patient.

Spanos (1996) created past-life personalities in a series of studies. [20] The subjects were hypnotically age-regressed into previous lifetimes. The subjects took new names and identities, often with elaborate details. A second experiment attempted to show how the experimenter/hypnotist's expectations could influence the contents of the memories and the images. Subjects who were given pre-hypnotic information about possible past-life identities were more likely to incorporate this information in the past-life narratives than those not receiving such information.

A third study by Spanos assessed whether the experimenter/hypnotist could influence the subject's memories regarding sexual abuse during a past life's narrative. Subjects in experimental conditions were told that children in past times had been abused. The other groups of subjects were not given this information. The past-life stories from subjects who had been told about childhood abuse contained more reports of sexual abuse compared to the control group.[21] Spanos et al. concluded that the memory reports from these subjects "are influenced by the beliefs and expectations conveyed by the experimenter."[22] Rather than evidence of reincarnation, these studies support the notion of a socially created identity reenactment. Information during these past-life sessions came from a multitude of sources including TV shows, novels and wish-fulfilling daydreams.[23]

Critique and Analysis of Past-Lives Therapy

There are no controlled research studies that demonstrate the viability of the underlying concept of reincarnation. None of the field studies to date has confirmed that people who are age-regressed to an alleged prior lifetime have veridical recollections. The use of suggestive techniques tends to taint the examination process and may produce artifactual responses. Thus, a person may confabulate, fantasize or speculate. Under hypnosis, suggestibility is heightened, and demand characteristics are rampant.

The lack of any type of experimental control or comparative research negates any conclusions that patients are improved as a result of Past-Lives Therapy. Assuming that there is even confirmed improvement in emotional functioning, Past-Lives Therapy for the time being remains no more than an interesting placebo.

Past-Lives Therapy cannot be considered a harmless treatment, however. Patients are informed or allowed to believe that horrible events occurred in a prior lifetime. Neither the therapist nor the patient knows whether the events are real or are fantasies. As a result, "the fiddling with memory that goes on in these sessions tends to leave some clients confused and dysfunctional."[24] Past-Lives Therapy is one of the unfortunate legacies of psychoanalysis in which there is an inexorable search for hidden psychopathogens.

During the last several decades, Past-Lives Therapy has evolved into a close cousin, if not a sibling, to Recovered Memory Therapy, where the search is for repressed memories of trauma without necessary regard for the truth or falsity of the alleged uncovered material. Intermixing Past-Lives Therapy with recovered memory of abuse only decreases the possibility of ascertaining the individual's actual psychosocial history. There is no reason to believe that combining various suggestive and untested techniques can help a person deal with the actual or root cause of emotional dysfunction.

CHRISTIAN THERAPY SPIRITUAL WARFARE

Biblically based Spiritual Therapy refers to the use of the New Testament scriptures to deal with emotional problems such as suicide and negative thoughts. An example of a biblically based therapy is found in *The Bondage Breakers*.[25] The book cover lists the author as the chairman of the Practical Theology Talbot School of Theology of Biola University. In Anderson's view, the cause of emotional problems relates to the invasion of demons. "Demons are like little invisible germs looking for someone to infect."[26] Satan carries on his evil and deceitful deeds through the use of emissaries such as demons, evil spirits or fallen angels.[27] Demons can have a number of negative effects, including drawing energy from several organs of the body, or they may live in the aura or surrounding energy field encompassing the physical body.[28] Demons may be somewhat different than entities or spirits in that they may be more solid and can even be physically seen.[29]

From this perspective, the cause of psychopathology and mental illness does not originate from within the psyche or the person's environment but rather from demonic influences. Demons are seen as real and not as symbolic or metaphoric. As gleaned from biblical scriptures, demons have several characteristics.[30] They may exist outside or inside humans; they can travel at will; they can talk to each other through humans, which reveals a taking over of the central nervous system; they have separate identities and have an intelligence. Demons may be manifested by blood-curdling screams, by being thrown across the room, and by ranting and raving and rolling around an office like a crazy man.[31]

The aim of spiritual counseling is to be free from Satan's bondage.[32] At each step of the journey to freedom, a person engages in prayers. Before beginning each step, a person prays out loud and makes a declaration to God and Christ. The prayer declares that God is in control and that Satan can be and will be banished. The person attempts to command Satan and the evil spirits to be released.

Christian Therapy Psychiatric In-Patient Programs

Christian Therapy in-patient programs in the United States combine the biblical approach with secular psychotherapy. The secular approach generally has a psychoanalytic framework, but there may be cognitive behavioral or other types of therapeutic orientations in the milieu of the in-patient treatment program.

In the 1980s, Christian psychotherapy attempted to merge with secular psychotherapy via special in-patient units. These units were first set up by psychiatrists from such institutions as Duke University and the University of Georgia. The next step was the initiation of a network of in-patient units across the United States. One of the largest organizations is the Minirth-Meier New Life Centers, which are in-patient treatment units.[33] Another large program is the Dr. Fred Gross Christian Therapy Program.

Minirth and Meier were trained in psychiatry at the University of Arkansas. Subsequently, they worked for a brief period with theological seminaries and later initiated an independent counseling center in Fort Worth, Texas. In a brief description, the magazine *Charisma* stated that Dr. Gross is considered the founder of Christian Therapy.[34] Over the previous 18 years, his approach "helped thousands of individuals become free from depression, compulsive behavior, substance abuse and dysfunctional family patterns."[35]

The in-patient programs are heavily marketed to evangelical Christians. The brochures and radio advertisements indicate that a number of emotional problems are treated. As noted, the mental disorders treated range from depression, chemical dependency, alcohol abuse and compulsive overeating. Part of the promotional material appeals directly to people who view the Bible as an infallible and literal guide. The Fred Gross Christian Therapy Program advertises a biblical approach but also mentions a psychoanalytic concept of defense mechanisms. The advertisement goes on to state that "by bringing together a born-again staff of clergy and mental health professionals, we offer more than in-depth therapy. We offer the opportunity to become reacquainted with Christian principles of love and forgiveness."[36]

The essence of the Christian Therapy Program is to provide a two- to three-week intensive program that combines a biblical approach with psychotherapy. Although the emphasis appears to be psychoanalytic with respect to the secular prong of the program, there is no restriction as to the nature or type of psychotherapy. Thus, any of the other multitudes of psychotherapeutic approaches can be utilized. In addition, the patients receive other modalities such as exercise; nutrition; living skills; recreation therapy; crafts and activities; outings to the community, such as Disneyland; and personal grooming. There are also personal devotional periods and Bible reading. The secular portion of the program appears to be virtually identical to the other in-patient programs.

On the Fred Gross in-patient unit, the patient is presented with a variety of written materials that combine the spiritual and secular approaches. A Christian psychotherapist will pray with the patient and invoke various biblical doctrines. For example, there is a short statement entitled "Authority of Satan" which cites the Gospel of John (5:19): "We know that we are of God and the whole world (around us) is under the power of the evil one."[37] The patient is informed which biblical scriptures are useful in counteracting demonic possession.[38] The therapist may engage in spiritual warfare in an attempt to have the patient's demons release their hold and stop oppressing the patient.

In discussing anger, the biblical and psychoanalytic approaches are integrated. Anger is viewed as hidden in unconscious denial, which leads to stuffing into the subconscious.[39] The biblical basis of anger as stated in the Fred Gross *Christian Therapy Program Manual* is found in Ephesians 2:3, namely, that a person is born angry or that anger may be learned,[40] which the *Christian Therapy Manual* cites as Proverbs 22:24–25.[41] Man's way of handling anger is contrasted with God's way. Thus, people may strike out or ventilate, clam up, internalize or pretend not to be angry. In contrast, God, as alluded to in Proverbs 29:11, states: "A fool always loses his temper, but a wise man holds it back."[42]

For group therapy, there are handouts that serve as guides. The 15-point handout relates to dealing with feelings and thoughts from within an eclectic therapeutic approach. There are tips that focus on body messages, such as being fidgety and sweating palms, but also the patient is asked to focus on whether others in the group remind them of someone else.

Case Reports

Barbara's Demons

Barbara was diagnosed as suffering from schizophrenia.[43] She was able to work but would suddenly resign after a few days or weeks due to stress. The patient believed that she was plagued by demons or evil beings that undermined her faith and made her do things she knew were wrong. She could hear the demons clearly, which caused her to lose her sense of concentration.

Her belief in demons seemed to disappear when she took medication. In addition, the therapist believed that the support she received from the local Christian community had reduced the number of psychiatric hospitalizations and the need for psychiatric care, other than medication.

Daisy: Paranoid Schizophrenia and Snakes

Daisy was described as a 26-year-old flower child from the 1960s.[44] She had been psychiatrically hospitalized three times within a five-year period, with a diagnosis of paranoid schizophrenia. After three weeks of spiritual counseling, she mentioned that snakes crawled on her at nighttime when in bed. When the snakes came, Daisy was instructed to say out loud, the following: "In the name of Christ, I command you to leave." After initial hesitation, Daisy was able to do so. The next week she reported that the snakes were gone. After a few months she was "free of demonic entanglements, and was ministering in the children's department at the church."[45]

Clinical Research

The question addressed here is: Does prayer affect emotional well-being and mental health? According to Dossey, a belief in a superior being can affect humans, as well as plants and animals.[46]

Several experiments have attempted to quantify the efficacy of prayer on physical and mental health. One of the earlier formal studies was called the Redlands Experiment.[47] The study took place at the University of Redlands in California. Volunteers were described as suffering from depression and fears and a variety of other problems. In Group One, no mention was made of religion during the therapy. The second group was comprised of subjects who prayed for themselves each night during the nine months of the study. Group Three consisted of a prayer and therapy group that lasted two hours each week.

All participants were given psychological tests, including the Rorschach and the Thematic Apperception Test (TAT). Nine months later, a new psychologist re-administered the tests. The results were as follows: Group One had 65 percent improvement, Group Two had no improvement and Group Three had 72 percent improvement. According to Dossey, the original researchers were pleased with the results and believed the patients in Group Three (group prayer and therapy) were healed of ailments, including migraine headaches, stuttering, ulcers and epilepsy.[48]

As Dossey noted, however, the study appears hopelessly flawed. Even assuming that the rates of improvement are accurate, it can be seen without statistical calculation that the no-religion group did as well as the group therapy and prayer group and vastly outperformed the individual prayer group. This study does not provide evidence of efficacy of prayer in resolving emotional and physical problems.

Of the 100 or so studies cited involving spiritual healing, none pertains to the effects of a belief in God and the effect on one's emotional condition. There may be some parapsychological components in some aspects of faith healing, but this does not necessarily implicate the relationship between the belief system and any alleged improvement in emotional functioning.

Critique and Analysis: Christian Therapy Spiritual Warfare

Apparently, no reports or research have documented the superiority of a Christian Therapy approach combining the secular therapies with the biblical approach.[49] Thus, there is no evidence at present to support the proposition that a synergistic effect develops when psychotherapy is mixed with Christian Therapy approaches.

One important distinction that needs to be made when integrating spiritual approaches with psychotherapy is to be able to differentiate a psychotic reaction from a "spiritual experience."[50] According to Mann, the spiritual experience can be characterized by the subtle energy of the superconscious.[51] Thus, "the superconscious flows from the higher centers of the brain and from the astral body."[52] Psychotic reactions, on the other hand, are attended by extreme feelings of agitation, anxiety and anger not seen in persons who are having a true spiritual experience. As noted in the snakes case example, the client, Daisy, was quite agitated. On the other hand, many psychotic patients can describe experiences while in a calm or tranquil state and with a sense of detachment. Thus, the distinction is tenuous at best.

One reason why no one has demonstrated dramatic results on the Christian Therapy units may be the cognitive overload that many patients may experience. At one moment a person is praying, based on very strict biblical doctrines. The next hour, the person could be receiving individual psychoanalytically oriented psychotherapy. Later in the day, a person could be in group therapy, which has a cognitive behavioral orientation. A patient must therefore integrate and juxtapose a set of possibly conflicting ideas in a matter of days or weeks.

In psychoanalysis, the patient is being asked to give allegiance to Freud's id, ego and superego. The patient may need to subscribe to the notion of unconscious determinants of behaviors. The intermingling of cognitive behavioral with psychodynamic approaches can present a patient with confusing perspectives. In spiritual warfare, the explanation shifts to demonic forces. Further difficulties may ensue if the patient does not adhere to the same biblical interpretation that is presented by the therapist/pastor.

With respect to the effect of prayer on emotional health, the research has not yet shown any positive findings in humans. No empirical support has been presented for the presence of demons, but rather only anecdotal reports. In the final analysis, the patient in Christian Therapy units is being bombarded with two types of religious healing approaches. Both psychoanalysis and spiritual warfare are faith-based. Although rapprochement has been argued,[53] it does not appear that integrating one faith-based system with another is a recipe for success.

ENTITY DE-POSSESSION THERAPY

Entity possession is another explanation of the cause of psychopathology. Unlike demons, which may be emissaries of Satan, entities are thought to originate from discarnate individuals. Thus, when people die, they may return in a spirit form to inhabit and possess another living person. The working hypothesis is that personality survives death.[54] Thus, entities are nonphysical beings or presences that become attached to human beings in a parasitic fashion and, as a result, cause emotional, mental and physical problems.[55] Entities, however, are not helpful like angels or beneficial as spirit guides may be. Entities are toxic and pest-like. The expression, "I don't know what's gotten into me," takes on a literal meaning in the context of entity therapy.

In spiritually oriented therapy, a major cause of psychopathology is hypothesized to be possessing entities. For example, in the case of obesity, the spirits are not only responsible for the weight gain but may not be particularly interested in weight loss or dieting. A patient's father-in-law, who craved chocolate, invaded his daughter-in-law and passed on the craving to her.[56] Anxiety, depression and even schizophrenia may be traceable to the alleged entity.

A case of phobia about highway driving was traced to a female spirit who had committed suicide by driving her car on the same highway that the patient had been driving on.[57] Thus, an entity may wander until it can locate a suitable host. Since a person has no awareness of the invasion, strange new behavior can be puzzling.

The identification of possession can be answered by several questions in the affirmative from a checklist.[58] The items include self-reports on mood swings and sudden changes in anxiety or depression, inner voices heard by the patient and problems with memory and concentration. Emotional or physical reaction to reading *The Unquiet Dead* also may be a sign of possession.

To alleviate possession, the therapist engages in de-possession therapy through the use of guided instructions while the patient is hypnotized. The use of hypnosis allows the therapist to communicate directly with the entities. If the patient seeks out an entity de-possession therapist, attention will likely focus on rooting out the entities. The therapist may interpret what the spirits are saying and transmit the information to the patient.

The entity is informed that it is not the patient but, rather, the entity that is dead.[59] The entity is persuaded to leave and go to another place. The procedure starts out with the therapist identifying and informing the entity of its existence. For example, the therapist might say, "You are inside Mary's body, but you are not Mary." The entity might be asked to go back to a time when it was inside its own body.[60] Later, the entity is asked to leave and go back to its own spiritual body.[61] Thus, the de-possession therapist also functions as a *channeler* and performs a kind of seance.

Case Reports

Anne and the Deadly Boss

A patient, Anne, indicated in her first session of de-possession therapy that she had dreamed about her boss. No formal psychosocial history was taken, nor was a psychodiagnosis formulated. A major problem seemed to be that her boss wanted to control the patient. Initially, the therapist explored the possibility that the relationship with the patient's father might have some bearing on her current problem with Bill, the boss.

In order to get to the root of the problem, the therapist attempted to contact Anne's entities. She was hypnotized, and the therapist began to talk to the alleged entities. When this happened, there was a noticeable shift in Anne's affect from a "blissful expression to one of total agitation."[62] According to Fiore, "this was my evidence" that Anne was invaded by a spirit. According to Anne, she felt as if a man's spirit had been with her. The therapist also engaged in Past-Lives Therapy in dealing with Anne's feelings toward Bill.

After one session, the patient appeared confident, relaxed and was impeccably groomed. She had a confident stride, smiled pleasantly and was less aggressive. Most significantly, her approach toward her boss was different. She had more energy and was putting more effort into her work. When the therapist inquired if the spirit had left, Anne answered that she was pretty sure that this had happened.

Jason: The Fiery Deaths

A 29-year-old patient named Jason entered therapy because of job stress and loneliness.[63] The therapist informed Jason that his problems were due to mental energy locked up inside an individual. He underwent hypnosis in order to release stress and to free himself from the invasion of various entities. As a result of the hypnosis, entities were located.

The initial sessions produced some confusion and a decrease in job performance. The therapist counseled that if all the entities were released, Jason would feel better. Thus, the patient was hypnotized and asked to visualize all his entities entering a barn. The barn was set afire by a bolt of lightning, burning all the entities in a fiery death. As a result of this experience, he felt a sense of unreality and estrangement. He thereupon sought emergency help at a psychiatric clinic.

Clinical Research

There appears to be no formal research on Entity De-possession Therapy. The only clinical outcome research materials are the numerous anecdotes reported by the various therapists. In Entity De-possession Therapy as well as other psychotherapeutic approaches, the clinician offers self-authentication. Thus, if the patient appears different after the alleged entities or demons have left, it proves the reality of the invasion and exorcism. No comparative research has been presented with placebo controls, nor have there been any critically examined follow-up studies on the thousands of patients who have undergone Entity De-possession Therapy.

Under these circumstances, it is predictable that "Spanos"-type research would demonstrate that subjects asked to role-play entity possession could readily do so. Being able to portray or experience entity possession doesn't necessarily negate the reality of such experiences; rather, it raises the possibility that the demand characteristics and suggestive use of hypnosis may play a major role in eliciting the entities.

At this point, there is only anecdotal evidence regarding the transmission of thoughts, feelings and emotions from a deceased person into a living person. There are reports that individuals who receive transplants may, at least initially, have certain cognitions or thoughts that originated from the person from whom they obtained the transplant. Although this would be an interesting line of future research, it may not have a significant bearing on the practice of psychotherapy for several reasons. First, there does not appear to be any proof at present that there are invading entities. Second, there has been no documentation that the alleged invading entities are in any way able to control a person's thoughts, emotions and behavior.

Critique and Analysis of Entity De-possession Therapy

The same criticism in Past-Lives Therapy pertains to entity de-possession. Namely, there is no clinical proof that a person is invaded by entities or that another person can help to eradicate their alleged presence. The therapist who espouses entity de-possession engages in self-validation of his methods. Second, the therapist makes an inappropriate use of hypnosis when he or she attempts to inculcate the patient with his or her belief system in the validity of discarnate entities.[64] The patient "experiences a type of trance mediumship with a form of modern-day exorcism."[65] Third, there is a focus on only one possible cause of a person's problem, which tends to ignore other, more relevant aspects of a person's mental functioning.

ANGELS AND SPIRIT GUIDES

As noted by the title of Brad Steiger's book *Guardian Angels and Spirit Guides*, some have postulated the existence of benevolent beings from the other side.[66] Angels are similar to personal spirits and can directly communicate with people.[67] Angels may have different forms, such as a human figure, with or without wings, a globe of light, or even a spiral of energy.[68] One view of angels is that they are "a benevolent being of light."[69] As in Entity De-possession Therapy, the angelic presences are considered to be literal and not figurative. Thus, when asking an individual to get in touch with her inner angel or to allow an angel to assist her, reference is made to an actual spiritual presence and not a symbol.

Stories abound of the influence of angelic forces that have assisted humans.[70] In Curry's view, "angels comfort me, protect me and make their presence known."[71] During one of her travels along a dusty path, she had trouble breathing, felt dizzy and was coughing up green phlegm.[72] Curry got in touch with her helping angels.[73] Within her mind's eye, she visualized a little green angel with green wings inside her lungs who was shoveling out fluid from her lungs. With the spiritual assistance of the angels, Curry reached a flat part of the trail.[74] At this point, a picture was taken, which now appears on the front cover of Curry's book. The angel is not immediately obvious. "You may need to expand your frame of reference, but if you choose to see her, the angel may appear."[75] The photographic lab could not explain how the "negative has more light than their equipment could normally match."[76]

Some individuals claim to have seen and heard angels.[77] Angelic figures were observed by a five-year-old girl who had a clear vision of a tall and strong-looking figure with long hair but no wings. Before the angel faded away, his voice could be heard identifying himself as a guardian angel. The guardian angel provided assistance later in her life, saving her from being stabbed in an elevator. She also reported that angelic forces helped her lose 150 pounds.

Guided imagery or hypnosis is one pathway to contacting the angelic helper.[78] For example, a patient is put in a relaxed state and asked to go to the bottom of the sea; the patient floats upward into her own body through the top of her own head. The therapist then counts from five to zero, and "she was at the main source of trauma in her body—the solar plexus."[79]

In group settings, an angelic circle is created wherein the participants can call for angelic assistance. The group, which is led by a psychotherapist, is in a candle-lit room "and scented with rose oil mixed with holy water."[80] As everyone holds hands, the group leader entreats the angels to enter the room. During the group session, the leader relates and interprets the angels' presence to the participants. It does not appear that there are actual visual or auditory manifestations of the angels in these sessions. The participants who bask in the angelic presence feel nourished and relieved of their problems.[81]

Case Reports

Angels

A patient underwent Past-Lives Therapy and discovered that she did not appropriately grieve, but rather was holding in a number of her feelings. She also had another traumatic experience related to her solar plexus wherein she was a young soldier killed in battle by a sword driven into that area of her body.[82] In her current life, she also experienced childhood trauma wherein she witnessed the shock of her mother being killed in a car accident.

The various traumas resulted in negative emotions of grief and feelings of loss and anger. The patient indicated that these various negative emotions were "dirty black and gray energy."[83] According to Rossetti, "The angels help to draw this dirty energy out of the body and aura and instantaneously transmuted the energies."[84] When the negative energies were released, the helpful angels were able to fill up the area with a divine healing energy.[85]

Spirit Guides

Spirit guides are contacted with the help of a healer or shaman. Native American Indians believe in the ability to make contact with spirit guides who may be on another plane of existence.[86] The spirits are very loving energies and are designed to protect individuals from other energies they may encounter in other universes.[87] The spirit guides or energies may appear as human or can be in the form of animals. At present, the work of a shamanistic healer appears to overlap with a variety of techniques commonly used by psychotherapists such as meditation, visualization and hypnosis.[88]

In order to meet one's protector, a ceremony is arranged for the "students."[89] All the participants stand in a circle for an opening prayer. They are then asked to sit with their backs straight up and go into a "meditative" state. Next, the participants are asked to focus on what they want to do and to ask the universe for guidance and assistance. The healing therapist lights a candle and may burn sage to clean the area.[90] Then, the shaman quiets her mind, breathes deeply, focuses her attention and steps into the center of "power."[91] Next is a prayer, which starts out as "Great Spirit, Universe Creator, we humbly ask for your love and your guidance. . . . We humbly come before you this day to meet our loving protectors so they may guide us on our journeys." Participants then close their eyes, allowing their minds to settle down and then proceed to say, "Universe, we come before you this day to introduce this person to his or her loving protector; we ask this energy to make itself known to us now."[92]

Clinical Research

There appears to be no clinical research documentation as to the presence of angel or spirit guides. Whether there are spirits in other dimensions has not been empirically verified. Clues as to the presence of angels, such as "pennies on the sidewalk, feathers in the air, the tinkling of bells, the flickering of lights," do not constitute evidence of the presence of angelic beings.[93] Nor have pictures or photographs authenticated the presence of angels or spirits. The interesting light form on the cover of *I Believe in Angels* cannot be distinguished from a photographic artifact.

Critique and Analysis

The presence of angels and/or spirits has not been clinically documented. Only anecdotal evidence tells us that there are other sources of energy forces in the universe. Also, there does not appear to be any evidence to indicate that people engaging in various ritualistic ceremonies have significantly improved their mental health. Hundreds, if not thousands, of testimonials may be available, but there does not seem to be any clinical evidence that people who undergo healing by way of a shaman have significantly altered their emotional condition. Furthermore, obviously no studies have compared and contrasted the potential placebo elements involved in these healing activities with other active forms of psychotherapy.

Angelic and shamanic healing is another example of the juxtaposition of secular and religious beliefs. The religious belief used in individual or group ceremonies may not be congruent with those of the participants. For example, in the case of angelic healing, there is a Buddhist flavor: "Spiritual consciousness allows me to enter into a dialogue with the sacred Presence. . . . The Buddha's arms open to embrace me."[94] The participant may have to reconcile lifelong religious beliefs with new ones imposed by the therapist.

The use of hypnosis and other types of suggestive techniques may simply be reinforcing a shared belief in that which is not provable. By the time a person enters into a group setting to work on contacting the inner angel or spirit guides, the demand characteristics of the situation, plus the reinforcement by other participants as well as the therapist, may tend to perpetuate the belief in what actually may be magical thinking. Not only does the patient not directly deal with his or her core issues, but there may be ethical problems as well. As Singer and Lalich have noted, techniques such as entity de-possession, as well as shamanistic healing for example, are "offering a quasi-religious/spiritual schema under the guise of scientific psychology."[95]

A COURSE IN MIRACLES

Many therapies have arisen from the research laboratory or in clinical practice. A Course in Miracles did not follow the usual pathway in which clinical research or trial runs with actual patients are performed. Channeling, the medium by which A Course in Miracles was produced, occurs when one person receives mental messages from another person. The provider of the messages is usually deceased or in some other dimension of time and space.

A Course in Miracles was written by an atheistic psychologist from Columbia University named Helen Schucman.[96] Dr. Schucman had a series of waking dreams and visions in which she heard an inner voice that eventually told her to take notes on a so-called course in miracles.[97] She identifies the author of the voice as Jesus Christ.[98] A Course in Miracles is held to be a biblically based text, which brings "a correction of traditional Christianity to the world in modern psychological language."[99] There were no field studies or experiments; rather, the material was presented by Jesus Christ by way of a psychologist who channeled his voice. The transcription led to a 1200-page, three-volume text.

Although A Course in Miracles can be considered psychotherapy, the teacher, guide or therapist does not have to be licensed or trained in psychotherapy. One of the popularizers of A Course in Miracles, Marianne Williamson, apparently had no formal training in mental health.[100] Since it is conducted as a spiritual journey, there is no restriction as to who can conduct the training.

Forgiveness is a key concept in A Course in Miracles. It is forgiveness that allows the transformation of the self.[101] For example, "*Forgiveness*, once complete, brings timelessness so close, the song of Heaven can be heard" [emphasis in the original].[102] It is also noted, however, that forgiveness is a type of illusion. "Forgiveness is release from all illusion, and that is why it is impossible to totally forgive."[103] All the writings are thought to be based in Christianity. Thus, such issues as sin, guilt, atonement and fear are all said to be congruent with the Christian Bible. A Course in Miracles teaches that fear is an illusion and that only love is real.

The purpose of psychotherapy is to remove the blocks to truth.[104] It attempts to restore the patient's ability to make his or her own decisions. The goal of psychotherapy is to help the patient deal with one fundamental error: "the belief that anger brings him something he really wants and that by justifying attack he is protecting himself."[105] There are no articles or texts regarding intake and diagnosis of a patient who is undergoing A Course in Miracles. The patient can be dealt with simply on the basis of alleged misperceptions that he or she is bringing to the psychotherapy table. There appear to be no published articles on ascertaining how a person would be treated during the course of A Course in Miracles. There are no articles indicating what the length of treatment might be.

A Course in Miracles deals with a variety of mental health issues and problems, including anxiety, obesity, addiction and depression. The patient obtains guidance through the texts and in verbal interaction sessions with a teacher/therapist, either in individual or group settings. In individual sessions, the patient may discuss clinical issues but will receive instruction by way of the principles enunciated in A Course in Miracles. There may also also be group discussions and lectures. It is vaguely similar to a cognitive approach in that both deal with distortions in thinking. In addition, there appears to be an Eastern influence in which the "metaphysics of the Course is thus more aligned with Eastern mysticism than traditional Western religion."[106]

Case Report: Seeing the Light

A self-report by Anne indicates that she was an atheist until she began A Course in Miracles. During her meditation, she began to communicate with people who had passed on. She believed these were real communications and not just fantasies.

As a result, she attempted to call on the spirit of Helen Schucman for career advice. Although Anne did not specifically get this advice, she was told to relax and focus on the "light." The light that was in vision was inside Anne's mind and filled her with a great sense of well-being.[107] The student received advice in her own voice, which was quite discordant. As it turned out, however, she decided to follow this advice.

Research

No research has been done on the effect of A Course on Miracles on one's mental health. There are numerous testimonials but no validation that studying the texts is a significant factor in altering one's emotional functioning.

The limited investigation into channeling should give one pause before Jesus Christ is accepted as the "author" of A Course in Miracles. For example, Singer and another author/researcher, Carl Raschke, independently listened to hundreds of hours of videotapes and audiotapes of alleged channelers from centuries ago.[108] Of particular note, the channelers spoke in a "pseudo-British accent"[109] at a time when the English language had not as yet arisen. The results of this investigation led Raschke to conclude that channeling is a form of a delusion that leads to the acceptance of the irrational.[110]

Critique of A Course in Miracles

To accept the notion that A Course in Miracles was channeled by an atheist psychologist, one would have to suspend a significant amount of belief. There appears to be no research that demonstrates the reality of channeling. Thus, the reality of the origins of the course itself could be based on an illusion.

Critics of the channeled materials have pointed out that A Course in Miracles may not actually be based on the teachings of Jesus Christ. It contains a number of significant deviations from biblical doctrines, and there also seem to be indications of Eastern religions that have entered into the course philosophy.[111] A supporter of A Course in Miracles claims that the course directly challenges "significant elements of contemporary Christianity."[112]

The question that arises is, if Schucman were literally channeling Jesus Christ, why are there apparent significant deviations from the biblical scriptures? It is as if Freud were being channeled, yet the text had elements of Jung, Adler or even Ellis.

Cognitive overload is one possibility when a participant is confronted with conflicting views between his own core religious beliefs and those of A Course in Miracles. Because of the impact on the individual, there may be confusion and disorientation.[113] Because of the lack of empirical data on any aspect of A Course in Miracles, it is not known to what extent the course may lead to negative outcomes.

Without any comparative research, it has not even been established that there are any positive outcomes more significant than a placebo or no treatment. Moreover, if the focus is on eliminating illusions but one is never able to do so, there may be no way for the therapy to end. There appear to be no objective criteria for determining the scope and nature of treatment. How does one know if one is in the middle or end of therapy? Moreover, how does the teacher know what is more real than this student? Who is going to verify the superiority of the teacher's reality over that of this student? No external criteria show that one's reality is any better than anyone else's. There is a circularity in that, if forgiveness is a release from an illusion, but it's impossible to totally forgive, then is one not trapped in an illusion? Thus, one is in an endless quest to search out the truth, which can never be achieved. The result is that therapy here, as in some cases of psychoanalysis, is interminable.

GENERAL CRITIQUE OF SPIRITUAL THERAPIES

An interesting parallel may be seen between Spiritual Therapy in particular and psychotherapy in general. The underlying causative factors in psychopathology are taken on an almost face value in Spiritual Therapy. In past lives, there is as yet no clinical verification of reincarnation. The alleged extracorporeal entities or beings have not been verified. In psychoanalysis, however, the alleged psychopathogens also have not been confirmed (see Chapter 2).

Therapists who engage in Spiritual Therapy implicitly or explicitly validate what the patient is telling them about the alleged pathogens. There are similarities with Recovered Memory Therapy and psychoanalysis in that the patient's narrative history is what is important rather than the actual truth of the matter. The patient, however, enters with perhaps a pre-conceived belief in the approach and encounters a hypnosis session from an authority figure. This interaction between therapist and patient tends to self-validate the reality of the factual basis of the therapy. At any rate, the patient feels that the entities are real, that demons exist and that there really is a past life. The patients are virtually never informed that the approach is controversial, untested and subject to alternative explanations such as demand characteristics, placebo or suggestion.

The outcome studies in Spiritual Therapy are virtually all of the anecdotal variety. Few studies have been done on the efficacy of prayer in promoting the mental health of humans. Studies on past lives implicate demand characteristics and suggestion. Group cohesion and other dynamics may be at play when people engage in de-possession therapy or use angelic guidance. Thus, even if improvement were demonstrated, without controlled studies there would be a serious gap in logic if one reached the conclusion that supernatural forces, entities or demons assist in helping persons or can be the cause of mental illness.

NOTES

1. Goldberg, G. (1982). *Past lives, future lives: Accounts of regression and progression through hypnosis.* North Hollywood, Calif.: Newcastle Publishing.

2. Woolger, R. J. (1988). *Other lives, other selves: A Jungian psychotherapist discovers past lives* (p. 41). New York: Bantam.

3. Woolger, *Other lives, other selves* (p. 95).

4. Woolger, *Other lives, other selves* (p. 52).

5. Woolger, *Other lives, other selves* (p. 54).

6. Woolger, *Other lives, other selves* (p. 63).

7. Woolger, *Other lives, other selves* (p. 65).

8. Woolger, *Other lives, other selves* (p. 353); Goldberg, *Past lives, future lives* (pp. 26, 27).

9. Goldberg, *Past lives, future lives* (p. 28).

10. Woolger, *Other lives, other selves* (p. 81).

11. Woolger, *Other lives, other selves* (p. 82).

12. Woolger, *Other lives, other selves* (p. 95).

13. Woolger, *Other lives, other selves* (p. 97).

14. Woolger, *Other lives, other selves* (p. 137).

15. Woolger, *Other lives, other selves* (p. 140).

16. Bernstein, M. (1956). *The search for Bridey Murphy.* Garden City, N.Y.: Doubleday.

17. Singer, M. T. & Lalich, J. (1996). *Crazy therapies: What are they? Do they work?* (p. 51). San Francisco: Jossey-Bass.

18. Spanos, N. P. (1996). *Multiple identities & false memories: A sociocognitive perspective.* Washington, D.C.: American Psychological Association.

19. Mann, R. L. (1998). *Sacred healing: Integrating spirituality with psychotherapy* (p. 191). Nevada City, Calif.: Blue Dolphin Publishing.

20. Spanos, *Multiple identities* (p. 135).

21. Spanos, *Multiple identities* (p. 135).

22. Spanos, *Multiple identities* (p. 140).

23. Spanos, *Multiple identities* (p. 140).

24. Singer & Lalich, *Crazy therapies* (p. 50).

25. Anderson, N. T. (1993). *The bondage breakers.* Eugene, Ore.: Harvest House Publishers.

26. Anderson, *The bondage breakers* (p. 77).

27. Anderson, *The bondage breakers* (p. 100).

28. Rossetti, F. (1992). *Psycho regression: A new system for healing and personal growth* (p. 62). York Beach, Maine: Samuel Weiser.

29. Rossetti, *Psycho regression* (p. 62).

30. Anderson, *The bondage breakers* (p. 102).

31. Anderson, *The bondage breakers* (p. 112).

32. Anderson, *The bondage breakers* (p. 185).

33. Blazer, D. (1998). *Freud vs. God: How psychiatry lost its soul and Christianity lost its mind* (p. 172). Downers Grove, Ill.: Intervarsity Press.

34. *Charisma*, August 1992.

35. *Charisma*, August 1992.

36. *Charisma*, July 1992.

37. Gross, Fred. *Christian therapy program in-patient manual* (p. 45), quoting 1 John 5:19.

38. Gross, *Christian therapy program in-patient manual* (p. 46).

39. Gross, *Christian therapy program in-patient manual* (p. 98).

40. Gross, *Christian therapy program in-patient manual* (p. 98).

41. Gross, *Christian therapy program in-patient manual* (p. 98).

42. Gross, *Christian therapy program in-patient manual* (p. 100).

43. Blazer, *Freud vs. God* (p. 26).

44. Anderson, *The bondage breakers* (p. 57).

45. Anderson, *The bondage breakers* (p. 58).

46. Dossey, L. (1993). *Healing words: The power of prayer and the practice of medicine.* San Francisco: Harper.

47. Dossey, *Healing words* (p. 172).

48. Dossey, *Healing words* (p. 174).

49. Blazer, *Freud vs. God* (p. 173).

50. Mann, R. L. (1998). *Sacred healing: Integrating spirituality with psychotherapy* (p. 186). Nevada City, Calif.: Blue Dolphin Publishing.

51. Mann, *Sacred healing* (p. 187).

52. Mann, *Sacred healing* (p. 187).

53. Blazer, *Freud vs. God.*

54. Fiore, E. (1987). *The unquiet dead: A psychologist treats spirit possessions* (p. 1). New York: Ballantine.

55. Sagan, S. (1994). *Entities: Parasites of the body of energy* (p. 1). Roseville, Australia: Clairvision School.

56. Fiore, *The unquiet dead* (p. 47).

57. Fiore, *The unquiet dead* (p. 42).

58. Fiore, *The unquiet dead* (p. 147).
59. Fiore, *The unquiet dead* (p. 133).
60. Fiore, *The unquiet dead* (p. 134).
61. Fiore, *The unquiet dead* (p. 135).
62. Fiore, *The unquiet dead* (p. 58).
63. Singer & Lalich, *Crazy therapies* (p. 68).
64. Singer & Lalich, *Crazy therapies* (pp. 84–85).
65. Singer & Lalich, *Crazy therapies* (p. 71).
66. Steiger, B. (1995). *Guardian angels and spirit guides: True accounts of benevolent beings from the other side*. New York: Penguin Group.
67. Ankerberg, J. & Weldon, J. (1996). *Encyclopedia of new age beliefs* (p. 30). Eugene, Ore.: Harvest House Publishers.
68. Rossetti, *Psycho regression* (p. 108).
69. Curry, J. (1995). *I believe in angels* (p. 17). Novato, Calif.: Win Publishing.
70. Curry, *I believe in angels* (p. 17); Steiger, *Guardian angels and spirit guides*.
71. Curry, *I believe in angels*.
72. Curry, *I believe in angels* (p. 92).
73. Curry, *I believe in angels* (p. 94).
74. Curry, *I believe in angels* (p. 94).
75. Curry, *I believe in angels* (p. 104).
76. Curry, *I believe in angels* (p. 104).
77. *Life Magazine*, Summer 1995 (p. 65).
78. Steiger, *Guardian angels and spirit guides* (p. 265).
79. Rossetti, *Psycho regression* (p. 113).
80. *Life Magazine*, Summer 1995 (p. 78).
81. *Life Magazine*, Summer 1995 (p. 78).
82. Rossetti, *Psycho regression* (p. 113).
83. Rossetti, *Psycho regression* (p. 114).
84. Rossetti, *Psycho regression* (p. 114).
85. Rossetti, *Psycho regression* (p. 114).
86. Steiger, *Guardian angels and spirit guides* (p. 52).
87. Gregg, S. (1997). *Find the sacred self: A shamanic workbook* (pp. 42–43). St. Paul, Minn.: Llewellyn Publications.
88. Ankerberg & Weldon, *Encyclopedia of new age beliefs* (pp. 537–538).
89. Gregg, *Find the sacred self* (p. 46).
90. Gregg, *Find the sacred self* (p. 47).
91. Gregg, *Find the sacred self* (p. 47).
92. Gregg, *Find the sacred self* (p. 48).
93. *Life Magazine*, Summer 1995 (p. 72).
94. Curry, *I believe in angels* (p. 114).
95. Singer & Lalich, *Crazy therapies* (p. 85).
96. Schucman, H. (1978). *A Course in Miracles*. Mill Valley, Calif.: Foundation for Inner Peace.
97. Miller, D. P. (1997). *The complete story of the course: The history, the people and the controversies behind A Course in Miracles* (p. 10). Berkeley, Calif.: Fearless Books.
98. Miller, *The complete story of . . . A Course in Miracles* (p. 4).
99. Miller, *The complete story of . . . A Course in Miracles* (p. 10).

100. Miller, *The complete story of . . . A Course in Miracles* (pp. 92–93).

101. Miller, *The complete story of . . . A Course in Miracles* (p. 3).

102. Schucman, *A Course in Miracles* (p. 579).

103. Schucman, *A Course in Miracles* (p. 470).

104. *Psychotherapy: purpose, process and practice: An extension of the principles of A Course in Miracles* (1976) (p. 2). Glen Ellen, Calif.: Foundation for Inner Peace.

105. *Psychotherapy: purpose, process and practice* (p. 4).

106. Miller, *The complete story of . . . A Course in Miracles* (p. 4).

107. Miller, *The complete story of . . . A Course in Miracles* (pp. 194–195).

108. Singer & Lalich, *Crazy therapies* (p. 76).

109. Singer & Lalich, *Crazy therapies* (p. 76).

110. Singer & Lalich, *Crazy therapies* (p. 77).

111. Ankerberg & Weldon, *Encyclopedia of new age beliefs* (p. 7).

112. Miller, *The complete story of . . . A Course in Miracles* (p. 4).

113. Miller, *The complete story of . . . A Course in Miracles* (p. 182).

Chapter 9

From Buddha Psychotherapy to Alien Abductions

In the open market, many new therapies are available. By now, the number of psychotherapies has more than likely surpassed the 500 mark. A glance at various periodicals and publications reveals that the permutations and combinations of therapies are endless. In this chapter, a sample of four modalities has been selected for review and analysis. Buddha Psychotherapy attempts to integrate Western psychotherapy, such as psychoanalysis, with Eastern religions and philosophies. Thought Field Therapy and Palm Therapy are also blends of the old and the new, ranging from acupuncture to a hypothesis about thought fields and energies. Finally, Alien Abduction Therapy focuses on the possible or actual abduction by extraterrestrial beings as a causative factor in a person's psychopathology.

BUDDHA PSYCHOTHERAPY

Interest in Eastern philosophies and religions can be traced back to the earlier part of the twentieth century and the writings of Jung and William James. Work in the areas of humanistic psychology and transpersonal psychotherapy resonates with some of the ideas of the Eastern religions and philosophies, particularly with the search for authenticity and identity-seeking.[1] Few formal attempts have been made to integrate Western psychotherapy with Eastern philosophies.

In 1995 Epstein attempted to blend psychoanalysis with Buddha psychology.[2] A second integrative approach arises from the middle-path analysis, which is in the "Buddhist tradition of applied philosophical psychology."[3] The middle-path analysis is similar to Rational Emotive Behavioral Therapy. The essence of the relationship between Buddhism and psychoanalysis is an interest in who a person is. "The question of the self has emerged as a cognitive focus of Buddhism and psychoanalysis."[4] The starting point for Buddha psychology is that a person's core sense of identity is confused.

Meditation is the underlying technique in Buddhist philosophy. Psychotherapy may be critical to expose and reduce a person's erotic and aggressive tendencies, but more is needed in order to deal with a person's restless and insecure self. According to Buddhism, it's the fear of experiencing one's self directly that causes suffering.[5] Through meditation, a person goes beyond the psychotherapeutic method and uses techniques of self-examination that are unknown in the West.[6]

Mental development is at the heart of meditation. Thus, there will be bare attention to various subtle phenomena, such as the breath coming in and out.[7] This concept seems at least somewhat reminiscent of the Gestalt Therapy approach, which focuses on a totality of experiences. Epstein notes that meditation and psychotherapy, though similar, are not identical. In psychoanalytic psychotherapy, the person tends to lead to experiences that bring up earlier emotional relationships, which *reconstruct* the person's history. On the other hand, Buddhist meditation intensifies a person's ego functions so that the sense of self is simultaneously magnified and deconstructed. In psychotherapy, the person may experience transference, which relates to how a person's earlier interactions may be reflected in current, ongoing perceptions of others. In meditation, however, the person does not come face to face with the therapist, but rather comes in contact with "various cherished images of self, only to reveal how ultimately lacking such images are."[8]

The person who meditates within the Buddhist perspective goes beyond therapy toward a plateau of self-understanding that is not ordinarily available just through psychotherapy alone. The essential element of meditation is that it "takes actual qualities of mind and cultivates them internally so that the person's powers of observation are increased."[9]

The Buddha Psychotherapeutic Approach

In combining Buddha Psychotherapy with meditation, the therapist may ask the patient to be involved in verbal psychotherapy, then meditate subsequently and bring back into the therapy session what may have emerged in the meditation. It is felt, however, that utilizing the two modalities has a synergistic and perhaps a multiplicative effect. Thus, the key concepts in the integration relate to Freud's notions of remembering, repeating and working through.[10] During meditation, a person may be able to remember material from early in his life that has been a major factor in coloring his behavior.[11] Thus, one of the primary purposes of integrating Buddhism with psychoanalysis is to help people deal effectively with the uncovering of hitherto repressed material. Because of emotional blocks, a patient may not be able to dredge up the repressed material, but rather is doomed to repeat past behavior. Thus, the patient is unaware of what he was doing.[12] Freud attempted to break through the repetition by analysis of the patient's resistance. The Buddha Psychotherapy approach helps the patient deal with his experiences by allowing him to come in touch with each moment.

The last element is termed "working through," which is a process of "repossessing that from which we have become estranged, of accepting that which we would rather deny."[13] A person who is meditating may be able to widen his view of what his difficult emotions are and may be more able to accept them as a present-day force.[14] By combining psychotherapy with meditation, a person may find it "possible to cultivate a mind that neither clings nor rejects" and is able to alter the way he experiences both time and himself.[15]

In the cognitive-Buddhist therapy approach, the aim is to increase the accuracy and appreciation of reality.[16] The goal is to be freed from all emotional problems, "to liberate all emotionally constricted energy and vitality."[17] Prior to initiating therapy, the participant meditates in order to develop a level of heightened focus. There are preliminary conversations with the therapist, who assists the patient with the sharpening of awareness and concentration.[18]

The patient undergoes a seven-step process with the aid of the therapist. First, the emotional problem is defined with an attempt to identify a feeling such as anger, fear or anxiety.[19] Next, it is shown that the so-called cause of the feeling or problem cannot be located. Thus, in a paradoxical fashion, the patient is shown that her perceived belief is the source of the emotion and cannot be the cause of the problem.[20] The therapist uses what is described as a systems cybernetics model in his dialogue with the patient to demonstrate the apparent logic of the therapist's position. The third step is to ascertain the conditions under which the feeling arises and is maintained.[21]

In the fourth step, the analysis concerns whether the emotional responses are in essence self-conditioned. The issue that is pursued is whether the consequences of an emotional reaction are not linked to an environmental factor.[22] In the fifth step, the therapist may expose external conditions that prompt the feeling or problem, such as issues at home or at work. Next the therapist explores whether the emotional problem "is conditioned by factors or influences that lie outside of the disturbance itself."[23]

The next step is to analyze the various factors that relate to the person's problems. Thus, a person may become angry when at home, feeling under pressure from a boss or already feeling annoyed. Through the therapist's logical discourse, the patient is shown that if no particular factor is responsible for her feelings, then neither is any combination.[24]

In the concluding step, the patient reaches the logical conclusion that there is no reason or cause to feel anxious, depressed, humiliated or a loss of self-esteem.[25] "We have seen that there is in fact nothing to make the client anxious."[26] The therapist explains to the patient that the reason she is anxious, for example, is that she is acting in the erroneous belief that there is a cause for her emotional problems.

Case Example

The healing power of releasing repressed memories is exemplified by a case involving a science teacher named Joe.[27] The patient was in psychotherapy for six years and participated in twelve-step recovery groups. He had an abusive upbringing by a "violent and rageful father, who had terrorized his wife and four children."[28] Joe appeared to be making adequate progress in his life and his career. After completing his first ten-day intensive meditation, however, he found that he was quite fearful of watching his breath. His breath felt dangerous and made him feel anxious. After first ignoring his breath and then attending to his breath, he had an experience that felt as if an iron band were constricting his abdomen; it hurt him and restricted his breath.

In this experience, through which he was trying to access his emotions, he began crying and shaking for several hours, and then a new childhood memory emerged. When he was a youngster, he would hide in the closet at home from his angry father and would put rags in his mouth so that his father would not be able to hear his sobbing. The realization that his somatic symptoms, as well as his fear, were related to this earlier episode emerged from the patient's experience with meditation. This is clearly an example of a therapeutic breakthrough through the use of meditation in conjunction with psychotherapy.

Clinical Research

No formal research studies have been done on the effectiveness of integrating Eastern philosophies with Western psychotherapy. In the case of the systems-cybernetic approach, it is not clear whether patients can withstand the onslaught of the philosophical/dialectic analysis or simply leave the therapeutic arena. There are no reported outcome studies or any data that relate to these therapeutic integrative approaches.

A large number of studies apparently indicate that meditation, as well as Yoga, is helpful in decreasing several psychological conditions, including anxiety. Benefits in terms of rehabilitation efforts may be seen in clinical populations that have suffered heart attacks. Positive effects have also been achieved in enhancing a person's confidence, self-esteem, empathy, marital satisfaction and academic achievement.[29]

On the other hand, a number of clinical reports of negative outcomes are also associated with meditation. For example, some meditators reportedly begin to depersonalize and feel that things are unreal. Other reports suggest that overuse of meditation could lead to psychiatric problems, ranging from depression to agitation to psychotic decompensation.[30] In addition, one investigator found that in some instances, meditation techniques can lead to symptoms of complex partial epilepsy, including experiencing visual abnormalities, hearing voices, feeling vibrations and exhibiting automatic behaviors.[31]

Some meditators who are involved in prolonged meditation may experience spontaneous movements. There may be dramatic energy flows, dream and time changes, out-of-body experiences and various psychic phenomena. Meditators may demonstrate twitching, involuntary jerks, violent shaking, drooling and arms flapping like wings.[32]

Critique and Analysis of Buddha Psychotherapy

First and foremost, it appears that the integration of psychoanalysis with Eastern philosophies is above all a personal approach. Thus, as Epstein notes, his "attempts at integration have been, above all, private ones."[33] Thus, no formal training institutes, centers or graduate courses can supervise or train persons in this attempted integration of therapies and approaches. There is no inherent reason why the psychoanalytic or cognitive behavioral techniques should be the therapy of choice to join forces with Buddhism.

Second, there does not appear to be a natural or inherent congruence between psychoanalysis and Buddha Psychotherapy. In some ways a Gestalt Approach seems to fit the emphasis on Buddha Psychotherapy's focus on body awareness.

In attempting to combine several approaches, it is critical to ascertain the efficacy of each individual component. Psychoanalysis as discussed in Chapter 2, however, is flawed. In Buddha psychoanalytic psychotherapy, a key concept is an attempt to uncover hitherto repressed material by way of psychotherapy and meditation. There is no check on the veracity of the memories that are bubbling up. Thus, Epstein accepts as the holy grail one of Freud's main concepts which has remained controversial, namely, that various childhood traumas may be antecedent to adult psychopathology.

In the case of Fenner's approach, he goes way beyond Rational Emotive Behavior Therapy. In advocating that there is no cause of emotional feelings, he appears to be saying that anyone who believes that some things may upset a person is thinking illogically. Ellis says that the basis of emotional dysfunction is irrational thinking, but he does not deny the possibility of specific antecedents to feeling upset or depressed. Fenner presents no data that even remotely support his position that meditating and giving up the erroneous belief of real causation of a mental problem leads to cessation of the problem.

Meditation, especially in the psychoanalytic merger approach, appears to offer patients an alternative to free association. Whatever thoughts seem to emerge that may seem significant can be brought up in the next session and be grist for the mill. The validity of free association is still open to question and appears to be speculative. Thus, there is no way to know whether the patient or the therapist has divined the truth or is just engaging in guesswork. No methodology is in place to assess whether the material emerging from the meditative state uncovers a deeper truth or reality.

The Buddha Psychotherapies appear to engage in secularization in that the various religious aspects may be negated or minimized. It is not clear to what extent, if any, some of the religious and spiritual aspects are to be integrated into the therapy. As noted in the context of spiritual therapies such as A Course in Miracles, there may cognitive overload, should a patient be exposed to new and dramatic beliefs, especially while attending an extended meditation retreat. Finally, although it appears that meditation, especially the pure secular type such as the relaxation response,[34] may be helpful, some research seems to suggest that prolonged meditation can have negative consequences. In the final analysis, Buddha Therapy appears to be a philosophical approach to dealing with life's problems. Without concrete information or clinical data, however, the blending of Western psychotherapies with Eastern philosophies is not any more helpful than either approach in isolation.

PSYCHOENERGY FIELDS

A number of therapies hypothesize that emotions are directly related to energy fields. One view is that subtle energies are voices of consciousness called *chakras*.[35] The energy flow is similar to the wave patterns seen emanating from the pavement on a hot day.[36] In *Thought Field Therapy* (TFT), it is asserted that acupuncture, like meridians, can be utilized to eradicate mental or emotional disturbances. In TFT, the patients touch points on their own bodies in an attempt to re-tune the psychoenergy imbalance. In *Palm Therapy*, the therapist makes a psychodiagnostic assessment and directly touches the meridians on the patient's palm.

Thought Field Therapy

If phobias, traumas and mental disorders can be cured in a few minutes, then Thought Field Therapy represents a miraculous new breakthrough. Thought Field Therapy did not emerge from the clinical laboratory but sprang from the efforts of one psychologist. The originator is Roger Callahan, who presents TFT training via workshops and seminars throughout the world.

Clinical interventions initially focussed on phobias. Thought Field Therapy, however, is used in the treatment of panic and anxiety disorders, depression, post-traumatic stress disorders and addictions, as well as multiple personality disorder. Thought Field Therapy has entered into the main-stream of Cognitive Behavior Therapy and appears to be routinely used by many therapists. Thought Field Therapy has been endorsed by Gary Emery, who stated that Thought Field Therapy was one of the most revolutionary and helpful therapies he had encountered in his endless search for better therapy.[37]

Thought Field Therapy offers a blend of Eastern concepts within a cognitive or a behavioral modality. It is hypothesized that there is a thought field, which contains negative emotions. The thought field may be imaginary, but one can project causal entities such as a *perturbation*.[38] All emotional upsets are thought to be caused by perturbations in the thought field. A perturbation is the basic causative entity of a negative emotion and is correlated with specific energy points on the body.[39]

On the behavioral side, Thought Field Therapy uses Subjective Units of Distress (SUD) on a ten-point scale introduced by Wolpe (see Chapter 6). The patient is asked to state how stressed he feels about a particular event or episode, with 10 being the most and zero being a virtual absence of stress or upset about the episode or event. In addition, advanced technology has been introduced to provide diagnosis and treatment. Thought Field Therapy uses what is termed *voice technology*. The so-called psychological perturbations in the thought field can be isolated or demonstrated in a holographic manner within the voice. As a result, a diagnosis can be performed within a fraction of a second.

Another major concept introduced by Thought Field Therapy is that of underlying *psychological reversal* correction. Psychological reversal is a type of emotional block that prevents, or interferes with, successful treatment because of the literal polarity reversal in the meridians.[40] The meridians referenced here are acupuncture meridians of energy. When adjustments are made for psychological reversal, it has been found by Callahan that the success rate is vastly improved.[41] The other concern in treating patients with Thought Field Therapy is the apex problem.[42] The apex problem refers to patients who are successfully treated but cannot or will not admit that their problem was helped by way of TFT; i.e., they do not credit the treatment for their improvement.

The treatment consists of a patient describing the incident or trauma and indicating the level of stress experienced at that moment. In other words, an initial SUD rating is obtained.[43] Neither an initial psychodiagnostic evaluation nor a history needs be taken. Then, the client is asked to tap with two fingers, starting with the beginning of the eyebrow, across the bridge of the nose. Five strong taps take place in order to "put energy into the system."[44] Next, the client taps under the eye about an inch below the bottom of the eyeball. Finally, other parts of the body are tapped, including the armpit and the collarbone. At this point, a second SUD rating is obtained. If there is no decrease in the SUD, a psychological reversal correction is performed. The patient hits or taps the outside edge of one hand into the palm of the other hand. While tapping the psychological reversal spot, the client says, "I accept myself, even though I have this problem."[45] The previous steps are then repeated.

If the rating is two or more points less, then a series of nine *gamut* treatments is offered. The gamut spot is a point on the back of the hand. The client taps this spot while simultaneously closing the eyes, opening the eyes with various eye moments and humming a few parts of a song, counting to five, and humming again. The back of the hand is to be continuously tapped during this period. By the end of the treatment, the SUD is generally reduced to a zero or one, at which point the client does not feel upset when thinking about the initial problem.

If difficulties are encountered in reducing the level of stress or other treatment difficulties, Callahan provides consultation on the phone. By way of *voice technology*, a patient can say a few words, and Callahan then informs the treating therapist of the proper sequence of tapping required to alleviate the problem.[46]

Case Report: Dissociative Identity Disorder

A patient suffering from dissociative identity disorder presented an overview of her treatment with Thought Field Therapy.[47] The patient related several "fantastic healing experiences" with Thought Field Therapy. The patient indicated that several months previously she had become overwhelmed by intense self-hatred emanating from several of her alters. She was constantly hurting herself and could barely function. At the beginning of the thought field session, the patient agreed that all of the affected alters would participate. "We went through a long sequence of locating and tapping the diagnosed points in proper order and the results were incredible."[48] The patient went from an intensity of nine on the SUD to zero. Her thoughts changed from hating herself and wanting to slice herself up to not hating herself. Furthermore, this patient indicated that she felt a lot of energy moving through her body like heat with sweat pouring down. The patient stated, "Even the child alters whom I couldn't access felt good!"

Another patient was helped by means of voice technology. The patient proved to be somewhat resistant to treatment by way of Thought Field Therapy, and so the treating therapist called Dr. Callahan on the phone. Dr. Callahan provided voice technology, supervision and treatment over the telephone to the patient. The patient was described as having manic experiences. She scored an 8 on the SUD. The patient was asked to state, "I want to be over this problem." The voice technology equipment analyzed this statement. The patient then was asked to do a number of finger taps such as touching her collarbone and counting to three. In a moment or two, she indicated that she was six on the SUD. She was next asked to say, "I want to be completely over this." Again, after the voice technology analysis, she was asked to touch her collarbone and count to three. After several other treatments were administered, she was then at four and, subsequently at the end of the treatment, she was at zero. The treatment appeared to take a matter of moments.[49] No follow-up was presented.

Clinical Research

In 1985 and 1986, Callahan treated 68 people on call-in radio shows. In 1995, Glen Leonoff of Monterey, California, replicated the earlier Callahan results. The average score before treatment in the Callahan study was 8.8 on the SUD; the average score after treatment was 1.9; and the average time for treatment was 5 minutes and 16 seconds. According to Callahan, his treatment dramatically and significantly helped all of the eleven public-speaking subjects. The call-in subjects experienced a wide variety of phobias, including fear of flying, heights, darkness, snakes, freeway driving and public speaking. Both in the original Callahan study and the follow-up study by Leonoff, the success rate was about 97 percent. Although there was no control group, Callahan regards all the patients he's ever treated during the prior 30 years as a type of control group. The drastic difference between his previous results and the results in the Callahan and Leonoff studies gives ample proof of the superiority of Thought Field Therapy, according to Callahan.[50]

No research has apparently been done on the nature of thought fields, the mental perturbations, meridians or interaction among any of these concepts. For example, a study is cited on the acceleration of fracture repair by electromagnetic fields. Callahan simply indicates that he believes that the same energy system is being tapped by what he calls Thought Field Therapy.[51]

Critique and Analysis of Thought Field Therapy

The mass marketing of the Thought Field Therapy psychotherapeutic approach without any relevant scientific documentation has led to exaggerated claims and unsubstantiated findings. Many mainstream psychotherapists have accepted the basic theory and techniques uncritically and almost blindly.

Callahan contends that his approach reveals revolutionary findings in clinical psychology.[52] What is not revealed is a total lack of any scientific basis for his results. None of the articles cited in his bibliography refers to research having anything to do with the efficacy of his psychotherapeutic approach.[53] One study refers to electromagnetism, and another to the controversial work of Sheldrake in 1981.[54] Callahan never explains how Sheldrake's theoretical approaches on biological formationism have anything to do with energy meridians.

No data have been presented to demonstrate the validity of voice technology. Callahan does not explain how a few seconds on the phone can identify the unseen mental perturbations. The voice technology apparatus apparently has never been subjected to any independent scientific review.

Thought Field Therapy, unlike EMDR (Chapter 6), is not grounded in serious academic research; virtually no peer-reviewed clinical research studies have been performed, nor do there appear to be any comparative studies containing control groups and treatment controls. Callahan bases his results on presumptive conclusions from a potpourri of various speculations originating from a variety of fields, including physics, biology and electromagnetism.

What has not been assessed in clinical research by neutral investigators who do not have a vested interest in the approach are the possible demand characteristics inherent in psychotherapy. Callahan claims that people rarely give a false improvement report during TFT.[55] It is not clear how this is independently validated. At this point, Thought Field Therapy appears to be somewhat akin to the *Consumer Reports* noted in Chapter 1. That is, a large number of people appear to state positive things about therapy and its outcome. It may very well be that Thought Field Therapy is a placebo. Like most placebos, however, once the excitement wears off, the positive results drastically diminish. Without any clinical follow-up studies, Thought Field Therapy must be considered an untestable and probably unprovable psychotherapy modality.

PALM THERAPY

Palm Therapy, developed in 1985 by Moshe Zwang,[56] is based on visible energy lines and energy pathways on the hand. Palm Therapy is defined as "the art and science of enhancing optimum potential self-growth, fulfillment and success in all aspects of life through the stimulation of specific areas and lines in the hands, which represent the various characteristics of the personality in brain/mind activities."[57] Stimulation of the palm sends direct suggestions to all of a person's existence. There can even be stimulation of success energy, which is essential for accomplishing life goals.[58]

In a five-day seminar offered by the International Palm Therapy Association, the participant can learn to recognize the following in their clients: "Hidden anger or aggression, introvert/extrovert, mood swings . . . depression, flexibility/stubbornness, hyperachiever/underachiever . . . addictive behavior patterns." In addition, a person who has experience with Palm Therapy will be able to deal with the following issues: anxiety, traumatic memories, severe fears, phobias, anger and grief.[59]

Through Palm Therapy, emotional pain such as grieving, anger, frustration and unhappy memories can be relieved in a very short time during the first session.[60] The course of sessions, however, can last several months. In the first session, there is no psychosocial intake; rather, the therapist reviews a questionnaire and a referral letter from the patient's therapist. In fact, Zwang, who is a naturopathic doctor, asserts that palm therapy is not psychotherapy. In the text, however, there are descriptions for diagnosing and treating a wide variety of mental disorders included in the DSM-IV, such as anxiety disorders, substance-related disorders, schizophrenia, eating disorders, tics and learning disorders.

With anxiety disorders, the following diagnostic signals are:
1. A break or an island on the heart line.
2. Hysteria lines.
3. A clear addiction or allergy line, which may appear on the mounts of Pluto.[61]

When the appropriate signs and symptoms are located on the hand and related to a particular mental disorder or disturbance, the palm therapist stimulates or manipulates the hands in order to effect an improvement in the condition.

Case Report: The Grieving Melissa

Melissa was a 26-year-old who was barely able to walk when first seen in the office. She had been crying and was in a depressed mood. She indicated that her husband had recently left her, and she had no means of support.[62]

After both of her hands were checked, the palm therapist stimulated certain lines in her palms for about five minutes. After this treatment, the look on her face changed, she became more relaxed, was comfortable and stated that her depressed feelings were gone and that the pain was gone.

Critique and Analysis of Palm Therapy

There are some superficial similarities between Palm Therapy and Thought Field Therapy. First, both TFT and Palm Therapy rely to some extent on energy fields and meridians. Thought Field Therapy, however, is thought to be successful in a very short period of time, whereas Palm Therapy can last several months or longer. Apparently, there is no problem that Palm Therapy cannot help. Although the scope of Thought Field Therapy is expanding in terms of its treatment, it appears there is no limit to what Palm Therapy claims it can accomplish. Virtually any mental disorder in the DSM-IV presumably would be covered by Palm Therapy.

Second, it is never made clear how a psychodiagnosis is made. With the advent of the DSM-IV, specific criteria and symptoms are listed that relate to the various clinical disorders. No explanation is given for the correlation between Zwang's diagnostic assessment and the traditional DSM-IV. Furthermore, it is quite disingenuous to claim that Palm Therapy is not psychotherapy when a mental diagnosis is made and treatment is offered to alleviate an emotional problem.

No clinical research supports any of the major tenets of Palm Therapy. Despite a 723-page tome, there is not one iota of support, either for the theory or for any of the clinical outcomes. Again, only a potpourri of anecdotal reports of success is known. From a scientific analysis, little distinction is made between Palm Therapy and palm reading.

ALIEN ABDUCTION THERAPY

Over the course of history, a wide variety of explanations have attempted to demonstrate the reason for adult psychopathology. A substantial number of mental health professionals have contended that unconscious forces are responsible for emotional conflicts. The Freudian notion of repression has evolved and been appropriated by clinicians who do recovered memory therapy and Past-Lives Therapy. One of the most unlikely legacies of psychoanalysis is the notion that a person can be plagued by a repressed or at least partly forgotten trauma related to alien abduction.

Beginning in the 1970s and continuing through the 1980s, a number of therapists sought to explain psychopathology as a result of alien abduction experiences. Perhaps the best known book in this area is *Abduction: Human Encounters with Aliens* by John E. Mack, M.D.[63] Alien Abduction Therapy, in essence, is a search for causative factors in a person's present-day life that tends to parallel the efforts in recovered memory therapy.[64] That is, the memories of alien abduction may not be immediately accessible to one's conscious awareness, but specialized techniques may be needed to unblock the experiences.

Similar to the checklists that have been developed to identify symptoms of childhood sexual abuse or satanic ritual abuse, those in the Alien Abduction Therapy movement also outline symptoms prevalent in persons who may have been abducted by aliens. Mack lists several symptoms that he claims are specifically related to the abduction experience: "Sinus pain, urological, gynecological complaints, . . . persistent gastrointestinal symptoms." Associated symptoms may include "odd rashes, cuts, scoop marks or other lesions."[65] Symptoms that might be indicative of a possible abduction history, though not necessarily definitive, include "a general sense of vulnerability, especially at night, a fear of hospitals . . . fear of flying, elevators, animals, insects and sexual contact."[66] Possible symptoms may also include insomnia and other types of phobias, as well as nightmares.

Mack further notes that abductees experience a sense of isolation from others and feel that they are different from other persons.[67] Although Mack can offer no explanation in terms of the ultimate explanation of how abductions occur with respect to possible violations of physics as they are now known, he accepts the experiential truth of the abduction experience.[68] In Abduction Therapy, as in Recovered Memory Therapy, it does not necessarily matter whether or not the patient is having a veridical experience; rather, it's the experience itself that counts. Instead of offering alternative hypotheses to the patients, Mack allows an exploration into the patient's abduction history as if it is actually and physically occurring. In an appendix Mack presents several alternative hypotheses as to what could account for the types of experiences the abductees have, but these alternatives are not presented to the patients.

The Alien Abduction Therapy sessions are conducted much as Past-Lives Therapy or Recovered Memory Therapy. Thus, in many instances, a patient is not only hypnotized but is hypnotically age-regressed to the time of a possible episode. A person could be in a less formal hypnotic state and be provided guided imagery as a pathway to the abduction experience. A person may have a speculation or an intuition that he or she has been abducted and may consult one of the alien abduction therapists for verification or validation. Although there may be an initial psychosocial history and/or psychological testing, it is not a necessary ingredient prior to beginning hypnotic age regression, guided imagery or even relaxation therapy. One of the most famous and controversial cases of an abduction experience, that of Barney and Betty Hill, was elicited by way of hypnosis.[69]

Case Reports

Peter's Journey

One of the cases in Mack's book was Peter's Journey. Peter, a former hotel manager and a recent acupuncture school graduate, was relatively intact psychologically.[70] In fact, during the hypnotic sessions, a psychologist administered several psychological tests, including the Wechsler Adult Intelligence Scale, Revised (WAIS-R), the Bender Visual Motor Gestalt Test, the TAT, the Minnesota Multiphasic Personality Inventory (MMPI) and the Rorschach Ink Blot Test and concluded that there was an absence of psychopathology. Between February 1992 and April 1993, Peter received seven hypnotic age-regression sessions. Peter was apparently not in psychotherapy at the time. He simply had a notion that he may have had an abduction experience, and he wanted to explore it by way of hypnosis. During the hypnosis session, Peter related that one day he got out of bed, walked over to a couch at the side of the room and was able to see aliens. They were thin and wore close-fitting body suits with hoods.[71] As is common in many abduction experiences, Peter floated out or was transported to a spaceship. During another session, Peter reported that, at about the age of nineteen, he was on a table where he was forced to ejaculate and sperm was taken from him.[72] Peter was informed at one point during the abduction experience that the babies he observed were his alien or hybrid babies.[73] He was breeding with aliens, and that was why they were taking his sperm.

Interestingly, on the psychological assessment, the TAT appeared to show that Peter was battling evil forces. His profile also suggested that he might have been sexually abused. He was showing visible anxiety as reflected on the psychological tests, but it is not clear whether this was related to the abduction experiences or whether some other underlying cause was present.

The Case of Marian

The case of Marian was presented by a skeptical psychologist.[74] Marian, who was 31, had been molested as a teenager by a male neighbor. She had not repressed this memory and had always remembered it. She sought out therapy when panic attacks developed after she was in a severe automobile accident. She exhibited several symptoms of panic attacks, including uncontrollable fear, rapid heartbeat and anxiety upon leaving the house out of fear of having a panic attack.

The psychologist Marian contacted did not focus on her panic attacks, nor was she referred for possible treatment by a psychiatrist for anti-anxiety medication. On the other hand, the psychologist was quite interested in her molestation by the male neighbor. The therapist told Marian that he had a background studying UFOs and extraterrestrials and their experimentation on humans. Next he told Marian that her childhood dreams were not normal but reflected themes related to extraterrestrials.

The therapist initiated hypnosis to elicit the repressed memories of an abduction experience. The therapist, however, impressed upon her that if she really wanted to get better, she should undergo this procedure. What followed was two years of hypnosis therapy sessions in which the therapist informed Marian of her various recovered memories. After each hypnotic session, Marian was barely able to recall what emerged and thought they were more like dreamlike images. Nevertheless, the therapist interpreted her recall as evidence that Marian was actually abducted by an ET. He went on to inform her that her parents were also programmed by extraterrestrials and that her father raped her, but because of the advanced technologies of the aliens, her memories of the rape had been eliminated.

Marian joined group therapy with this therapist's other patients who also had been abductees, as well as victims of incest. The patients were informed that they needed to be cautious "because secret government agencies were trying to find out" what others knew about extraterrestrials.[75] He also told his patients to confront their parents and not to have any more contact with them.

Subsequently, Marian went to another therapist for her panic attacks and agoraphobia, which was not treated by the alien abduction therapist. She had also become quite paranoid because the first therapist had told her that government people might be following or spying on her.

Marian retracted her belief in the alien abduction narratives that emerged during the course of her two years of hypnosis therapy. She subsequently recontacted her family.

Clinical Research

There is no documented research as to the literal or physical veridicality of an alien abduction experience. The first step that would be helpful in proving such experiences in a physical sense would be the presentation of some tangible, verifiable, physical evidence such as a subcutaneous implant, a bodily cut or chemicals not from this earth that are at or nearby an alleged ET landing. Such physical evidence, as Mack notes, is "subtle, elusive and difficult to prove."[76] The therapist is left with the subjective account of the patient without any corroborating physical evidence.

Spanos (1993) examined the relevance of a person's subjective account of the alien abduction experience.[77] People in this study claimed to have had UFO experiences and were given questionnaires and objective psychological tests as well as a semi-standardized review. Two other groups of individuals had not reported any UFO experiences. On the basis of the inventory, the UFO subjects were divided into two groups. In one group, the individuals reported some distant lights or objects in the night sky that they interpreted as UFOs.[78] The individuals in the other UFO group, however, reported that they had close contacts with alien spaceships or extraterrestrials and had been occasionally abducted by aliens. The subjects who reported the more extensive UFO experiences "were much more likely to report that their experiences were sleep-related than were those who reported more mundane (i.e., lights in the sky) experiences."[79] Many of the subjects in the elaborate UFO group reported night dreams, hypnogogic imagery, full-body paralysis and vivid, multi-sensorial imagery.[80]

According to Spanos, the types of experiences that some of these subjects reported could be explained as sleep paralysis. That is, while still in the process of falling asleep, a person is still conscious but suddenly realizes he or she is unable to move. "Sleep paralysis is typically associated with extreme fear and a feeling of suffocation and sometimes it is also associated with complex auditory and visual hallucinations and a sense of a presence."[81]

In the Spanos study, the subjects who had the more elaborate UFO experiences were more likely to have unusual bodily sensations and to be more fantasy prone. The individuals who had explicit alien experiences were more likely to be predisposed to beliefs such as reincarnation, astrology and channeling and to interpret unusual bodily sensations and imagination as evidence of an alien incident.[82]

According to Spanos, a wide variety of phenomena could explain the UFO experiences: day or night dreams, intrusive fantasies, screen memories, fairies, mental illness, demonic attacks, memories from a past life, witchcraft and aliens.[83] In the case of someone with UFO experiences, a belief in aliens may serve as a template to mold ambiguous information into the shapes of alien encounters that are perceived as real.

Critique and Analysis of Alien Abduction Therapy

The same criticism leveled at Recovered Memory Therapy can be applied to Alien Abduction Therapy—namely use of highly suggestible techniques such as hypnosis (Chapter 7). When a patient enters therapy with someone who is likely to validate his belief system, the possibility increases that the alien abduction interpretation is going to be the most likely outcome. A patient arrives, basically believing in the potential and possibility of an alien abduction episode, and encounters a sympathetic therapist who does not challenge his belief system.

Although hypnosis is readily used in Recovered Memory Therapy and alien abduction work, other suggestive methods are employed. For example, guided imagery can provide the same effect. There may be priming preliminary interviews along with leading questions, and the patient may be encouraged to try to relive the abduction experience.[84] Repeated interviews and carefully tailored questioning are "undoubtedly important in the construction and augmentation of abduction narratives."[85] Since the therapist generally does not challenge the material that is forthcoming, the patient reports are implicitly being validated by an authority figure. This scenario can produce and maintain memories and experiences that may or may not be literally true.

In some instances, the therapist may launch an independent investigation along with the patient to prove that the patient, for example, has an alien implant. The patient and therapist may go to visit a medical doctor who surgically removes a subcutaneous implant for analysis. If the results are ambiguous, the quest nevertheless continues.

The patient is not told that this is a controversial area and that there could be three, four or five different explanations for the purported alien abduction experience such as sleep paralysis, current hyperspace intrusions by time travelers, ghosts and other entities, as well as imagination. The patients are not told about the possible suggestive affects of hypnosis or that the checklist of symptoms which may have been elicited by the therapist may be a catchall type of questionnaire, such as found in the areas of multiple personality and childhood sexual abuse. As noted, demand characteristics can sometimes produce self-reports that are suggested by the situation and may include sensory distortions.[86]

Just as in Recovered Memory Therapy, the alien abduction therapist has no tools to differentiate fantasy from reality. It may be that no patients have ever been abducted by aliens, or only one patient has been, or perhaps hundreds of thousands of individuals have been abducted. The tools available to the alien abduction therapist are too crude to make any differentiation as to what is veridical and what is not. What is most astounding is that no clinical research as yet indicates that bringing this troubling alien abduction experience to the person's consciousness has reduced any person's mental suffering.

One negative consequence of selecting an alien abduction therapist is the unilateral focus. For example, in the case of Peter, the major attention was on the individual's experiences with extraterrestrials. In some instances, as reflected in the case report on Marian, other, perhaps more severe or serious, problems affecting a person's everyday activities are ignored or not dealt with.

A more sinister consequence of entering into Alien Abduction Therapy is finding a therapist who, unbeknownst to the patients, is indoctrinating them to believe in not only the "reality" of alien abductions but also in government conspiracies, cover-ups and a host of unprovable or untestable notions. It is well beyond the therapist's job to try to explain or investigate the possible role of the CIA, FBI or other secret governmental agencies who may or may not be in cahoots with the alleged aliens. To promote such ideas only fuels the flames of the patient's fantasies.

Finally, in many instances, there is an intermixture, not only of Alien Abduction Therapy, but also other types of Recovered Memory Therapy, which includes Past-Lives Therapy and postulating satanic ritual abuse and childhood sexual abuse. The cumulative effect of suggestive procedures will not likely lead to actual memories and provide clinically relevant treatment.

NOTES

1. Walsh, R. (1995). Asian psychotherapies. In Corsini, R. J. & Wedding, D. (Eds.), *Current psychotherapies* (5th ed.) (pp. 387–398). Itasca, Ill.: Peacock Publishers.

2. Epstein, M. (1995). *Thoughts without a thinker: Psychotherapy from a Buddhist perspective* (p. 6). New York: Basic Books.

3. Fenner, P. (1995). *Reasoning into reality: A system-cybernetics model and therapeutic interpretation of Buddhist middle path analysis* (p. xvii). Boston: Wisdom Books.

4. Epstein, *Thoughts without a thinker* (p. 6).

5. Epstein, *Thoughts without a thinker* (p. 17).

6. Epstein, *Thoughts without a thinker* (p. 45).

7. Epstein, *Thoughts without a thinker* (p. 110).

8. Epstein, *Thoughts without a thinker* (p. 129).

9. Epstein, *Thoughts without a thinker* (p. 130).

10. Epstein, *Thoughts without a thinker* (p. 159).

11. Epstein, *Thoughts without a thinker* (p. 164).
12. Epstein, *Thoughts without a thinker* (p. 192).
13. Epstein, *Thoughts without a thinker* (p. 204).
14. Epstein, *Thoughts without a thinker* (p. 205).
15. Epstein, M. (1998). *Going to pieces without falling apart: A Buddhist perspective on wholeness* (p. 62). New York: Broadway.
16. Fenner, *Reasoning into reality* (p. 164).
17. Fenner, *Reasoning into reality* (p. 166).
18. Fenner, *Reasoning into reality* (p. 196).
19. Fenner, *Reasoning into reality* (p. 196).
20. Fenner, *Reasoning into reality* (p. 198).
21. Fenner, *Reasoning into reality* (p. 198).
22. Fenner, *Reasoning into reality* (p. 199).
23. Fenner, *Reasoning into reality* (p. 201).
24. Fenner, *Reasoning into reality* (p. 205).
25. Fenner, *Reasoning into reality* (p. 206).
26. Fenner, *Reasoning into reality* (p. 206).
27. Epstein, *Thoughts without a thinker* (p. 168).
28. Epstein, *Thoughts without a thinker* (p. 168).
29. Walsh, Asian psychotherapies (pp. 387–398).
30. Singer, M. T. & Lalich, J. (1995). *Cults in our midst: The hidden menace in our everyday life* (p. 141). San Francisco: Jossey-Bass.
31. Singer & Lalich, *Cults in our midst* (p. 142).
32. Ankerberg, J. & Weldon, J. (1996). *Encyclopedia of new age beliefs* (p. 396). Eugene, Ore.: Harvest House Publishers.
33. Epstein, *Thoughts without a thinker* (p. 1).
34. Benson, H. (1975). *The relaxation response.* New York: William Morrow.
35. Mann, R. L. (1998). *Sacred healing: Integrating spirituality with psychotherapy* (p. 87). Nevada City, Calif.: Blue Dolphin.
36. Mann, *Sacred healing* (p. 143).
37. *APA Monitor*, December 1996, Advertisement (p. 17).
38. Callahan, R. J. & Callahan, J. (1996). *Thought Field Therapy (TFT) and trauma: Treatment and theory* (p. 126). Indian Wells, Calif.: Thought Field Therapy Training Center.
39. Callahan & Callahan, *TFT and trauma* (p. 121).
40. Callahan & Callahan, *TFT and trauma* (p. 11).
41. Callahan & Callahan, *TFT and trauma* (p. 17).
42. Callahan & Callahan, *TFT and trauma* (p. 47).
43. Callahan & Callahan, *TFT and trauma* (p. 10).
44. Callahan & Callahan, *TFT and trauma* (p. 10).
45. Callahan & Callahan, *TFT and trauma* (p. 12).
46. Callahan, R. J. (Speaker). (1996). *Voice technology demo* (Cassette recording). Indian Wells, Calif.: Callahan Techniques, Ltd.
47. Fenstemaker, D. & Callahan, J. (Eds.) (1996, November 4). The Callahan techniques. *The thought field.* Vol. II, No. 4 (pp. 2–3).
48. Fenstemaker & Callahan, The Callahan techniques, p. 3.
49. Callahan Techniques audiotape (1996).
50. Callahan & Callahan, *TFT and trauma* (p. 41).

51. Callahan & Callahan, *TFT and trauma* (p. 137).

52. Callahan & Callahan, *TFT and trauma* (p. 59).

53. Callahan & Callahan, *TFT and trauma* (p. 137).

54. Sheldrake, R. (1981). *A new science of life: The hypothesis of formative causation*. Los Angeles, Calif.: J. P. Tarcher.

55. Callahan & Callahan, *TFT and trauma* (p. 96).

56. Zwang, M. (1995). *Palm therapy: Program your mind through your palms—a major breakthrough in palmistry*. Los Angeles, Calif.: Ultimate Mind Publishers.

57. Zwang, *Palm therapy* (p. 118).

58. Zwang, *Palm therapy* (p. 36).

59. Seminar brochure of International Palm Therapy Association (1998).

60. Zwang, *Palm therapy* (p. 36).

61. Zwang, *Palm therapy* (p. 465).

62. Zwang, *Palm therapy* (p. 61).

63. Mack, J. E. (1995). *Abduction: Human encounters with aliens*. New York: Ballantine Books.

64. Sagan, C. (1995). *The demon-haunted world: Science is a candle in the dark* (pp. 158–159). New York: Random House.

65. Mack, *Abduction: Human encounters with aliens* (p. 16).

66. Mack, *Abduction: Human encounters with aliens* (p. 15).

67. Mack, *Abduction: Human encounters with aliens* (p. 29).

68. Mack, *Abduction: Human encounters with aliens* (p. ix).

69. Fuller, J. G. (1966). *The interrupted journey*. New York: Dial Press.

70. Mack, *Abduction: Human encounters with aliens* (p. 286).

71. Mack, *Abduction: Human encounters with aliens* (p. 290).

72. Mack, *Abduction: Human encounters with aliens* (p. 300).

73. Mack, *Abduction: Human encounters with aliens* (p. 314).

74. Singer & Lalich, *Crazy therapies* (p. 91).

75. Singer & Lalich, *Crazy therapies* (p. 92).

76. Mack, *Abduction: Human encounters with aliens* (p. 425).

77. Spanos, N. P., Cross, P. A., Dickson, K. & DuBreuil, S. C. (1993). Close encounters: An examination of UFO experiences. *Journal of Abnormal Psychology, 102* (pp. 624–632).

78. Spanos, N. P. (1996). *Multiple identities and false memories: A sociocognitive perspective* (p. 120). Washington, D.C.: American Psychological Association.

79. Spanos, *Multiple identities* (p. 120).

80. Spanos, *Multiple identities* (pp. 120–121).

81. Spanos, *Multiple identities* (p. 121).

82. Spanos, N. P. et al. (1993). Close encounters: An examination of UFO experiences. *Journal of Abnormal Psychology, 102* (pp. 624–632).

83. Spanos, *Multiple identities* (p. 122).

84. Spanos, *Multiple identities* (p. 125).

85. Spanos, *Multiple identities* (p. 125).

86. Orne, M. T. and Scheibe, K. E. (1964). The contribution of nondeprivation factors in the production of sensory deprivation effects: The psychology of the "panic button." *Journal of Abnormal and Social Psychology, 68* (pp. 3–12).

Chapter 10

The Death of Psychotherapy: Conclusions

Based on the evidence presented in this book, it appears that psychotherapy in its present form will not survive as a viable and reliable form of assistance to people with emotional problems.

Several signs lead to the conclusion that psychotherapy is dead as a scientific enterprise. First, rather than relying on experimental research, mass marketing merging with modern technology has resulted in a proliferation of untested therapies and unsubstantiated claims as to their effectiveness.

As a method of helping people who have mental or emotional problems, psychotherapy functions much like religious healing. Thus, both psychotherapy and religious healing are based on faith. Furthermore, the so-called active modes of psychotherapy do not appear to be any more effective than a placebo.

The most fundamental symptom pointing the way to the death of psychotherapy is the total lack of adequate scientific evidence that it is effective. Despite the amount of clinical research that has been conducted, because of the severe methodological flaws, including generalizability, irrelevance of expertise and lack of fidelity to methods, few psychotherapy modalities will likely survive more than a decade or two.

THE MASS MARKETING OF PSYCHOTHERAPY

Psychotherapy is a business. The success of psychotherapy or growth seminars is judged not by clinical research but by the profit margin and satisfied customers.[1] The ominous trend affecting psychotherapy is evidenced by the proliferation of permutated and amalgamated psychotherapies, which are based on slogans and exaggerated claims. Finally, with the advent of telephone psychotherapy, mass marketing is merging with technology.

Since there are virtually no First Amendment restrictions or other controls on who can do what, anybody can do anything in the field of psychotherapy, such as make exaggerated claims about improving one's emotional well-being. As demonstrated in earlier chapters, a person does not have to be licensed in order to perform psychotherapy.

One of the most intensely mass-marketed therapies is Thought Field Therapy (TFT). As demonstrated in Chapter 9, absolutely no evidence supports its underlying theoretical mechanisms, let alone its effectiveness. Some of the techniques and especially the apparatus of voice technology are apparently shrouded in a veil of secrecy.

In the early 1990s, Gary H. Craig, a Stanford University engineering student, developed the *Emotional Freedom Technique* (EFT) after studying TFT with Dr. Callahan. He then launched his own cloned version of TFT. The title of his brochure announces boldly, "New Therapy Brings Lasting Relief in Minutes!"[2] Elsewhere he claims that there is "no limit to the variety of applications for Emotional Freedom Technique." EFT promises that clients' lives will change dramatically after EFT; they will have independence from negative emotions, and as participants, they will personally blossom and rise above hidden hurdles that keep them from performing to capacity. They will also have greater freedom to "approach people with ease, become a public speaker, singer, or comedian, eliminate the anxiety that causes them to take those pills, drink that alcohol, smoke that cigarette and raid that refrigerator, express love easily, earn larger income, make those business calls, improve golf scores, lose weight and say goodbye to years of self-doubt."[3]

Needless to say, if TFT has not been validated, how is it possible that the Emotional Freedom Technique or any other clones or palm-offs of TFT can be considered a success? The only so-called data presented by TFT or the Emotional Freedom Technique are testimonials and anecdotal case reports. In the case of TFT and Emotional Freedom Technique, mass marketing of their therapy has overtaken any concern with verifying any of their claims.

Another case in point is the *Silva Method* (formerly called Silva Mind Control). The Silva Method has been offered to millions of people in hundreds of countries. The instructors can teach a person to:

• Solve more problems
• Have fewer fears
• Have better health
• Have less anger
• Be more productive
• Have a better memory

- Make better goals
- Be more motivated
- Control pain
- Stop headaches
- Direct dreams
- Have less stress
- Develop psychic ability
- Stop harmful habits.[4]

Clearly, it would be a major revolutionary breakthrough if a few weekend seminars could produce such dramatic results. There is no documentation, however, that any element of the Silva Method is responsible for changes in a person's mental functioning.

Another therapeutic technique that is being mass marketed through advertisements and local newspapers, brochures and seminars is the *Sedona Method*.[5] Advertising material claims that scientific studies conducted at Harvard Medical School have validated the effectiveness of the "Release Program," which "eliminates stress at its source." According to the ad, the method is "scientifically proven." (The Release Program refers to the Sedona Method.) The brochures indicate that the Sedona Method shows significant reduction in heart rate and diastolic blood pressure. In addition, with respect to short- versus long-term gains, the advertisements state that the overall findings show that it is effective "in promoting and maintaining stress reduction months after the training." It is claimed that over 16,000 people in the world have used this method, including some well-known figures in both the entertainment and mental health arenas. A testimonial is offered stating that when more of a person's negative energy is discharged, that person will experience more positive feelings.

What does a weekend seminar in Los Angeles offer? It helps you "get rid of fear, get rid of failure, feel love anytime you want it, learn how to trust yourself, reduce self-worry, how to access answers from your higher self, clear away years of accumulated confusion, have abundant health, joy and riches, and be in total control of your life with ease." The Sedona Method is also useful in business and industry in that it applies to team-building. The Sedona Method is purported to be "a complete learning system that combines an original process of cognitive inquiry and problem solving with an innovative relaxation technique."[6]

What research substantiates the effectiveness of the Sedona Method? There is an abstract of a study by Richard Davidson at the State University of New York conducted over ten years ago entitled "The Impact of Sedona Training on Stress Responsivity: A Psychophysiological Study." The purpose of the study was to evaluate the effectiveness of the Sedona Method in reducing stress. The study employed three conditions: the Sedona Group, a group of individuals trained in progressive relaxation, and a no-treatment group. They were tested on three occasions prior to any training, followed by a post-test approximately two to three weeks after the pre-test and a second post-test approximately three months following the first pre-test. The study involved the presentation of three stress challenges during which physiological activity was recorded: a film depicting an industrial shop accident; "a self-generation of emotional injury associated with an extremely negative experience from the subject's recent past; and "a word association to stimuli related to themes of death, violence and sex."[7]

The physiological measures in the study that were measured before, during and after the three stress challenges were heart rate, blood pressure and frontalis EMG. In addition, there was a behavioral task designed to measure the degree to which individuals could concentrate in the face of distracting emotional stimuli.

The results generally indicated that the Sedona group showed larger drops from pre-test to post-test one and two and physiological arousal in response to the stress challenges in comparison with the other two groups. This finding was most noteworthy in the reduction of heart rate and diastolic blood pressure. The results also indicated that, in comparison to the no-treatment group, the progressive relaxation group showed many significant changes in the direction of decreased stress responsivity, especially in measures of the frontalis EMG. In addition, the differences between the Sedona Group and the progressive relaxation group on the second post-test for most measures was smaller than in the first post-test. Whether there was a statistical significance is not indicated. There is no description of what happened to the subjects given the behavioral task, which was to measure their degree of concentration. Also, the subjects in the Sedona group initially had a higher heart rate at the first testing than the other two groups. This would tend to reduce the degree of matching that is generally utilized in these kinds of studies. The problem here is that a person starting with a higher heart rate would be expected to show a larger reduction. Thus, this may be a severe artifact in this study.

The major weakness in the study is that it does not present any statistical data showing whether any practical or statistical differences exist between progressive relaxation and the Sedona Method.

The particular research quoted in the advertising literature has never been presented in a peer-reviewed article. It was apparently presented as a paper at a conference. Furthermore, there is nothing more than about a page and a quarter write-up, which is simply an abstract of the findings. The author[8] indicated that the results were never published and that they were never followed up. He also stated that the results, though intriguing, were inconclusive. The implication is that the results of the Davidson study have been grossly misused as a basis for claiming some experimental support for the efficacy of the so-called Sedona Method. Obviously, the claims made in the advertisements have little relationship to this one type of study.

What has occurred in many types of therapies—not only those mass marketed but the more traditional types of psychotherapy as well—is that they attempt to go beyond their initial scope and to encompass the entire range of mental disorders.

NLP and Beyond

One major example of the broadening vista is NLP. NLP has been reinvigorated and transformed into "IDEA Seminars." These seminars were devised by Rex Sikes, who is known as a master NLP trainer.[9] He is described as a speaker, business consultant, writer, expert in accelerated learning and brain-based learning. He has also studied Eastern religions, including Zen masters. In a fourteen-day NLP education seminar, a person can:

• Obtain tremendous personal growth,

• Learn to communication [*sic*] better with one's family and avoid misunderstanding,

• Eliminate stress, fears and anxieties,

• Create more loving and supportive relationships,

• Communicate with precision,

• Learn to control emotions and stop them from gaining control,

as well as a number of other skills and forms of awareness.

The brochure for the seminars states that "IDEA Seminars' unique approach to NLP unlocks the keys to creating rapid and lasting change without going through long hours of painful therapy or divulging private information."[10]

There is only one problem with the claims made by NLP and the IDEA Seminars: not one iota of clinical research supports any of the claims. Apparently, no peer-reviewed research has been published for over a decade. Moreover, there has been virtually no comparative research recently that assesses NLP's effectiveness. Word of mouth, reputation, charisma and neatly packaged seminars seem to constitute proof of NLP's favorable outcome. If such incredible results had truly been achieved, why haven't they been documented and presented to the scientific community and the general public? The various mass-marketed approaches to therapy may be nothing more than a mass placebo.

TELEPHONE PSYCHOTHERAPY

Another sign of the decline of psychotherapy as a serious professional enterprise can be seen with the introduction of so-called telephone psychotherapy. Over the last several years, psychologists and other entrepreneurs have presented the option to the public of calling an 800 or 900 number in order to receive psychotherapeutic advice or counseling. Advertisements indicate that one or more counselors or therapists with expertise in treating anxiety, depression, relationships or other issues are available. A mental health professional agrees to offer psychotherapy at certain times of the day or night and in essence is on call. When a potential patient calls, he or she is automatically routed to one of the psychotherapists. Some of the services do not allow the patient to re-contact the same therapist. Thus, if such a patient calls back again, he or she will get a new psychotherapist.

In order to join such a phone panel, a therapist need only be licensed. There is no requirement for any particular expertise with any type of population or any type of therapy. Thus, two strangers are talking for a brief period of time, and one of those strangers is offering advice to the other. No attempt is made to match a patient's problem or diagnosis with a particular therapist's expertise. Furthermore, the panel member is not required to have expertise on any mental health issue. In California, for example, a psychology license is generic and does not require any training or experience in psychotherapy. Telephone conferencing is somewhat similar to the rent-a-friend notion talked about by Campbell.[11] In the case of telephone therapy, however, at the end of the conversation both the therapist and the patient basically go their separate ways, never to interact again. Thus, when the patients call back they will have to retell their story. It is hard to conceptualize making random calls to an unknown therapist as being within the orbit of a professional arena.

DEVELOPMENT OF NEW PSYCHOTHERAPIES

A new psychotherapy technique can be introduced almost with the snap of a finger or, in the case of EMDR, with the alleged magic finger waving in front of a patient. In the blink of an eye therapies emerge contending that the way to better health is through the newly devised psychotherapy. In the case of EMDR, the new discovery and techniques are serendipitous, accidentally leading to revelations in how to treat emotional trauma. Next, the innovator writes an article or book that extols the virtues of the positive results.[12] A series of seminars may be initiated, along with the institution of a clinic and a national organized training program that will teach therapists how to perform the newly discovered technique. With the success of the new method, a marketing strategy is devised to attract even more patients.

Generally missing in this formula is that the psychotherapeutic techniques are not subjected to serious scientific investigation by neutral outsiders. If negative research has been conducted and published, it is ignored. Unreliable positive research and testimonials are misused for marketing purposes. Therefore, the new technique takes on a life of its own as witnessed by the spawning of unfettered *crazy therapies*.[13]

With the introduction of computers and the Internet, mass mailings and cable television, underground psychotherapies are spreading like wildfire. With no controls on free speech in the marketplace with respect to puffery, practically anybody can do or say almost anything under the guise of psychotherapy. Unlicensed mental health providers or personal growth counselors may have little concern about the risks of exaggerated and false claims.

Because of the gullibility and vulnerability of prospective patients, there is little ability to separate what may be a reasonable claim from the totally unwarranted and unverifiable assertions of success.

PSYCHOTHERAPY AS RELIGIOUS HEALING

Another indication that psychotherapy falls outside the walls of science is that, in many ways, psychotherapy can be envisioned as a form of religious healing. As Szasz indicated, psychotherapy may be a modern pseudoscientific name for religion. Without a scientific basis, psychotherapy has many apparent similarities to religion and religious healing. Szasz goes on to say that one of the supreme ironies of modern psychotherapy is that "it is not merely a religion that pretends to be a science, but it is actually a fake religion that seeks to destroy true religion."[14] The line between psychotherapy and religion has become increasingly blurred over the last several decades. For example, as noted in Chapter 8 on spiritual therapies, several approaches actively integrate the spiritual approach with the so-called secular psychological approach. In Buddha Psychotherapy, the religious aspect is integrated with a secular psychological approach, which might be psychoanalysis or Cognitive Behavior Therapy. In the case of Dianetics, what initially appears to be a psychotherapeutic technique seems to have evolved into the Church of Scientology.[15]

COMMON ELEMENTS IN PSYCHOTHERAPY AND RELIGIOUS HEALING

A look at the first common element in psychotherapy and religious healing (see Table 1) reveals that both have unseen forces. For example, in psychoanalysis there are the id, superego and ego, which are not tangible and may not be measurable or amenable to scientific scrutiny. The notion of unconscious forces has not yet been adequately tested. Therefore, acceptance of the etiology of psychopathology in most psychotherapies is accepted on the basis of faith. Similarly, unseen forces are utilized in religious healing, mainly

Table 1
Common Elements in Psychotherapy and Religious Healing

Common Elements	
PSYCHOTHERAPY	**RELIGIOUS HEALING**
Basis of Mental Illness	
Unconscious or repressed forces, distorted thoughts	Demon v. God Good v. Evil
Healer	
M.D., Ph.D. or someone called a psychoanalyst or psychotherapist.	Dr. of Divinity, Ph.D. or someone called Reverend or an equivalent title.
Description of Office	
Contains a couch, diploma and books, one of which may be the DSM-IV.	Office may be in a church and contain religious symbols and Bibles.
Techniques	
Free association, hypnosis, catharsis, alteration of thinking.	Exorcism, prayers and ceremonies.
Results	
Innumerable positive cases, reports, anecdotes and testimonials.	Innumerable positive cases, reports, anecdotes and testimonials.
Philosophical Disagreements	
Therapists are rejected or banned from group.	Individuals are labeled as heretics.
Research	
No research has demonstrated the efficacy of psychotherapy.	No research has demonstrated the efficacy of religious healing.

spirits, angels or other entities. In the Christian religion, the notion that demonic forces may be present is not amenable to ordinary measures or scientific investigation. Some of the Eastern religions have as their key concept the notion that a person must get in touch with a higher level of awareness. This would presumably help to eliminate distorted cognitions. At present it is not at all clear that cognitive distortions as alleged by the cognitive behavior therapist are at the root of many of the mental disorders such as depression or anxiety. Across the broad array of hundreds of psychotherapies, most clinicians are accepting their underlying rationale essentially on a faith basis.

Psychoanalysts accept as a given fact that, by analyzing transference, the unconscious motivation of a child can be deduced from how an adult is currently interacting with his or her analyst. Since there is virtually no documentation for such a broad statement, this is really a myth-based assessment. The psychoanalyst is relying on clinical intuition.

In the case of the thousands of therapists who utilize TFT, it is accepted as a given fact that psychoenergy fields can be tapped into. Thousands of therapists have also accepted the idea that waving a finger in front of a patient who is traumatized is a key element in reducing anxiety and stress. To date, these notions have not been confirmed. The therapists are simply accepting someone else's word. The patient, in turn, accepts the word of the therapist as to the underlying theoretical rationale for the therapist's approach. In one case, there are mystifying forces, and in the other, there are mystifying explanations.

With regard to the healer in psychotherapy, generally the person who is the therapist is regarded as an authority figure or at least wears the cloak or mantle of someone who has some superior knowledge. Even when a person has virtually no training at all, having attended a university and rendering advice in itself may be enough to warrant the cloak of authority and authenticity. In the case of spiritual healing and counseling, the healer may be both a secular therapist and a religiously oriented person. In the case of shaminism, for example, there may be a combination of traditional secular techniques along with various spiritual approaches.[16]

In many instances, the person who originates the psychotherapeutic approach is extremely charismatic and influential. Names that come to mind are Freud, Ellis, Rogers and Perls. Today the term *psychoanalysis* or Cognitive Behavior Therapy carries with it a certain magic. In spiritual healing, which has been around for thousands of years, there is a certain in-built credibility. For example, the names of Jesus Christ and Buddha will provoke in certain individuals a positive response. As with God, the therapist's words and actions may be thought to be inerrant.

With respect to psychotherapy, the healing usually occurs in a psychotherapist's office. In the early days of psychoanalysis, the patient would be on the proverbial couch. Even nowadays, a minority of therapists may still use the couch. In the office, there will be diplomas, and perhaps a DSM-IV will be in the therapist's bookshelf along with other authoritative books in the field. In the church or synagogue, there may be various religious symbols, Bibles or other religious artifacts. Interestingly, the DSMs have been called the "bibles" of psychodiagnosis. They may be viewed as infallible but only until the next edition.

Regarding the practice of psychotherapy, there are techniques such as free association, hypnosis, catharsis and, in Cognitive Behavior Therapy, there may be an attempt to alter a person's distorted cognitions. A spiritual or religious healer will attempt to fight a person's demons and improve the patient's mental health through prayer, exorcism, possibly hypnosis and, in many instances, through the use of various religious ceremonies.

As to the results of psychotherapy, no empirical study has shown the effectiveness of psychotherapy. Particularly in the case of psychoanalysis, the theory appears to be fatally flawed. Numerous case reports and anecdotes support the alleged improvement of patients who undergo psychoanalysis or psychotherapy. There does not appear to be any confirmed research, however, that demonstrates how psychotherapy works or that it is more effective than a placebo. Similarly in the instance of religious healing, there is no way to verify that demons have been exorcised other than through case reports and anecdotes. Clearly, the scientific approach cannot reveal any supporting data for religious healing.

De-possession therapy, exorcism, Past-Lives Therapy and other spiritual approaches have not generally been amenable to the scientific approach. Thus, both psychotherapy and religious healing must be taken on a faith basis.

With regard to persons who disagree with the basic tenets of a theory, especially in the case of psychotherapy, if the therapist tends to dispute the underlying philosophy of his mentor or supervisor, he will be rejected from the group or institute. There is a long history in psychoanalysis of people who disputed some of Freud's original theoretical contentions and were either abruptly or later rejected from the fold. If the Freudian gospel is not accepted, an analyst may simply set up his own theoretical tent. To date, there are at least 40 different flavors of psychoanalysis. Because of the constant modifications and alterations in the psychotherapeutic arena in general, there may now be well over 500 types of psychotherapeutic techniques. With increasing rapidity, each new generation of therapists, which is now about every year or so, produces a new form of psychotherapy somehow claiming that it is better than anything else preceding it. In the case of religion, if a cleric or parishioner rejects a basic tenet of the religion, he or she may be labeled a heretic. Similarly, a rebellious or banned clergyperson is free to initiate a new religion or to spin off from an old one.

In summary, it appears that psychotherapy can be viewed at least in part as a form of secular religion. Little, if any, scientific basis has been presented to support the major propositions in virtually all of the psychotherapies. The basic theoretical formulation of psychotherapy and the alleged effectiveness are without any demonstrable proof. This state of affairs is congruent with what happens in religion. The similarity between psychotherapy and spiritual healing is striking. Thus, in the case of faith healing ceremonies, there is a "climactic union of the patient, the family, the larger group and the super-natural world by means of a dramatic, emotionally charged, aesthetically rich ritual that expresses and reinforces a shared ideology."[17] The same factors appear prominent in the healing that occurs in psychotherapy.

PSYCHOTHERAPY AS A PLACEBO

Numerous therapies have been developed over the last several decades. Many of these new therapeutic techniques are incredible or even bizarre, yet the proponents of the methods claim positive outcomes and in some instances miraculous cures. For example, in the case of TFT, it is claimed that this technique brings about an almost instantaneous reduction in phobias even after just a few minutes are spent with a patient. What may lead to the positive testimonials is not only the power of expectation within the patient's mind, but also the effect of the charisma and the hope generated by the therapist. Patients who enter into psychotherapy generally expect improvement and look for signs of improvement. They may look for and be willing to "exaggerate any scintilla of evidence as indicating improvement. Their willingness to do so demonstrates the power of suggestibility and the influence of their therapist."[18] If this is the case, psychotherapy may also be a placebo which incorporates various rituals along the lines of religious healing.

To date no scientific support has been presented showing that a so-called active treatment is more effective than supposed placebo controls. In ruling out artifacts, the "gold standard" has been the double-blind study used in drug research. It may be difficult, however, to transpose the double-blind methods from drug research to that of psychotherapy.[19] For one thing, it is unlikely that the people in the control group, who are not receiving treatment, would be unknown to the experimenter or the therapist. Furthermore, the so-called subject/client would also have some awareness that he or she was not involved in a therapy program. Obviously, an individual on a wait-list who is not even in therapy cannot be said to be blind to the fact that he is not receiving therapy.

When an attempt at placebo control is offered by providing a mini-treatment, and when comparing the differences between the placebo and active treatment group the results turn out to be less than dramatic, it has been retroactively argued that the placebo group was actually in active treatment.[20] This type of observation and speculation raises the tantalizing proposition that a whole variety of interpersonal interactions can produce changes in one's self-report in terms of one's mental status. As Parloff notes, "If the positive effects of psychotherapy are attributable primarily to such mechanisms as suggestion, attention or common sense advice, then the credibility of psychotherapy as a profession may be impugned."[21]

Underlying improvement in both one's medical condition and mental health may be based on the patient's positive expectations. When both the patient and healer believe there will be improvement, positive feelings are generated that can lead to improvement, especially when there is an under-lying psychological emotional component.[22]

Examples in the medical arena include the removal of a carotid body (a whitish mass at the bifurcation of the carotid artery) in the treatment of bronchial asthma.[23] First, it appeared there was a significant improvement when this operation was performed as a cure for patients who had intractable asthma. But despite a number of positive results, subsequent studies with different types of experimental designs indicated that this procedure was no better than a sham.

When double-blind studies were instituted, no differences were found between the treated and the control subjects. Interestingly, two-thirds of the patients in each group felt that the treatment had made a significant difference in their illness. By 1968, the American Thoracic Society indicated that the procedure "had not proven to be an effective treatment for asthma."[24] The operation was discontinued in all major clinics in the United States.

Another example of the possible placebo effect relates to gastric freezing of duodenal ulcers. Numerous studies published in the 1960s indicated that between 98 and 100 percent of patients experienced significant or complete relief immediately following treatment and for up to six weeks following freezing.[25] By the late 1960s, at the end of the six-week follow-up little or no significant difference was found between a treatment group and a control group. By 1969, one investigator concluded that gastric freezing was no better than a sham procedure as reported in Roberts.[26]

The classic example of the placebo's power in psychotherapy may be found in the well-known national NIMH study on depression.[27] The most striking conclusion is that the placebo group, which contained the clinical management component, did as well as a so-called active group.[28] "When the clinical significance of the various treatments was compared using measures of depressive symptomatology . . . , no statistically significant differences among the groups were found."[29]

Thus, at the present time, research does not support the contention that psychotherapy exceeds the effectiveness of placebos in mentally ill patients.[30] In the case of depression, exercising may be as beneficial as Cognitive Behavior Therapy or meditation/relaxation therapy.[31] To argue that credible and effective placebos are active treatments is to conclude that, first, the real treatment is no more effective than the so-called placebo, and second, that support, encouragement and generally speaking about the problem in a warm environment is as effective as any of the other 499 methods that have been developed to alleviate mental health problems.

EMPIRICALLY UNSUPPORTED THERAPIES

In part because of the explosion in psychotherapy techniques in the 1980s and 1990s and the controversy over the effectiveness of psychotherapy, a task force formed by Division 12 of the American Psychological Association promoted and disseminated so-called empirically validated therapies.[32] Because the term "empirically validated" was perhaps oversold and severely criticized, the phrase has been replaced by "empirically supported" therapies.[33] In order to be a well-established empirically supported treatment, there must be at least two good comparison group experiments that demonstrate efficacy in one or more of the following ways:

1. Superiority to a pill or a psychological placebo or to another treatment;
2. Equivalence to an already established treatment in experiments with adequate statistical power; or
3. A large series of single-case design experiments that demonstrate efficacy.

These experiments must have used a good experimental design and compared the intervention to another treatment. Additional criteria for an empirically supported treatment include use of treatment manuals, clearly defining the characteristics of the patients and demonstrating the therapeutic effects by at least two different investigators and investigatory teams.[34]

Using these criteria, it was concluded that cognitive behavioral therapies have been empirically supported in the treatment of panic disorders, agoraphobia, generalized anxiety disorder and other types of anxieties and depression. What is astounding is the striking absence from the list of empirically supported treatments not only of psychoanalysis but of virtually all other treatment modalities except the cognitive and behavioral. There is mention of the likely effective treatment of chemical abuse and opiate dependence by means of brief dynamic therapy.

When examining the examples of empirically supported treatments, however, it becomes apparent that no research supports the other 490 or so therapeutic modalities.[35] Garfield stated that the Division 12 report is "overly strong and the recommendations [are] premature."[36] He stated that it is too early to view therapies as being validated.

In looking at the scientific confirmation in psychotherapy, it is instructive to examine the recent Supreme Court case decision in *Daubert v. Dow Pharmaceuticals*.[37] The United States Supreme Court in the *Daubert* decision identified several factors that need to be considered in order to admit expert witness testimony.

1. The general acceptability of the method or technique in the scientific community.
2. The question of the published findings have been subjected to peer review.

3. The issue of whether the technique can be and has been tested.

4. The fact that the acceptable rate of potential error is known.

In order for evidence to be admissible, there has to be a rational explanation or methodology and an external source to validate the methodology.

Recently, the recovery of repressed memory has come under intense scrutiny in the legal system. In *State v. Hungerford*, the Supreme Court of New
Hampshire wrestled with the problem of acceptability or admissibility of the
testimony because an individual's recovered memory "may be actual recollections of actual traumatic events, manufactured narratives of events that
never occurred or some combination of these."[38] In looking at the totality
of the circumstances under the *Daubert* prism, the New Hampshire Supreme
Court stated in *Hungerford* that, although there was support for the phenomenon of repressed memory in a therapeutic setting, "scientists rest their
rejection of recovered and repressed memories on the absence of confirming
laboratory results."[39]

According to the New Hampshire Supreme Court, the experimental research supporting the notion of recovery of previously completely repressed
memories was subject to methodological flaws. This court did not believe
that the phenomenon of recovered memory of traumatic episodes had
gained general acceptance in the psychological community. Thus, although
certain peer-reviewed articles support the concept of repressed memory,
other factors should cause some skepticism. Part of the reasoning of this
court had to do with the demand characteristics of the therapy situation as
well as the therapist's influence in validating so-called recovered memories.

We are especially concerned with the influence of therapy on the recovery of memory
as in the instant cases. The process of therapy is highly subjective, with its purpose
"not the determination of historical facts, but the contemporary treatment and cure
of the patient." . . . Within the environment of a therapy, a patient may report memories in response to the perceived expectations of the therapist. (citations omitted)[40]

Therefore, because of the uncertainty as to the reliability and validity of the
recovery of repressed memories, this Court rejected the expert witness testimony on this decision.

What if the *Daubert* decision were applied to psychotherapy? In general,
looking at psychoanalysis, as pointed out in Chapter 2 that there is a virtually
non-existent scientific basis for the theoretical rationale and any significant
positive outcomes. As yet, no external confirmation exists for some of the
metaphysical concepts enunciated by Freud. No experimental research has
been done to show that free association can penetrate into the person's
unconscious and lead to the actual cause of a person's psychopathology.
Similarly, no validated research has been presented to indicate that dream
analysis is "the royal road to the unconscious." There has been no confir-

mation as to what the hit or miss rate is in assessing whether or not transference leads to accurate interpretations. The only thing that would fall in line with the *Daubert* decision is the great abundance of publications.

It is not controversy alone that renders psychoanalysis unverifiable, but rather, there have been no well-controlled studies to indicate that the underlying concepts have scientific merit. Perhaps even more significant, there have been no studies demonstrating the efficacy of psychoanalysis. According to case reports, some individuals have been in therapy for five, ten or fifteen years, but it is highly questionable whether these people have improved as a result of psychoanalysis.

The legacy of psychoanalysis has fared no better. In the last 25 years or so, there has been an outgrowth of psychoanalysis such as Past-Lives Therapy, Recovered Memory Therapy, Alien Abduction Therapy, and a whole host of therapy modalities that rely on the notion that unblocking the unconscious will lead to an improvement in mental health. As argued in this book, there has been no clinical proof that any of these therapies have any scientific merit whatsoever. There have been no adequate experimental or clinical studies to demonstrate that the underlying concepts of these theoretical approaches are accurate. Nor have there been any adequate outcomes studies.

Under the *Daubert* and *Hungerford* analyses as well as the announcement from Division 12 of the American Psychological Association, psychoanalysis and its successors should be regarded as unverified and unsupported.

A large number of psychotherapeutic techniques have not been subjected to peer review but rather have originated from within the office or clinic of a particular clinician. For example, Primal Therapy has not been subjected to any serious research effort either by Janov or by anybody else. In Thought Field Therapy, for example, there appears to be only in-house verification as well as publication. Furthermore, as noted previously, Thought Field Therapy and its offshoot, Emotional Freedom Technique, do not even pretend to be involved in any clinical research. Thus, no studies support underlying theoretical concepts relating to energy fields or meridians, nor have there been any serious attempts to study the efficacy, especially with respect to long-term outcomes.

The cognitive behavioral therapies appear to be more promising in terms of someday providing a scientific standard of reliability and replicability. A number of problems remain, however, before too much optimism should be generated. For example, few studies in the last several decades have matched the sophistication of the Paul study in 1967.[41] Unfortunately, as noted earlier, the Paul study was conducted with a relatively healthy population, most of whom were complaining of speech anxiety. Some of the difficulties with the cognitive behavioral studies relate to the small number of patients, especially those who drop out of the studies. Perhaps most important, the key question is whether these studies that seem to support the effectiveness of Cognitive Behavior Therapy can be generalized outside of the clinical or laboratory situation.[42]

In treating people with severe emotional problems, a number of approaches have been devised that deal with anxiety and depression, for example. Modalities that are no more effective than a placebo do not warrant acceptance in the scientific arena. Furthermore, in the absence of reliable and replicable research, there is virtually no basis for accepting the scientific principles alleged in the practice of psychotherapy. Thus, just looking at the *Daubert* and *Hungerford* decisions alone, it appears that the overwhelming majority of the 500 psychotherapies would have to be considered as unverifiable and not even worthy of being accepted into a court of law as clinically supportable approaches providing help to people with mental disorders.

Another problem with the research that allegedly supports the effectiveness of psychotherapy deals with the patient's or client's diagnostic variability. The incredible increase in the number of psychodiagnoses has not been accompanied by any improvement in the reliability of the diagnoses. The DSM-III published in 1980 was used as the benchmark in terms of reliability. The problem is that the data appeared to be faulty. There are no scientific criteria for establishing "a new diagnosis." The recent diagnoses have no scientific validity and are based on perhaps myth-making diagnoses. As Caplan notes, some of the research on the DSM-III that allegedly is proof of its scientific foundation apparently has never been published. The research that has been published is of extremely poor quality.[43] The appendix to the DSM-III published reliability data on various psychodiagnoses. The DSM-III-R and DSM-IV have no new reliability data however. Examination of the appendix in the DSM-III indicates that the diagnostic categories add up to well over 100 percent. Therefore, it is not clear how this reliability data was obtained. In the last 20 years or so, there has never been any explanation for this discrepancy or apparent flaw in the presentation of diagnostic data. With a faulty diagnostic system, it will not be clear who is profiting from what type of psychotherapy. The lack of reliability in determining whether or not a patient has a particular diagnosis will greatly undermine the strength of any particular research finding and reduce any generalizability.

Only a handful of studies have used stringent diagnostic procedures; these would include the NIMH study and several of Beck's clinical studies. Thus, unless different researchers are talking about the same phenomena under question, it is unclear as to whether any of the studies are comparable. Where there has been no serious attempt to perform psychodiagnosis, little can be said about the outcome. Literally hundreds of psychotherapies have been embarked upon wherein no particular psychodiagnostic procedure is attempted. For example, in Thought Field Therapy, to some extent in the humanistic therapies, and a whole host of therapies, the therapist initially embarks on therapy without specifically attempting to refine and define the diagnosis.

In the classic case of Freud's patient Dora, there is a total disconnect between Dora's diagnosis and Freud's theoretical approach. Clearly, no empirical support can be generated for a psychotherapeutic modality when there are questions as to the initial or subsequent psychodiagnosis.

Another issue of major concern has to do with the generalizability of the results obtained in a clinical research study. The studies are generally antiseptic or conducted under close supervision and monitoring and may utilize a manual. In private practice nobody is as closely watched as in an on-going research project, especially those that are funded by the federal government. In private practice, anyone is free to do whatever he or she wants.

Over the years, psychoanalysis, for example, has evolved into well over 40 permutations.[44] Some psychoanalysts may mix and merge what are thought to be incompatible approaches. It is extremely unlikely that any therapist in private practice is going to perform psychoanalysis in the same exact manner as do the clinical researchers in a research project. The use of manuals is of no avail since clinicians in private practice tend to do what they think might be helpful and make many innovations over the months and years of their practice. Furthermore, few reports show that the therapists who adhere more strictly to the training manuals have better results than those who conform less.

Finally, if there were something special about the active or necessary ingredients in psychotherapy that provides clinical improvement, not only psychotherapists but also those with more expertise would be expected to be the most effective. Thus, in many instances, experience is not a necessary requirement in rendering psychotherapy to mentally ill individuals. As Dawes argues, there is little relationship between a person's level of training in clinical psychology or psychiatry and improvement as a result of psychotherapy.[45] In a well-known study by Strupp and Hadley,[46] the therapeutic effectiveness of psychologists was compared to that of university professors who had no training in psychotherapy. The professors were selected on the basis of their presumed ability to form "understanding, warm and empathic relationships." The main hypothesis was that, if technical skill is uniquely effective, then people with training should produce more improvement than those interacting with college professors.

The patients in this study had a number of problems, such as depression, that are usually seen in an outpatient clinic. All subjects were given the MMPI and were selected on the basis of a similar personality profile. The subjects were described as suffering from "a sense of loneliness, isolation, depression and anxiety."[47] Ratings were made of a number of assessments initially, at termination, and at follow-up therapy.

The results of the study were unequivocal: "Patients undergoing psychotherapy with college professors showed . . . as much improvement as patients treated by experienced professional psychotherapists."[48] Thus, there was no difference between people who were licensed and trained in psychotherapy and the untrained. The therapist's technical skills did not produce greater therapeutic change than the therapist's presumed relationship skills.

Even more disheartening, an analysis of 32 studies comparing professionals and paraprofessionals found that, when treatment was of longer duration, paraprofessionals appeared to be more effective. Thus Berman and Norton[49] conclude that professional training does not yield more positive effective treatment. As Dawes notes, no clinical evidence supports the position that psychotherapy works. "There is no *positive* evidence supporting the efficacy of professional psychology" (emphasis in original).[50]

Therapists may argue that because of innovation and the uniqueness of their approach, the results in the formal studies are unrepresentative of actual private practice. At first glance, this argument appears to have much merit. As Prochaska and Norcross note, eclectic therapists "seek to improve our ability to select the best treatment for the person and the problem."[51] The term "technical eclecticism" has been coined to describe what a majority of therapists really do—namely, therapists employ technical procedures from a wide variety of sources without necessarily endorsing the underlying theoretical rationale.[52]

It is precisely the alleged technical eclecticism that prevents any of the research findings from having any relevance to private practice. Under careful supervision and monitoring in a clinical study, the therapist must adhere to a treatment manual and protocol. The findings in such a closely controlled study may have little applicability to what really happens in private practice. The reason is that each therapist devises his or her own procedure, which may deviate in small or large ways from the psychotherapy that was under investigation in the research study. Thus, technical eclecticism is somewhat of an oxymoron. The more eclectic, the less technical and less scientifically reliable a procedure may be. When the techniques are borrowed, there is no guarantee as to their technical purity. Thus, when eclecticism runs rampant, no quality control is possible. When the product is different from therapist to therapist, clinical investigation and testing of the therapeutic modality is meaningless.

For example, Ellis talks about elegant and inelegant Rational Emotive Behavior Therapy (REBT—see Chapter 6). There is no guarantee that the typical practitioner of REBT is performing the type of therapy advocated by Ellis. Severe problems with fidelity and purity may arise even with a seemingly straightforward procedure. Thus, within the cognitive behavioral sphere, there may be mixing and matching of various techniques.

Clearly, it may be impossible to vouch for the purity or adherence to any form of therapy, let alone therapies that attempt to integrate cognitive with psychodynamic approaches. There is no real guarantee that the same therapy is being provided by different therapists. When a drug is manufactured, if it carries the same label, there is a high degree of assurance that each capsule contains the same formula. The same cannot be said for psychotherapy. Psychotherapists add their own ingredients into the mixture of what they perceive as an appropriate and effective therapy.

It is virtually impossible to compare therapies with different elements that are composed of different orientations blended in an idiosyncratic manner. How or why therapy works can't be gleaned from studies on eclectic and blended therapies with unknown variations.

The ultimate conclusion at this point is that there are no empirically supportable therapies. What remains are rhetorical exchanges between two people that can't be distinguished from religious healing or a placebo. As a scientific enterprise, psychotherapy should be declared dead.

NOTES

1. Dineen, T. (1998). *Manufacturing victims: What the psychology industry is doing to people* (2nd ed.) (p. 201). Montreal: Robert Davies.

2. Craig, G. H., Held, M. J. & Jordan, J. R. *New therapy brings lasting relief in minutes!* Advertising brochure for "EFT Home Study Course." San Francisco.

3. Craig et al., *New therapy brings lasting relief in minutes!*

4. *Los Angeles Times* (July 8, 1998), Advertisement (p. A4).

5. *Los Angeles Times* (August 8, 1998), Advertisement.

6. Sedona Method brochure (1998), p. 2.

7. Davidson, R. (ca. 1987). *The impact of Sedona training on stress responsivity: A psychophysiological study.* Unpublished abstract, Purchase, N.Y.: State University of New York.

8. Personal communication with Richard Davidson, September 8, 1998.

9. IDEA Seminar brochure (1998), p. 4.

10. IDEA Seminar brochure, p. 8.

11. Campbell, T. W. (1994). *Beware of the talking cure: Psychotherapy may be hazardous to your health* (p. 20). Boca Raton, Fla.: Upton Books.

12. Bobgan, M. & Bobgan, D. (1997). *The end of "Christian psychology"* (p. 14). Santa Barbara, Calif.: East Gate.

13. Singer, M. T. & Lalich, J. (1996). *Crazy therapies: What are they? Do they work?* San Francisco: Jossey-Bass.

14. Szasz, C. (1979). *The myth of psychotherapy: Mental healing as religion, rhetoric and repression* (p. 27). Garden City, N.Y.: Anchor Press/Doubleday.

15. Hubbard, L. R. (1968). *Dianetics: The modern science of mental health.* Sussex, England: Publication Organization Worldwide.

Hubbard, L. R. (1987). *Scientology: A new slant on life.* Los Angeles, Calif.: Bridge Publications.

16. Ankerberg, J. & Weldon, J. (1996). *Encyclopedia of new age beliefs* (pp. 537–538). Eugene, Ore.: Harvest House Publishers.

17. Frank, J. D. & Frank, J. B. (1991). *Persuasion and healing: A comparative study of psychotherapy* (3rd ed.) (p. 108). Baltimore, Md.: Johns Hopkins University Press.

18. Campbell. *Beware of the talking cure* (p. 22).

19. Parloff, M. B. (1986). Placebo controls in psychotherapy research: A sine qua non or a placebo for research problems. *Journal of Consulting Clinical Psychology, 4* (pp. 79–87).

20. Elkind, I. et al. (1989). National Institute of Mental Health Treatment of Depression Collaborative Research Program. *Archives of General Psychiatry, 46* (pp. 971–982).

21. Parloff, Placebo controls (pp. 79–87).

22. Frank & Frank, *Persuasion and healing* (p. 132).

23. Roberts, A. H., Kewman, D. G., Mercier, L. & Hovell, M. (1993). The power of nonspecific effects in healing: Implications for psychosocial and biological treatments. *Clinical Psychology Review, 13* (pp. 375–391).

24. Roberts et al., The power of nonspecific effects in healing.

25. Roberts et al., The power of nonspecific effects in healing.

26. Roberts et al., The power of nonspecific effects in healing.

27. Elkind et al., National Institute of Mental Health Treatment of Depression Collaborative Research Program.

28. Ogles, B. M., Lambert, M. J. & Sawyer, J. D. (1995). Clinical significance of the National Institute of Mental Health Treatment of Depression Collaborative Research Program data. *Journal of Consulting and Clinical Psychology, 63* (pp. 321–326).

29. Ogles et al., Clinical significance of NIMH Treatment of Depression.

30. Prioleau, L., Murdock, M. & Brody, N. (1983). An analysis of psychotherapy versus placebo studies. *Behavioral and Brain Sciences, 6* (pp. 275–310).

31. Klein, M. H. et al. (1985). A comparative outcome study of group psychotherapy vs. exercise treatment for depression. *International Journal of Mental Health, 13* (pp. 148–177).

32. Task Force on Promotion and Dissemination of Psychological Procedures. (1995). Training in and dissemination of empirically-validated psychological treatments: Report and recommendations. *Clinical Psychologist, 48* (pp. 3–24).

33. Garfield, S. L. (1996). Some problems associated with "validated" forms of psychotherapy. *Clinical Psychology: Science and Practice, 3* (pp. 260–263).

34. Dobson, K. S., Craig, K. D. (Eds.) (1998). *Empirically supported therapies: Best practice in professional psychology* (p. 6). Thousand Oaks, Calif.: Sage Publications.

35. Chambless, D. L. et al. (1995). An update on empirically validated therapies. *Clinical Psychologist, 49* (pp. 5–18).

36. Garfield, Some problems associated with "validated" forms of psychotherapy.

37. *Daubert v. Dow Pharmaceuticals, Inc.* 113 Supreme Court 2786 (1993).

38. *State v. Hungerford*, 697 Atlantic Rptr.2d 916 at 920 (1997).

39. *State v. Hungerford*, 926 (1997).

40. *State v. Hungerford*, 923 (1997).

41. Paul, G. L. (1967). Insight versus desensitization in psychotherapy two years after termination. *Journal of Consulting Psychology, 31* (pp. 333–348).

42. Garfield, Problems associated with "validated" forms. (pp. 260–263).

43. Caplan, P. J. (1995). *They say you're crazy: How the world's most powerful psychiatrists decide who's normal* (p. 197). Reading, Mass.: Addison-Wesley.

44. Mitchell, S. A. & Black, M. J. (1994). *Freud and beyond: A history of modern psychoanalytic thought* (p. 15). New York: Basic Books.

45. Dawes, R. M. (1994). *House of cards: Psychology and psychotherapy built on myth* (p. 150). New York: Free Press.

46. Strupp, H. H. & Hadley, S. W. (1979). Specific versus nonspecific factors in psychotherapy. *Archives of General Psychiatry, 36* (pp. 1125–1136).

47. Strupp & Hadley. Specific versus nonspecific factors.

48. Strupp & Hadley. Specific versus nonspecific factors.

49. Berman, J. S. & Norton, N. C. (1985). Does professional training make a therapist more effective? *Psychological Bulletin, 98* (pp. 401–407).

50. Dawes, *House of cards* (p. 58).

51. Prochaska & Norcross, *Systems of psychotherapy* (p. 430).

52. Lazarus, A. A., Beutler, L. E., & Norcross, J. C. (1992). The future of technical eclecticism. *Psychotherapy, 29* (pp. 11–20).

Selected Bibliography

Bass, E. & Davis, L. (1988). *The courage to heal: A guide for women survivors of child sexual abuse.* New York: Harper & Row.

Campbell, T. W. (1994). *Beware of the talking cure: Psychotherapy may be dangerous to your health.* Boca Raton, Fla.: Upton Books.

Corsini, R. J. & Wedding, D. (Eds.) (1995). *Current psychotherapies* (5th ed.). Itasca, Ill.: Peacock Publishers.

Crews, F. (1995). *The memory wars: Freud's legacy in dispute.* New York: New York Review.

Dawes, R. M. (1994). *House of cards: Psychology and psychotherapy built on myth.* New York: Free Press.

Dineen, T. (1998). *Manufacturing victims: What the psychology industry is doing to people* (2nd ed.). Montreal: Robert Davies.

Frank, J. D. & Frank, J. B. (1991). *Persuasion and healing: A comparative study of psychotherapy* (3rd ed.). Baltimore, Md.: Johns Hopkins University Press.

Grünbaum, A. (1993). *Validation in the clinical theory of psychoanalysis: A study in the philosophy of psychoanalysis.* Madison, Conn.: International Universities Press.

Loftus, E. & Ketcham, K. (1994). *The myth of repressed memories: False memories and allegations of sexual abuse.* New York: St. Martin's Press.

Masson. J. M. (1994). *Against therapy.* Monroe, Maine: Common Courage Press.

Prochaska, J. O. & Norcross, J. C. (1994). *Systems of psychotherapy: A transtheoretical analysis* (3rd ed.). Pacific Grove, Calif.: Brooks/Cole.

Singer, M. T. & Lalich, J. (1996). *Crazy therapies: What are they: Do they work?* San Francisco: Jossey-Bass.

Spanos, N. P. (1996). *Multiple identities and false memories: A socio-cognitive perspective.* Washington, D.C.: American Psychological Association.

Szasz, T. (1979). *The myth of psychotherapy: Mental healing as religion, rhetoric, and repression.* Garden City, N.Y.: Anchor Press/Doubleday.

Index

Abrams, J., 123
Accelerated Information Processing, 122
Acrophobia, 147
Acta Psychiatrica Scandinavica, 50
Adams, R., 63
Adler, Alfred, 22, 127, 180
Agoraphobia, 199, 217
Alcoholics Anonymous, 16
Alien Abduction Therapy, 2, 4, 185, 196–201
Alters, 71, 72, 86, 87
Anal phase, 22
Anderson, N. T., 167
Anxiety, 3, 5, 6, 15, 47, 49, 54, 57, 62, 70, 107, 118, 119, 120, 121, 122, 123, 124, 125, 126, 131, 137, 156, 165, 171, 172, 178, 188, 190, 195, 198, 210, 213, 219, 221
Applied muscle aphonia, 30, 31
Applied Muscle Relaxation, 125
Asthma, 29
Astral body, 171
Atonement, 178
Attack Therapy, 3, 45, 57–60
Attention-placebo, 107, 119

Aura, 167, 176
Automatic thoughts, 132

Bachrach, H. M., 35, 36
Bandler, R., 153, 155, 157, 158
Bass, E., 68, 69, 70, 87
BCBT. *See* Cognitive Behavior Therapy
Beck, A. T., 8
Beck Depression Inventory, 8, 13, 16, 121, 132, 133, 136
Becker, L. A., 124
Behavior Therapy, 6, 13, 37, 95, 117–127
Bender Visual Motor Gestalt Test, 197
Beutler, L. A., 107, 108
Bias, 9, 10, 12, 14, 16, 24, 78, 102, 108, 110
Bibliotherapy, 74
Bioenergetic Analysis, 3, 45, 52–57, 73
Bipolar disorder, 47, 107
Body work, 55, 67, 73
Bondage Breakers, The, 167
Borderline personality, 54
Borderline Personality Disorder, 7–8
Boston Psychoanalytic Institute, 35
Bower, G. H., 6
Bradshaw, John, 68, 74

Brown, L. S., 70
Buddha Psychotherapy, 4, 185–190, 211
Buddhism, 164, 185, 186, 189
Bulimia, 71

California Business and Professions Code, 1
Callahan, R., 190, 191, 192, 193, 194, 206
Campbell, T. W., 210
Carpenter, R., 124, 126
Case study report, 14
Castration, 22, 34, 35, 40, 55
Cathartic therapies, 3, 45–63
Cayce, Edgar, 164
Ceci, S. J., 81, 82, 88
Chakras, 190
Channeling, 178, 179, 199
Charisma, 168
Childhood sexual abuse, 3, 68, 69, 70, 71, 73, 75, 76
Claustrophobia, 111
Cline, F. W., 60
Cognitive Behavior Therapy, 2, 57, 127–133, 134, 135, 136, 137, 191, 211, 212, 213, 216
Cognitive overload, 171, 180, 190
Cognitive Therapy, 13, 117, 118–121
Collective unconscious, 163, 164
Columbia Psychoanalytic Center, 35
Communication systems. *See* Strategic Family Systems Therapy
Confluence, 104
Congruence, 96, 97, 99, 100, 101
Consumer Reports, 7, 15, 17, 130, 194
Conversion disorder (hysteria), 28–33, 190, 195
Cooper, N. A., 120, 125
Cornell Medical Index, 136
Correire, R., 49
Corsini, R. J., 1, 2
Countertransference, 23, 24, 36, 98, 101
Courage to Heal, The, 68, 74, 77
Course in Miracles, A, 163, 177–180, 190
Craig, G. H., 206

Crazy Therapies, 46, 211
Crews, F., 70
Crum, G. A., 120, 125
Cryptoamnesia, 164
Curry, J., 175

Daubert v. Dow Pharmaceuticals, 217–220
Davidson, R., 207
Davis, L., 68, 69, 70, 87
Dawes, R. M., 9, 221, 222
Demand characteristics, 10–12, 39, 62, 78, 79, 83, 84, 88, 119, 138, 167, 174, 177, 181, 194, 200, 218
Demons, 163, 167, 168, 169, 170, 172, 174, 181, 214
Depression, 5, 6, 15, 31, 47, 52, 53, 62, 67, 70, 86, 131, 132, 133, 134, 135, 136, 137, 138, 152, 164, 168, 170, 172, 178, 189, 190, 195, 210, 216, 217, 219, 221
Design Human Engineering (DHE), 154
Diagnostic and Statistical Manual of Mental Disorders, 7, 8, 13, 28–31, 56, 71, 86, 107, 125, 132, 134, 165, 195–196, 213, 220
Dianetics, 211
DID. *See* Dissociative identity disorder
Direct Exposure Therapy, 121–122, 125
Dissociative identity disorder, 68, 69, 71, 74, 77, 86–88, 192
Dora, 26–33, 38–39, 85, 221
Dossey, L., 170
Dream interpretation, 21, 25, 27, 32, 34, 37, 38, 52, 55, 67, 218
Dryden, W., 129

Eastern religions, 60, 163–164, 185, 209, 212
EFT. *See* Emotional Freedom Technique
Ego, 21, 22, 38, 63, 171, 186, 211
Elich, M., 158
Ellis, Albert, 97, 127–128, 129, 130, 180, 189, 213, 222

EMDR. *See* Eye Movement
  Desensitization-Reprocessing
Emery, Gary, 191
Emotional Freedom Technique, 206,
  219
Empathy, 96, 97, 99, 100, 110, 158
Empty-chair technique, 105, 107, 108
Entity de-possession therapy, 172–174
Ephesians, Book of, 169
Epstein, M., 185–186
Erhard Seminars Training. *See est*
Erickson, M., 144, 145, 146, 147, 151,
  152, 153, 154
Erikson, E., 22
est, 60–63, 86
Exorcism, 59, 174, 214
Experiential Therapy, 95, 107, 110–
  112
Experimental controls, 11, 14, 18, 125
Exposure Therapy, 117, 120–122, 125,
  126, 131
Eye Movement Desensitization-
  Reprocessing, 117, 122–126, 194,
  210
Eye-scanning, 157–158

False memory syndrome, 69
False Memory Syndrome Foundation,
  69
Farmer, K., 68
Feeling therapy, 58
Feldman, G. C., 69, 75, 76, 88
Fenner, P., 189
Field psychology, 109
Field report, 15
Fliess, W., 28
Flooding, 120, 121
Forum, 60
Frank, J. D., 2
Fredrickson, R., 68, 70, 71, 72, 73, 87
Free association, 21, 25, 33, 37, 38,
  74, 164, 189, 190, 213, 218
Freud, Sigmund, 3, 4, 6, 21, 22, 24,
  25, 26, 27, 28, 29, 30, 31, 32, 33,
  34, 35, 37, 38, 39, 45, 50, 57, 67,
  68, 70, 73, 85, 87, 88, 103, 105,
  159, 171, 180, 186, 187, 189, 213,
  214, 218, 221

Freyd, Pamela, 69
Frogs into Princes, 153
Future Lives Therapy, 163

Garfield, S. L., 217
Gating, 46
Generalization, 4, 125
Genital stage, 22
*Gestalt Approach and Eye Witness to
  Therapy*, 153
Gestalt psychology, 109
Gestalt Therapy, 52, 60, 95, 97, 103–
  110, 158
Glass, G. V., 100
God, 168, 169–171, 213
Goldstein, E., 68
Gould, C., 72
Greenberg, L. S., 107
Grinder, J., 153, 155, 157, 158
Gross, F., Christian Therapy Program,
  168, 169
Group therapy, 47, 77, 78, 107, 137,
  169
Grünbaum, A., 34
Guardian Angels and Spirit Guides,
  175, 177
Guided imagery, 60, 72, 73, 131, 164,
  175, 197

Haken, J., 63
Haley, J., 143, 144, 145, 146, 147,
  148, 149, 150, 151, 152, 153, 154
Hamilton Rating Scale for Depression,
  132, 136, 170
Hanly, John P., 61
Hart, J., 49
Healing the Shame that Binds You, 75
Henle, M., 109
Herman, J. L., 68, 78, 79, 85
Hilgard, E. R., 6
Homework assignments, 131, 133
Hopkins Symptoms Checklist, 136
Hull, C. L., 6
Human potential movement, 60, 61
Humanistic Therapy, 37, 95, 103, 117,
  143
Hypnosis, 6, 25, 29, 50, 67, 72, 73,
  75, 76, 78, 79, 83, 88, 112, 147,

148, 154, 155, 164, 165, 166, 172,
173, 174, 175, 181, 197, 198, 200,
213

I Believe in Angels, 177
Id, 21, 47, 171, 211
IDEA Seminars, 209
Image Habituation Training, 125
Imipramine, 135–136
Implant, subcutaneous, 199, 200
Implosion Therapy, 3, 45, 117, 120,
121, 128
Informed consent, 60, 88, 151, 153
Insomnia, 61, 131, 132, 134
Institute of Rational-Emotive Therapy,
129
International Palm Therapy Association,
194
Interpersonal Therapy, 127, 134–138
Interpretation of dreams, 23, 25, 27,
32, 39, 55, 56, 70, 100, 108, 110,
119, 146, 154
Interpretation of Dreams, The, 25

Jacobson, N. S., 133
James, William, 185
Janov, Arthur, 45, 46, 47, 48, 49, 50,
51, 67, 219
Jesus Christ, 163, 168, 170, 178, 179,
180, 213
Journaling, 67, 74
Jung, C. G., 22, 34, 127, 163, 164,
180, 185

Karle, W., 49
Karma, 164
Kazdin, A. E., 14
Klerman, G. L., 135, 136
Kovacs, A. L., 7

Lalich, J., 158, 177
Latency stage, 22
Lazarus, A. A., 118
Leonoff, G., 193
Lessons in Evil, Lessons from the Light,
69
Life Spring, 60, 61, 63
Loftus, E., 69, 81, 82

Lowen, A., 52, 53, 54, 55, 56, 57
Luborsky, L., 36
Lyons, L. C., 129

Mack, J. E., 196, 197, 199
Magid, K., 58, 59, 60
Mahrer, A. R., 104, 110–111, 112
Malpractice, 58
Manic depression, 47
Masochistic character, 54
Mass marketing, 159, 193, 205, 206,
207
Massage, 52, 73
Masson, J. M., 31, 37, 68, 102
Masturbation, 28, 32, 146
Maternal deprivation, 59
McKelvey, C. A., 58–60
Meditation, 2, 136, 176, 179, 186,
187, 188, 189, 190, 216
Meier, P., 168
Melzack, R., 46, 50
Memory and Abuse, 69
Menninger Project, 36
Mental telepathy, 32
Meyer, Adolph, 134
Michelle Remembers, 88
Mind-control, 69, 72, 88
Minirth, F., 168
Minirth-Meier New Life Centers, 168
Minnesota Multiphasic Personality In-
ventory, 62, 121, 197, 221
Mirroring, 154
Multimodal Therapy, 118
Multiple personality disorder. *See* Disso-
ciative identity disorder
Murphy, Bridey, 165
Muscular armor, 52, 55
Myth of Repressed Memory, The, 69

Narcissistic character, 54, 56
National Institute of Mental Health,
135, 137, 138, 216
Native American Indians, 176
Negative transference, 24
Neswald, D., 88
Neurolinguistic Programming, 3, 86,
153–159, 209

Neurosis, 23, 25, 28, 30, 34, 45, 46, 104, 127, 128
New Testament, 167
NLP. *See* Neurolinguistic Programming
Norcross, J. C., 103, 150, 151, 152, 222

Obesity, 172, 178
Oedipal conflict, 22
Oedipal fantasies, 34
Ofshe, R., 69, 81, 82, 87
Oral character, 53
Oral phase, 21
Orgasm, 52
Orne, M. T., 10, 11, 79, 84

Paivio, S. C., 107, 109
Palm Therapy, 4, 185, 190, 194–196
Panic disorder, 123, 190, 198, 217
Paranoid personality, 54
Parloff, M. D., 215
Past-Lives Therapy, 163–167, 197
Paul, G. L., 119, 125, 219
Pendergrast, M., 68, 69
Penfield, W., 46, 50
Perls, Fritz, 52, 95, 97, 103, 104, 105, 106, 109, 110, 153, 213
Person-Centered Therapy, 95–103, 104, 142, 145
Personality disorder, 7, 8, 56, 107
Perturbation, 191
Phallic-narcissism, 54
Phallic stage, 22
Phobia, 15, 111, 112, 124, 153, 156, 157, 164, 172
Placebo, 10, 11, 12, 18, 39, 51, 62, 89, 99, 100, 107, 112, 119, 120, 122, 133, 136, 138, 139, 153, 158, 167, 174, 177, 180, 181, 194, 205, 209, 215, 216, 217, 219, 223
Pope, K. S., 70
Post-traumatic stress disorder, 70, 120, 123, 124, 125
Prayer, 168, 170, 176, 181, 214
Prebirth memories, 50
Primal pain, 46, 51
Primal Therapy, 3, 45–52, 58, 61, 86, 87, 219

Principles of Behavior, The, 6
Prochaska, J. O., 103, 150, 151, 152, 222
Progressive relaxation, 131, 208
Projection, 104
Proverbs, Book of, 169
Prozac, 130
Psychoanalysis, 3, 4, 13, 14, 21–40, 45, 56, 57, 62, 85, 88, 95, 100, 102, 103, 112, 117, 137, 143, 145, 159, 163, 164, 167, 171, 180, 185, 186, 189, 196, 211, 213, 214, 217, 218, 219, 221
Psychobbable, 51
Psychodiagnosis, 6, 8, 31, 47, 51, 96, 110, 156, 173, 196, 213, 220
Psychodrama, 60
Psychopathic personality, 54
Psychosexual theory of development, 21
Psychotic decompensation, 189
PTSD. *See* Post-traumatic stress disorder

Quinn, R., 102

Rage Reduction Therapy, 57–60
Ramona, Holly, 71, 84
Raschke, C., 179
Rat-Man, 33, 34
Rational Emotive Behavior Therapy (REBT), 97, 127–130, 131, 134, 222
Recovered Memories of Abuse, 70
Recovered memories of abuse, 69, 78, 79, 80, 81, 82
Recovered Memory Therapy, 67–89, 167, 180, 197, 200, 201, 219
Redlands Experiment, 170
Reframing, 111, 154, 155, 156
Reich, Wilhelm, 52, 56, 103
Reichian Therapy, 52, 56
Reincarnation, 164, 166, 180
Relaxation, 60, 107, 119, 121, 123, 124, 131, 136, 190, 197, 208, 216
Religious healing, 205, 211, 212, 214, 215, 223
Replication, 4, 6
Repressed childhood memories, 21

Repressed Memories, 68
Repressed memories, 67, 68, 69, 71,
    72, 73, 79, 80, 85, 143, 167, 218
Repression, 2, 3, 21, 27, 35, 46, 49,
    51, 52, 68, 75, 80, 81, 196
Resentment game, 105
Retroflection, 104
Reversal, psychological, 191
Rigid character, 54, 56
Roberts, Jane, 164
Rogers, Carl, 3, 13, 95–96, 97, 98, 99,
    100, 101, 102, 104, 213
Role-playing, 83, 88, 107, 128, 131
Rolfing, 73
Rorschach Ink Blot Test, 9, 170, 197
Rosen, J. N., 58
Rosen, R. D., 51
Rosenzweig, S., 35
Rossetti, F., 176

Sampling bias, 16
Sanderson, A. A., 124, 126
Satan, 163, 167, 168, 169
Satanic ritual abuse, 69, 70, 72, 83, 87,
    88, 196, 201
Satir, V., 153
Schatzow, E., 78, 79
Scheibe, K. E., 10, 11, 79, 84
Schizoid character, 53
Schizophrenia, 101, 107, 144, 152,
    155, 169, 170, 195
Schucman, H., 178, 179, 180
Scientific method, 4, 17, 18
Scientology, 211
Sedona Method, 207, 208, 209
Self-actualization, 96, 102, 111, 156
Self-concept, 96, 101
Seligman, M.E.P., 12, 15
Seminars, 60, 61, 63, 109, 154, 158,
    190, 205, 207, 209, 210
Sensory deprivation, 10, 11, 84
Shaman, 176
Shapiro, F., 122, 124, 126
Sharpley, C. F., 157, 158
Sheldon, W. H., 53
Sheldrake, R., 194
Sikes, R., 209
Silva Method, 206

Singer, M. T., 158, 177
Skinner, B. F., 6
Sleep paralysis, 199
Smith, M. L., 100
Sodium amytal, 67, 75, 78, 79, 82, 84
Spanos, N. P., 82, 83, 88, 166, 194,
    200
Spence, D. P., 25, 26
Sperry, R. W., 50
Spirit guides, 163, 172, 175, 176
Spiritual Therapy, 163–181
Spiritual warfare, 167–172
Spitz, R. A., 5
Spontaneous remission, 16
St. John, Gospel of, 69
Stampl, T., 120, 125
State-Trait Anxiety Inventory, 124
State v. Hungerford, 218, 219, 200
Steiger, B., 175
Strategic Family Systems Therapy, 3,
    143–153
Subjective Units of Distress, 122, 124,
    126, 191, 192, 193
Substance abuse, 107, 168
SUD. *See* Subjective Units of Distress
Suggestions of Abuse, 69
Sullivan, Harry Stack, 22, 134
Sulloway, F., 34
Superego, 21, 105, 171, 211
Survey reports, 6
Symptom Check List, 124
Systematic desensitization, 112, 117–
    120, 123, 125, 126
Szasz, T., 2, 211

TAT. *See* Thematic Apperception Test
Telephone psychotherapy, 205, 210
Terr, L., 69, 71
Thematic Apperception Test, 170
Thought Field Therapy, 190–194, 195
Thought transference, 32
Three Approaches to Psychotherapy, 97
Tinker, R. H., 124
Toilet training, 27
Top Dog/Underdog, 105–106
Torrey, E. F., 35
Transference, 21, 22, 23, 24, 28, 34,
    35, 36, 37, 38, 52, 55, 95, 96, 110,

119, 126, 127, 134, 143, 146, 186,
  213, 219
Trauma and Recovery, 68, 69
Traux, C. B., 101, 102

UFOs, 198, 199, 200
Uncommon Therapy, 147, 153
Unconditional positive regard, 96, 99,
  100, 102, 127
Unquiet Dead, The, 172

Validity of Cognition Scale, 124
Vegetotherapy, 52
Victims of Memory, 69
Voice technology, 191, 192, 206

Wall, P. D., 46
Watters, E., 69, 81
Way to Vibrant Health, The, 57
Webster, R., 70
Wechsler Adult Intelligence Scale, 147
Wedding, D., 1–2

Weight loss, 5, 157, 172
Weinrach, S. G., 98, 101
Wheeler, D. L., 85
Whitfield, C. L., 69
Williams, L. M., 79, 80, 81
Williamson, Marianne, 178
Wilson, S. A., 124
Wolf-Man, 33, 34–35, 39
Wolpe, Joseph, 117, 118, 119, 123,
  191
Woods, P. J., 129
Woolger, R. J., 165, 166
Word game, 34
Working through, 187

Yapko, N. D., 69
Yoga, 2, 137, 188

Z-therapy, 57
Zaslow, R. W., 58, 59
Zung Depression Scale, 121
Zwang, M., 194, 195

About the Author

DONALD A. EISNER is a licensed psychologist and a practicing attorney in Encino, California.

ISBN 0-275-96413-2

9 780275 964139

HARDCOVER BAR CODE